W9-BML-093

MELISSA GRAHAM researched and wrote the first edition of *Trans-Canada Rail Guide* back in 1995, an undertaking which saw her travel from the Atlantic to the Pacific and north to Hudson Bay, covering 15km by dog sled, 40km on foot, 45km by bus, 60km by car and over 12,000km by rail. Melissa is also the co-author of *The Rough Guide to Chile* and *The Rough Guide to Ecuador*. She lives in London with her husband and three children.

Melissa's sister **HELEN GRAHAM** researched and updated the fifth edition of this book with Elizabeth Kent. Like Melissa, Helen was born in Sunderland, UK, and has loved travelling from an early age, spending much of her childhood holidaying in France. In 2005 she travelled further north to study History of Art at Edinburgh University, spending a year in Paris studying at the Sorbonne. Helen currently works in Product Management for Berghaus in North-East England and looks forward to returning to Canada to test some of her outdoor gear!

Inspired by travelling and learning about other cultures, **ELIZABETH KENT** studied French at the University of Birmingham. After spending a year in Paris, she took the opportunity to travel through Canada and use her French in another, very different, Francophone country, researching and updating the fifth edition of *Trans-Canada Rail Guide*. Currently teaching in Leicestershire, she is planning further writing excursions.

Trans-Canada Rail Guide
First edition 1996; this fifth edition 2010

Publisher
Trailblazer Publications
The Old Manse, Tower Rd, Hindhead, Surrey, GU26 6SU, UK
Fax (+44) 01428-607571, info@trailblazer-guides.com
www.trailblazer-guides.com

British Library Cataloguing in Publication Data
A catalogue record for this book is available from the British Library

ISBN 978-1-905864-33-1

© **Melissa Graham 1996, 2000, 2003, 2007, 2010**
Text, maps and photographs (unless otherwise credited)

The right of Melissa Graham to be identified as the author of this work has been
asserted by her in accordance with the Copyright, Designs and Patents Act 1988

Reproduced by permission of VIA Rail Canada (**VRC**), the cover photo and photos
opposite p16 (btm), p17 (top), p64 (top and middle); by permission of Rocky Mountaineer
Railtours (**RMR**), the photo opposite p17 (btm); by permission of Tourism BC (**TBC**),
Manitoba Tourism (**MT**) and Jim Manthorpe (**JM**), the photos between p64 and p65;
by permission of VIA Rail Canada and Matthew G Wheeler (**MGW**) the photo opposite
p17 (middle); by permission of VIA Rail Canada and Melanie Fordham (**MF**) the photo
opposite p64 (btm); by permission of VIA Rail Canada and Steven J Brown (**SJB**) the
photo opposite p225 (top); by permission of Helen Graham (**HG**) the photos opposite p96
(top) and 224 (top); by permission of Elizabeth Kent (**EK**) the photos opposite p16 (top),
p96 (btm), p112, p113 (top), p225 (btm); all other photos © Melissa Graham (**MG**)

Editor: Henry Stedman
Series editor: Bryn Thomas
Typesetting and layout: Nick Hill
Proof-reading: Nicky Slade
Cartography: Nick Hill
Index: Jane Thomas and Nicky Slade

All rights reserved. Other than brief extracts for the purposes of review no part of
this publication may be reproduced in any form without the written consent of the
publisher and copyright owner.

Every effort has been made by the author and publisher to ensure that the information
contained herein is as accurate and up to date as possible. However, they are unable to
accept responsibility for any inconvenience, loss or injury sustained by anyone as a result
of the advice and information given in this guide.

Printed on chlorine-free paper by
D2Print (☎ +65-6295 5598), Singapore

Trans-Canada
RAIL GUIDE

MELISSA GRAHAM

Fifth edition researched and updated by
HELEN GRAHAM and ELIZABETH KENT

TRAILBLAZER PUBLICATIONS

KALAMAZOO PUBLIC LIBRARY

Acknowledgements

From Helen and Elizabeth: Firstly, a huge thank you to the author, Melissa Graham, for her support and guidance in updating this fifth edition of *Trans Canada Rail Guide* and to the publisher, Bryn Thomas, for giving us the opportunity to be part of such a brilliant project.

Many thanks to everyone at VIA Rail, especially Diane Garth, a fantastic service manager who patiently answered lots of our questions, and Lee George, in the UK, whose assistance was invaluable when arranging the trip.

We are also hugely grateful to Melanie Childs, who arranged accommodation in many of the Fairmont Hotels across Canada and to the employees of Fairmont Hotels who looked after us so well.

We are indebted to the tourist board representatives across Canada who assisted us in so many ways: Kylie Toner in Halifax and everyone at Halifax City Hall, Richard Séguin in Quebec, Marie Jose and Peggy Wilson in Montreal, Michele Simpson in Toronto, Yvonne Dupuis in Winnipeg, the brilliant Kelly Bertoncini in Edmonton, Maude Laliberte in Calgary and Lena Lin in Vancouver. A huge thank you, also, to Pamela Trofenko in Jasper and Scott Eady and Christian at Jasper Raft Tours for taking such good care of us.

We had a fantastic time travelling across Canada, which was all the more special because of all the wonderful people we met, be it in hostels, restaurants or on the train – thanks, everyone, for your help and advice.

Finally, a huge thanks and lots of love to our families the Grahams and the Kents for their invaluable support.

From Melissa: A very big thank you to Malcolm Andrews and Ashley Doyle of VIA Rail; to Henry Stedman for another sterling edit; to Nick Hill for great map work; and to Helen and Elizabeth for all their hard work.

A request

The author and publisher have tried to ensure that this guide is as accurate and up to date as possible. Nevertheless things change. If you notice any changes or omissions that should be included in the next edition of this book, please write to Melissa Graham at Trailblazer (address on p2) or email her at melissa.graham@trailblazer-guides.com. A free copy of the next edition will be sent to persons making a significant contribution.

Cover photo: VIA Rail's *Skeena* service between Jasper and Prince Rupert is a two-day journey through the heart of the Rockies. Photo © VIA Rail Canada.

CONTENTS

INTRODUCTION

The overwhelming thing about Canada is its sheer size. How can one train ride in a single country take three whole days and three whole nights? And you've still got further to go. No other mode of transport conveys such an acute sense of Canada's vastness, of its beautiful, desolate, wide-open spaces. Endless stretches of track take you through a wilderness scarcely touched by man. You can travel for hours without seeing a road or a house, or indeed any sign of habitation – it's an incredible, almost haunting, experience. Back in 1872 an early traveller wrote a book about Canada's interior called *The Great Lone Land*. It captured the North American imagination and became an instant bestseller. Today, much of Canada is still a 'great lone land' that continues to fire the imagination of the modern traveller; the huge iron artery stretching across the continent is truly the best way to cross it.

It is also the reason why this massive country exists at all. When the Dominion of Canada was created in 1867 it was no more than a set of loosely connected colonies with no sense of unity or nationhood. It was, moreover, under a very real threat of being swallowed up by its powerful southern neighbour. The railroad was the single most important reason why this never happened: it gave the new country its life-blood and bound the provinces together into a transcontinental nation. When the last spike was driven in on 7 November 1885 it paved the way for rapid expansion, mass immigration and economic boom. Urban development ran parallel to the tracks and the stops along the line became the backbone of a new nation – which makes a rail trip today a fascinating journey into this young country's history.

What you'll probably remember about the trip more than anything, though, is the dazzling scenery you travel through. In 1885 the General Manager of the Canadian Pacific Railway Company realized that travellers would flock from all corners of the world to ride through such magnificent landscape. 'If we cannot export the scenery,' he declared, 'we shall have to import the tourists!' And tourists have quite joyfully been imported ever since. Imagine the snow-capped peaks towering right over the tracks; the sweeping panoramas of lakes, waterfalls and glaciers gliding past you. Better still, imagine looking out of the window onto a jade-green lake to find yourself staring at a moose. The whole thing takes your breath away.

On top of all this, a rail ride across Canada is a supremely relaxing experience, a rare joy in today's climate of rapid communications and jet-travel. In the words of Robert Louis Stevenson, 'the train disturbs so little the scenery through which it takes us, that our heart becomes full of the placidity and stillness of the country'. Nowhere is this more true than in Canada.

PLANNING YOUR TRIP

1

Routes

Travel a thousand miles up a great river; more than another thousand miles along great lakes; a thousand miles across rolling prairies; and another thousand through woods and over the great ranges of mountains, and you have travelled from Ocean to Ocean. **Rev Grant**, *Ocean to Ocean*

ROUTE OPTIONS

Canada's **transcontinental through service** is operated by VIA Rail (the national passenger rail network) three times a week between **Toronto** and **Vancouver**. You can take **connecting trains** to extend or alter your route in several ways. For a start, if you want to make it a truly transcontinental journey from coast to coast, you can begin or end it in **Halifax** on the Atlantic. Alternatively you can make **Montreal** or **Quebec City** the eastern terminus of your trip. Another option is to start or end in **Prince Rupert** on the Pacific instead of Vancouver; this is very popular with travellers who want to combine their rail trip with the Inside Passage ferry ride between Prince Rupert and Vancouver Island. Finally, if you're short of time you may choose to do not the whole trans-Canada trip but only a portion of it, such as the scenic leg between Jasper and Vancouver.

❏ **Routes at a glance**
Each scheduled service is given a different name by VIA. The most famous is *The Canadian* from Toronto to Vancouver but there are several other services that we cover in this guide; we also include a couple of privately owned lines not operated by VIA.

The Ocean: Halifax to Montreal (21 hours; about the train p17; route guide p189); *The Corridor*: Montreal to Toronto (from 4hr 34min; about the train p18; route guide p196); *The Canadian*: Toronto to Vancouver (4 days; about the train, p12; route guide p199); *The Skeena*: Jasper to Prince Rupert (2 days; about the train p18; route guide p214); *The Hudson Bay*: Winnipeg to Churchill (2 days; about the train p19; route guide p221); *The Rocky Mountaineer*: four privately run daylight-only services between Vancouver and Banff/Calgary, Jasper and Whistler, and between Whistler and Jasper (about the trains p20; route guides pp228, 234 and 237).

Which direction?

Once you've chosen your route, the next thing to decide is in which direction to do it. By and large you see the same scenery whichever direction you travel in, though on some services the eastbound and westbound trains travel through slightly different sections of the journey at night. There's no doubt that the approach to the Rocky Mountains is far more dramatic from the prairies than from the Pacific. Furthermore, if you're interested in charting Canada's history on your rail trip, travelling from east to west follows the direction of railway development and settlement across the country. It's worth noting, however, that westbound trains get booked up far earlier than eastbound trains.

BREAKING YOUR JOURNEY

Few people want to spend their entire holiday sitting on a train; fortunately, the railway takes you through some superb cities where you can break up your journey. Some of the best, notably **Vancouver**, **Toronto** and **Montreal**, are conveniently located at the beginning or end of a line, so spending time there is no problem as far as your ticket's concerned. In addition, all VIA Rail tickets include one free **stopover** per journey, which can be for as many days as you wish. The single most compelling stop on *The Canadian* is undoubtedly **Jasper**, in the heart of the Rocky Mountains.

If you want to make more than one break you need to buy either **separate tickets**, which works out more expensive than a through ticket, or a **rail pass** (see box opposite), which allows **unlimited stops** within a given time period. In this case, **Winnipeg** makes a good place to stop off, being right in the middle of the county – though some travellers find **Edmonton** more appealing.

If you're travelling on *The Ocean* (Halifax–Montreal), you should try to stop off at **Quebec City** (served by Charny station), perhaps the most beautiful city in Canada. The daylight-only *Skeena* has an obligatory overnight stop at **Prince George**, with no other stops allowed on a through ticket.

Services and fares

If you take the train right across Canada you'll notice that different sections of the route use different types of train and offer slightly different services. By far the longest through train is VIA's flagship, *The Canadian* – the tri-weekly transcontinental between Toronto and Vancouver.

The other trains/routes covered by this book are *The Ocean* (Halifax to Montreal), *The Corridor* (Montreal to Toronto), *The Hudson Bay* (Winnipeg to Churchill), *The Skeena* (Jasper to Prince Rupert) and the privately run *Rocky Mountaineer* (Vancouver to Jasper, Banff/Calgary or Whistler, and Whistler to Jasper).

❏ BUYING YOUR TICKET

The classes: economy, sleeper and business

There are two main classes on Canadian trains: **economy class** and, on transcontinental trains, **sleeper class** (known as Sleeper Touring Class on *The Canadian*). Regarding the latter, sleeping accommodation comes as an upper or lower berth (double seats that convert to bunk beds), or a single, double or triple bedroom (called cabins for one, two or three); see p12 for more details. Shorter services (eg Montreal to Toronto) where there is no need for a sleeping car instead offer **business class** as an alternative to economy class.

Advance purchase discounts

VIA offers a wide range of **advance-purchase discounts** (eg 'supersaver' or 'special' fares), available to all passengers year-round. These fares have to be booked at least three to seven days in advance depending on the train, though in peak season you should book long before then to secure the cheapest fares. There are other restrictions and conditions attached too, for example a fee is usually charged if you wish to change the dates or cancel the ticket. Nevertheless, the savings can be considerable: eg a Toronto-Vancouver ticket in high season is $442 if purchased in advance, as opposed to $603 for the full fare.

Other discounts

Seniors (aged 60 and over) are entitled to a discount (normally around 10%) on all regular fares. **Students** (aged 12–17, or 18+ with an ISIC card) and **youths** (aged 18–25) receive a discount (normally around one-third) on economy-class tickets. Youths also get a 10% discount on business class or sleeper tickets. **Children** aged two to eleven are given a 50% discount in economy class and a discount (normally around 25%) on business class or sleeper tickets; under-twos travel free when not occupying a seat. Older children are classed as 'students' (see above). To find out the exact discounted fare for the dates and journey you want to travel on, check 🖥 www.viarail.ca.

CANRAIL pass

The CANRAIL pass gives 12 days of economy-class travel throughout the VIA national network within a 30-day period. Up to three extra days can be bought (for travel within the 30-day period) and in some cases passengers can upgrade to sleeper class. Unlimited stops are allowed on the pass. **Note that these prices do not include taxes (13% extra).**

	High season (1 June–15 Oct)		Low season (all other dates)	
	Basic pass	extra day	Basic pass	extra day
Adult	$941	$81	$588	$50
Concessions	$847	$73	$529	$45

Fares

Fares that are listed in the following pages **include all taxes** (with the exception of the fares for CANRAIL passes, to which 13% must be added; see above). Fares given under 'Berths' refer to upper berths; a supplement is added for lower berths (the exact amount depending on the length of journey and the type of ticket). 'Room' refers to a private bedroom per person in sleeper class.

Useful websites

Check out schedules, fares and special offers for VIA services on 🖥 www.viarail.ca.

Visit Rocky Mountaineer Vacations' website at 🖥 www.rockymountaineer.com for their latest prices and schedules.

THE CANADIAN

Renovation

The Canadian was first introduced by the CPR in 1955. At that time the stream-lined, stainless-steel trains, designed and built in America, were considered ultra modern, representing the latest in railway technology. Thirty-seven years later VIA reinvented *The Canadian*, this time marketing its nostalgic appeal, elegant appearance and the luxurious comforts of old-style, long-distance rail travel.

❏ Sleeping accommodation

There are four types of sleeping accommo-dation available to **Sleeper Touring class** passengers.

● **Berths** These are wide double seats facing each other which convert to bunk beds at night. It's an open section of the train and people will be wandering up and down the carriage all day on their way to the dome or the dining car. You do get a bit of privacy at night time, however, when the bunks are enclosed by heavy curtains. There's always a toilet close by.

● **Cabin for one** Until recently known as 'Roomettes', these ingenious little one-per-son rooms contain your seat, a private loo (doubles up as a leg rest) and your own cor-ner sink and mirror.

   You sleep on a pull-out bed which slots into position on top of your seat and the toilet. If you need the loo in the night it can be a lit-tle tricky sliding back the bed to get to it quickly; it is advisable to practise this handy manoeuvre before going to sleep.

● **Cabin for two** These private rooms con-tain two armchairs by day and pull-down bunks by night.

   Unlike the single bedrooms and the berths, these beds lie along the width instead of the length of the train which apparently induces a pleasant rocking or cradling sensa-tion as the train chugs along.

   Each bedroom is equipped with its own washbasin and a private loo in an adjoining little room.

● **Cabin for three** Like the cabins for one, but for three people. They are the most spa-cious private compartments on the train.

At night the upper berths are folded down

Service attendants make up the bunks which are enclosed by curtains

Bunks are comfortable and well-equipped with reading lights and pockets for your belongings

Before launching a new service aboard *The Canadian*, VIA carried out a massive renovation project on the 190 trains. Steam heating was converted to electric; new wiring and lighting were installed; air conditioning was introduced; showers were fitted in each sleeping car; ventilation was improved; mechanical components such as brakes and bogies were completely overhauled and the interiors were recarpeted and reupholstered throughout. The total cost of the project was over $200 million.

Economy or Sleeper Touring Class?

There are two ways of travelling on *The Canadian*: in economy class or in Sleeper Touring class. In **Economy class** you get reclining seats where you sleep overnight, with pillows and blankets provided (main lights go off at 10pm). The seats have pull-down trays, overhead lights, leg rests, and very generous leg room. You also have access to a panoramic dome car (see p16), though competition for space there is fierce. **Sleeper Touring class** is for passengers travelling in sleeping cars and is much more luxurious than economy class. This section has its own dome car and lounges and passengers have exclusive use of the dining cars.

Staff on the train

VIA's on-board staff are almost without exception helpful, efficient and friendly. They also tend to be very knowledgeable about the train and the places it takes you through, particularly the older people who've worked on the railway for many years. Don't feel shy about asking them questions – they're usually more than happy to talk about anything to do with the journey. During the peak season, however, *The Canadian* gets packed out and things can get rather hectic, which leaves the staff with little time to sit around and chat.

Boss of the train is the **Service Manager**. He or she will usually introduce him/herself to Economy-class passengers at the beginning of a trip, and explain the layout of the train, the facilities on board and give a brief description of the highlights of the scenery or towns you'll pass through. Next in line are the **assistant service coordinators**, who mainly work in the sleeping cars, where they'll see passengers to their seats and explain the facilities and service.

The staff you'll meet most, whether in Economy or Sleeper Touring class, are the **service attendants**, who generally run around making sure everything's okay. The staff are attentive in both sections of the trains but Sleeper Touring

---

❏ **Baggage on the train**

Each passenger is allowed to check in three items of **baggage** on *The Canadian* and most other trains (four on *The Ocean*), and to take two items of carry-on baggage with them on the journey (only one on *The Ocean*). The combined weight of your checked baggage should not exceed 32kg (70lb). Label each item clearly with your name, address and contact telephone number, and leave all checked baggage with VIA staff at the station at least one hour prior to departure, so that it can be loaded onto the baggage car.

You can check in **bicycles** for $20 per trip; VIA will supply a free bicycle box, and you must turn the handlebars and remove the pedals. This being Canada, you can also check in canoes, kayaks and dog sleighs at $50 per train ride.

class passengers are particularly well looked after, with drinks and snacks brought to their seats as and when they please.

Bathrooms
Each sleeping car has its own piping hot shower, but these are not available to Economy-class passengers, who have to make do with the wash basins. You might expect this part of the train to get a bit whiffy by the third day but this rarely seems to be the case. The passengers seem happy to improvise with the basin – or else the air conditioning is extremely effective. Moreover, the toilets/washrooms are given a thorough clean at each main stop.

Eating and drinking
If you're travelling in **Economy class** during the peak season (June–October) you'll be feeding yourself at the 'Coffee Shop' in the Skyline Car, which serves snacks you can take back to your seats (sandwiches, crisps, and the ubiquitous Oh Henry bars) or warm meals you can eat at the tables. These are usually very

---

❑ FARES ON *THE CANADIAN*
The cheapest type of ticket on the Canadian is the economy-class '**supersaver**' fare, with the next cheapest being '**discounted fare**' (not listed below), which is also available in Sleeper Touring class (with different peak and off-peak rates). Finally there's the '**full fare**', with no discounts. Supersaver and discounted fares come with various **restrictions** and penalties (typically a $100 service charge) on changing the date of travel or cancelling your journey; the booking page on VIA's website specifies restrictions for each fare quoted.

Economy class

	Peak (June–Oct 21) full fare / supersaver	Off-peak (rest of year) full fare / supersaver
Toronto to:		
Winnipeg	$395/$256	$296/$217
Edmonton	$587/$381	$440/$322
Jasper	$661/$430	$497/$364
Vancouver	$803/$522	$603/$442
Edmonton to:		
Jasper	$175/$114	$131/$97
Vancouver	$328/$213	$246/$181
Jasper to:		
Vancouver	$244/$159	$183/$134

Sleeper Touring class

	Peak (June–Oct 21) full fare / cheapest fare		Off-peak (rest of year) full fare / cheapest fare	
	Berth §	Room *	Berth §	Room *
Toronto to:				
Winnipeg	$770/$485	$1164/$734	$577/$485	$874/$734
Edmonton	$940/$592	$1414/$891	$704/$592	$1060/$891
Jasper	$1040/$655	$1570/$989	$780/$655	$1177/$989
Vancouver	$1390/$876	$2097/$1321	$1043/$876	$1573/$1321

tasty (pot roast, wild mushroom ravioli, grilled salmon to name but a few typical items from the menu), and cost around $12. Alcohol is served here, too, as well as in the Skyline Bar. You can't, however, take your booze back to your seat: you must drink it where you bought it. Outside the peak season, Economy-class passengers also have access to the dining car, where all meals must be paid for as you go along (around $20–30 for three courses plus a drink).

Over in **Sleeper Touring class** meals are included in the price of your ticket and during the peak season you have exclusive use of the **dining car**, with its crisp linen tablecloths and efficient service. You're given a choice of three sittings, which are rarely on time in the busy summer months. The food is usually very good: typical main dishes might be 'Atlantic fish chowder', 'rainbow trout with caper beurre blanc', or 'Canadian prime rib of beef, slow roasted', to give a few examples from the menu. Breakfast is hearty – usually toast, bacon and eggs, or pancakes with maple syrup – while at lunch you'll normally have the choice of a fish or meat dish, or a large salad. The menu always includes vegetarian options

Sleeper Touring class continued

	Peak (June–Oct 21) full fare / cheapest fare		Off-peak (rest of year) full fare / cheapest fare	
	Berth §	Room *	Berth §	Room *
Edmonton to:				
Jasper	$487/$306	$737/$464	$365/$307	$553/$464
Vancouver	$718/$453	$1082/$682	$539/$453	$812/$682
Jasper to:				
Vancouver	$623/$393	$939/$591	$467/$393	$705/$591

§ Supplement for lower berths applies.
* 'Room' refers to a private bedroom per person in sleeper class
Fares include all meals on the train.

PRIVATE SUITES ON *THE CANADIAN*

For the ultimate in train-travel luxury, book your own private suite on *The Canadian*. Two bedrooms are joined together so that instead of sleeping in bunk beds, couples can sleep in a queen-size bed, beneath a cosy down duvet instead of the usual grey blankets. Fresh flowers and a bottle of chilled sparkling wine in each room add to the sense of luxury; extra pampering is offered by way of breakfast in bed. When this service was first launched it was aptly named 'Romance by Rail' – and it really is a romantic way to travel. Perhaps the most memorable way to do it is on the stretch from Jasper to Vancouver in winter, when the Rocky Mountains are enveloped in snow and ice – a dazzling view to behold from the comfort of your own double bed.

Fares	Peak (June–Oct 21)	Off-Peak (rest of year)
Toronto to Jasper	$6130	$3513
Jasper to Vancouver	$3626	$2063

Price is per couple, not per person.

(let VIA know when booking if you are vegetarian or have any other dietary requirements, so they can make sure all passengers are properly catered for).

The dining car also has a good range of alcohol on sale which you'll be billed for at the end of your meal. Be warned that the dining-car experience can be a little manic in the middle of peak season as the harassed staff work flat out to serve three sittings of three meals a day to hundreds of hungry people.

In Sleeper Touring class you can also help yourself to complimentary tea, coffee, biscuits and fruit in the Park Car and activity dome car (at the very back of the train), or get a service attendant to bring a cup to your seat.

Note that smoking is not permitted on any of VIA's trains.

The dome cars

The glass-roofed, panoramic observation domes are probably the most famous feature of *The Canadian*. There's one in the sleeping-car section and one in the economy-class section, and seats are at a premium in both.

Passengers tend to treat the dome the way holidaymakers treat pool-side sun loungers: they get there early, they stake their claim and they stay there. They do get hungry, though, so you can usually find a free seat at mealtimes and in the early morning or late evening. The best time to sit in the dome is at dawn. No one's around, the only sound is the movement of the train and Canada's vast, wide open space is at its most haunting.

Life on the train

If you're travelling in Economy class you'll doubtless find yourself surrounded by a young and cosmopolitan crowd. Fellow travellers are often backpacking or hostelling and there are a lot of Europeans on board in the summer months. Strangers strike up conversations quite easily and meeting new people is all part of the enjoyment of the trip. Between scanning the horizon for bears you can stretch your legs by wandering to and from the café or hover around the dome car in the hope that someone will offer you their seat.

Sleeper Touring Class passengers are a particularly convivial lot. The service is inevitably patronized by slightly older and wealthier travellers who all

---

🚂 The CP Holiday Train

Every winter Canadian Pacific runs a special **Holiday Train** from Montreal to Vancouver, to collect food and money to donate to food banks for homeless people across the country, as part of the National Food Sharing initiative. The train – dubbed the **Food Bank Express** – is a freight train decked out in thousands of Christmas lights and incorporates a box-car stage on which a line-up of musicians provide fundraising entertainment to the communities the train passes through. Since the launch of the Holiday Train in 1997 it has raised over $4 million in funds and collected over 2 million pounds of food for Food Banks Canada (💻 http://food bankscanada.ca), the national charity dedicated to providing emergency food for Canada's neediest people. Find out more about the Holiday Train on 💻 www8.cpr.ca (select 'General Public' from the main menu, and then 'Holiday train').

(**Opposite**) VIA's flagship is *The Canadian*, its iconic dome cars offering unrivalled views of the Rockies. (Photos: top © EK, bottom © VRC).

appear (when thrown together three times a day in the dining car) to get on extremely well. There is a shared preoccupation with nocturnal comforts. Conversations at breakfast tend to focus on the previous night's sleep, and conversations at dinner on the impending night's sleep.

Sleeper Touring Class passengers may also pursue a social life in the bullet lounge or the mural lounge, where they can discuss the merits of the specially commissioned artwork on display. The original murals, painted by artists from the Group of Seven (see p121), are now in a museum in Ottawa. There's also an activity car where movies are shown in the evenings and, if you're lucky, there may be a wine-tasting session, concentrating on Canadian wines from southern Ontario.

THE OTHER TRAINS

The Ocean
Between Halifax and Montreal you'll most likely travel aboard the same stainless-steel trains as *The Canadian*, though some services are on modern, spacious 'Renaissance' trains – check before booking if you'd like to travel old-style. Again, you can travel either in **Economy class** or in sleeping cars, though here you have a choice of two types of sleeper class. **Sleeper class** (formerly known as Easterly Class) is available year-round; you have full use of the dining car, though your meals are not included in the price of the ticket. **Sleeper Touring class** is a peak-season tourist service, including on-board commentary from guides, exclusive access to some areas of the train and priority access to

---

❏ **FARES ON *THE OCEAN***
Economy class

Peak (mid-June to mid-Oct)		Off-peak (rest of year)	
full fare	supersaver	full fare	supersaver
$251	$138	$251	$125

Sleeper class

Peak (mid-June to mid-Oct)		Off-peak (rest of year)*	
full fare	cheapest fare	full fare	
Room‡	Berth	Room	
$481/$290	$323/$167	$423/$218	

*During off-peak period there are usually only rooms, and no berths, available on this train, except when demand is a bit higher than normal eg, during the Easter period

Sleeper Touring class (mid-June to mid-Oct)*
Room‡

full fare	cheapest fare
$554	$333

* Sleeper touring class includes all meals, on-board commentary and other extras. For more details, see below. ‡ 'Room' rates are based on double occupancy, per adult.

(Opposite) Top: *The Ocean* passing a typical Acadian village in Nova Scotia. (Photo © VRC). **Middle**: The *Skeena* (see p18) and its panorama dome car. (Photo © MGW). **Bottom**: Operating since 1989, the *Rocky Mountaineer* (see p20) now offers three two-day routes through the Rockies. (Photo © RMR).

the dining car (meals included in the ticket). Renaissance cars have private showers in about half of the cabins; otherwise, there are shared hot showers in each sleeping car.

The train never gets as hectically busy as *The Canadian* and the 21-hour journey proceeds at a leisurely, relaxed pace.

The Corridor

Moving on from Montreal to Toronto you'll take the aptly titled 'Corridor' route. The LRC (light, rapid and comfortable) trains operating along The Corridor carry the highest volume of passenger traffic in Canada. The trains are sleek, modern and very fast – downtown Montreal to downtown Toronto takes just four and a half hours on the fastest trains. The train offers Business class travel, and Economy class. Business class is super luxurious: you get to sit in a posh lounge before boarding; delicious three-course meals are served to you at your seat and you're plied with wine or liqueurs during and after each meal.

Economy class has the usual roomy seats and the attendants periodically bring round refreshments for which you have to pay. The journey is more functional than recreational and you're not likely to walk around the train meeting people. It gets you from A to B good and fast but it's probably the least memorable train ride you'll take in Canada.

❏ FARES ON THE CORRIDOR ROUTE

On the Montreal–Toronto line the cheapest tickets are known as 'special fare', which are completely non-refundable and non-exchangeable, followed by 'supersaver fare' and 'discounted fare' (not listed below). All advance-purchase discounts have **limited availability**, so tickets should be bought as far in advance as possible.

Montreal-Toronto

	Full fare	Special fare
Economy class:	$148	$78
Business class:	$233	$146

Tickets are the same price year-round

Wi-fi on the trains and in stations

At the time of writing, the only **trains** to offer **wi-fi** are those on *The Corridor* route, for example from Montreal to Toronto, or the services to Quebec City, Ottawa or Windsor. These trains also have electrical sockets next to the seats, in both Economy and Business class. Wi-fi is not offered on *The Canadian*, mainly because the train passes through very remote areas with no cell phone coverage or wi-fi network available.

Wi-fi is, however, offered at a number of **train stations**, including Halifax, Quebec City, Montreal, Toronto, Winnipeg, Edmonton, Jasper and Vancouver. Wi-fi access costs $9 per day, or you can buy unlimited access for 30 days from $30.

The Skeena

The *Skeena* service from Jasper to Prince Rupert, completed in 1914 by the Grand Trunk Pacific Railway, is a two-day daylight-only journey, in direct competition with the privately operated *Rocky Mountaineer* (see p20). *The Skeena* is arguably the most beautiful rail journey in Canada, taking you through the

❑ FARES ON *THE SKEENA*

Economy class is available year-round; during the off-peak period (mid-September to May), Economy-class passengers have access to an observation dome. During the peak period (from June to mid-September), **Touring class** is offered, which includes access to the observation dome car as well as meals served at your seat.

Jasper to Prince Rupert

Economy	Supersaver	Touring class
Year-round	Year-round	June to mid-September
$199	$110	$486

Touring class includes three meals a day and access to a dome car. There are no advance-purchase discounts in Touring class on The Skeena.

heart of the Rocky Mountains and ending in the misty, deep-green fjordland of north-west British Columbia. You're on board the train for about 21 hours.

Passengers spend a night in Prince George en route and must arrange accommodation there themselves. You can call VIA for assistance with hotel bookings: ☎ 250-562-3700 for Prince George and ☎ 250-624-5637 for Prince Rupert. We also give some suggestions on p216 and p220.

The trains are the same stainless-steel ones used by *The Canadian*.

The Hudson Bay

The train that takes you on the 1000-mile journey up to Churchill has rather gone to seed. Operated by VIA, it's as old as *The Canadian* but lacks its elegance and expensive renovations. All the same it has a charm and character all of its own and travelling aboard *The Hudson Bay* is a magical railway experience.

For a start, there'll be very few of you on the train unless you go in the middle of the polar bear season. This creates a camaraderie among the passengers and by the second night you may find yourself playing poker, drinking whiskey, swapping spurious anecdotes, telling obscene jokes and singing Abba songs.

Life on the train gets particularly interesting north of The Pas as you're joined by Cree and Chepewyan natives, or wizened fishermen and trappers. For once you're travelling not only with fellow tourists or elderly Canadians but face to face with an entirely different culture. The railway provides a vital link for the small communities along this northern stretch of the route.

The crew on *The Hudson Bay* is uniformly relaxed and friendly and, to tell the truth, a little on the eccentric side. This is no doubt due to the fact that most of them have been working this lonely line for many, many years. They know the route inside out, back to front; they will happily tell you

The Canadian gets a washdown during its 70-minutebreak at Jasper station
PHOTO © MELISSA GRAHAM

❏ FARES ON *THE HUDSON BAY*

Winnipeg to Churchill
Economy class

Full fare	Supersaver
$299	$170

Sleeper class

Upper Berths		Room	
Full fare	cheapest	Full fare	cheapest
$497	$298	$562	$338

Tickets are the same price year-round on the Hudson Bay.

everything they know about the land you're travelling through and will point out osprey, geese, teal and ducks, giving you the names of all the wild flowers, trees and lakes that you're passing. In winter it's also worth keeping an eye out of the window even when it's dark, as this is the place to catch the spectacular northern lights.

The journey on *The Hudson Bay* takes 43 hours, setting out from Winnipeg around noon, arriving in Churchill at around 7am two days later.

The Rocky Mountaineer

In 1989, the Armstrong Group took over *The Rocky Mountaineer* from VIA Rail and launched Rocky Mountaineer Railtours (now Rocky Mountaineer Vacations). It subsequently (and with some justification) dubbed its daylight-only routes as 'the most spectacular train trips in the world', becoming a roaring success.

The flagship ***Rocky Mountaineer*** train travels along three two-day routes, each with an overnight stop in Kamloops or Quesnal included in the package: the 'First passage to the West' from **Vancouver to Banff/Calgary**; the 'Journey Through the Clouds' from **Vancouver to Jasper**; and the 'Rainforest to Goldrush' from **Whistler to Jasper**. In addition, the 'Whistler Sea to Sky Climb' is a three-hour trip on the old BC Railway lines from **Vancouver to Whistler**. All train rides can be taken in either an eastbound or westbound direction.

There are two ways of travelling on *The Rocky Mountaineer*: Red Leaf or Gold Leaf service. **Gold Leaf** passengers travel in an ultra-luxurious dome car – and pay a few hundred dollars extra for the privilege. The dome area seats 74 people who are assigned seating there for the whole of the journey. Downstairs there's an open-air observation platform and a dining area which serves hot gourmet meals (included in the price).

At either end of the dome car are the ordinary coaches where you'll be if you're travelling **Red Leaf**. These are nowhere near as stylish as VIA's stainless-steel fleet and you might be disappointed by the absence of a dining car or observation dome if you've already taken *The Canadian*, although there are complimentary snacks and large picture windows from which to admire the views.

The Rocky Mountaineer, moreover, excels in other ways, primarily with their onboard **service attendants**. Each carriage has its own attendant who

❏ **FARES ON *THE ROCKY MOUNTAINEER***

Note: These fares **do not include tax**, which is an additional 2.5% if you book your tickets from outside Canada, or 5% if you book the tickets from within Canada.

	Peak June–Sept	**Mid-Season** May & early Oct	**Off-peak** April
Vancouver–Calgary			
Red Leaf:	$989	$809	$709
Gold Leaf:	$1919	$1739	$1379
Vancouver–Jasper			
Red Leaf:	$889	$709	$609
Gold Leaf:	$1769	$1589	$1229
Whistler–Jasper			
Red Leaf:	$889	$709	no service
Gold Leaf:	$1769	$1589	no service

Prices are per person, based upon double occupancy. Fares include overnight accommodation in Kamloops or Quesnal and meals on the train.

Vancouver–Whistler (mid-May to Sept)

	Classic service	**Dome service***
One Way:	$129	$219
Round Trip:	$219	$329

* Dome service includes assigned seating in a dome coach; both services include access to an open-air observatory car.

(ingenious recruitment policies ensure) will almost certainly be warm, outgoing and charismatic, putting passengers at their ease and taking excellent care of everyone. His or her duties include serving you breakfast, lunch, snacks and soft drinks at your seat (included in the price of the package) and providing you with commentary about the route. This is one of the highlights of the trip: the attendants have obviously been required to learn large volumes of information by heart, as their knowledge of the history of the railway and the landscape you pass through is encyclopaedic. They also do a good line in amusing anecdotes and corny jokes. Our attendant told us the railway workers constructing the line from Kamloops to Revelstoke were so fed up with the local fare – moose for breakfast, moose for dinner, moose for tea – that they expressed their frustration in the name they chose for the next station we were to pass. It was Sicamous. One attendant is also known to switch out the lights and recite Shakespeare through the five-mile Spiral Tunnels.

The Rocky Mountaineer is essentially group travel and the service attendants encourage everyone to join in, getting people to look out for mile markers or shout out to the others if they see any wildlife. This makes for a highly enjoyable atmosphere (even if group travel isn't normally your cup of tea), though the real draw is, of course, the magnificent **scenery** and the luxury of travelling through it all in daylight.

Overall costs

The overall cost of a rail trip across Canada can vary enormously, depending mainly on when you go, how many nights you spend off the train (and the kind of accommodation you choose to stay in), the length of your rail journey, the type of ticket you buy and how you get to Canada; see p11 for details on how to book your ticket and take advantage of the many discounts and special fares on offer.

There are several major expenses to consider, including travel to and from Canada, train tickets within Canada, accommodation and day-to-day living.

Getting to Canada

The first is **getting to Canada**; the exact price of this depends on where you are coming from, of course, but for those heading from outside North America it will probably be a significant portion of your overall budget. From the UK, expect to pay from around £300 (low season) or from £550 (summer) flying into Toronto and out of Vancouver; and from £600 (summer) into Halifax and out of Vancouver. For more on flights, see pp25-6. Note that if you're on a package your flights should be included.

Train tickets

The box on p11 has some useful advice on obtaining discount tickets but, even if you do manage to secure the cheapest possible tickets you are still looking at a fairly hefty sum. From **Halifax to Vancouver**, the cheapest fare would be with a Canrail Pass for $588 (plus 13% tax) during the off-peak season, and $941 (ditto) at peak period. Sleeper class tickets on this route would cost from around $700 off-peak, and from $1250 during peak period.

Hotel costs

Prices are nearly always per room rather than per person, with most doubles only a few dollars more expensive than singles. This makes travelling in a pair extremely good value but lone travellers can end up feeling rather hard done by. Bear in mind that room rates are often quoted before taxes are added on (typically an extra 13% – see p54).

Upmarket hotels tend to offer exceptionally good value compared to their European counterparts, with rooms going from around $240 – just $120 (about £70) each if there are two of you. Note that it's usually cheaper to stay in these places at weekends, since weekday 'rack rates' are designed with business travellers in mind – and the cheapest deals are usually available only online.

❏ **Room rates – high season, double occupancy**
Unless otherwise stated, the hotel room rates given are for high-season double rooms, before tax. Prices in most hotels drop a lot in low season (around November to April).

Typical **mid-range accommodation** will give you a double with a private bathroom for around $80-130, though prices can vary significantly depending on location and the general state of the place.

Budget travellers can count on paying about $25 for a youth hostel bed in the smaller cities and about $28 in the bigger places (more for non-members). Single rooms in university residences usually cost around $50-60, with discounts normally given to students.

PACKAGE TOURS

When you add the cost of accommodation to these prices, it can sometimes work out cheaper to get a **package deal**, particularly if you plan to stay in upmarket hotels. In the UK, packages start at around £1600 for a two-week trip in the low season, including flights into Toronto and out of Vancouver, the rail journey between the two, and all hotel accommodation. This price is closer to £3000 in the peak season, going up around £4000 for the more expensive luxury holidays. In the US and Canada, trans-Canada packages start at around $2000 (note all prices quoted are in Canadian dollars) for ten days out of season (and from around $3400 in peak season), and usually exclude the cost of transport to and from Toronto and Vancouver (or alternative start/end points). We list selected UK **rail tour companies** on p26, and Canadian companies on p28.

When to go

Corny as it may sound, Canada is beautiful in every season. Autumn is a tourist attraction in itself as the country's forests turn into a glorious blaze of reds and golds, especially in eastern Canada. In winter the snow-covered landscapes are dazzling, but best experienced from the comfort of a train; you have to be pretty hardy to cope with sightseeing in sub-zero temperatures. Canadians, like hedgehogs, tend to hibernate in these cold months so city centres can be depressingly empty. Spring is lovely in Canada (as spring usually is anywhere) with May temperatures averaging 13-15°C/55-59°F in most cities. The warmest and sunniest months are July and August when temperatures average around 25°C/80°F in places on the line.

Of course, there's more than the weather to take into account in deciding when to go. An important consideration is the cost of the trip: rail fares and hotel rates are considerably cheaper out of the tourist season (with off-season generally considered to be between October/November and April). It's also

---

❏ **Prices in the book – Canadian $**
Note that all prices in this book are given in Canadian dollars unless otherwise indicated. At the time of writing, the exchange rate was Canadian$1 to US$0.94 or UK£0.62.

Halifax
Max/min temperatures

Toronto
Max/min temperatures

Winnipeg
Max/min temperatures

Churchill
Max/min temperatures

Calgary
Max/min temperatures

Vancouver
Max/min temperatures

much easier to get train reservations in the quieter months, whereas peak period sleeper tickets should be booked five to six months in advance. Something else to bear in mind is the number of fellow tourists you can expect to be surrounded by on your visit: July and August are very, very busy, so if you're going to Canada for its tranquillity and big empty spaces, give these months a miss.

Making a booking

WITH A TOUR OR ON YOUR OWN?

Canada is one of the easiest and most hassle-free countries in the world to travel in and arranging a trans-Canada rail trip is an extremely uncomplicated process. You can **book your tickets online** on VIA's website from anywhere in the world, and collect them from your departure station on arrival in Canada (or arrange to have them sent to your home address). This is the best way to make a booking as you can see which discounted tickets are available on which dates of travel. Alternatively, if you don't like the idea of booking online, VIA have a number of **overseas booking agents** (see box p27) who can make a reservation for you over the phone. Similarly, booking flights and accommodation is a much easier process than it once was, thanks to the internet.

In light of this, it hardly seems worth taking a package tour, particularly as you can decide exactly how much time you want to spend where if you organize it yourself, whereas this decision will usually be taken for you on a tour.

Moreover, independent travel invariably works out cheaper if you plan to stay in mid-range or budget accommodation.

Where **tours** come into their own is if you want to stay in upmarket hotels. Many tour operators put you in luxurious establishments such as the former Canadian Pacific hotels now owned by Fairmont; they make block bookings which means they get big discounts, so you often end up paying less than if you booked the accommodation yourself.

Escorted tours take most decision-making and the responsibility of getting from A to B out of your hands, which can be a good or a bad thing depending on what you're after. Bear in mind, though, that the pace of some tours can be considerably more gruelling than that of independent travel as you will be whisked off on countless sightseeing trips in between your days on the train.

MAKING A BOOKING IN BRITAIN AND IRELAND

Booking your rail tickets

It's very easy to book your tickets using VIA Rail's **online booking** engine (🖳 www.viarail.ca), which allows you to compare the various fares available for different dates of travel. When you make an online booking, you will receive confirmation by email, which you use to collect your tickets from your departure station. If you prefer to receive your tickets in advance by post, you can arrange for them to be sent to you for a small extra cost.

Alternatively, VIA's UK sales agent is **1st Class Holidays** (☎ 0844-499 0771 or 0161-877 0432, 🖳 www.1stclassholidays.com). They should be able to answer all queries relating to fares, routes and availability and can book all your tickets for you, both for VIA and *The Rocky Mountaineer*. If you want to get in touch with VIA Rail directly you can send an email via its website or call them on ☎ +1 514-989-2626.

Getting to Canada from mainland UK

If you're organizing your rail reservations yourself you'll need to sort out your **flights** as well. Note that the sample fares we quote here are for **return flights** from London, including airport taxes.

The obvious choice is **Air Canada** (☎ 0871-220 1111, 🖳 www.aircanada .com), as they have more flights to more places in Canada than any other airline. Like most airlines, they offer 'open jaw' tickets which allow you to fly into one point and out of another; the fare is calculated by halving the cost of a return to each destination and adding them together. As a rough guide, typical Air Canada fares to Halifax go from £550 in winter and £850 in summer, to Montreal and Toronto from around £370 in winter and £570 in summer, to Calgary from £490 in winter and £670 in summer, and to Vancouver from around £530 in winter and £730 in summer.

Other scheduled airlines flying to Canada from the UK include **British Airways** (☎ 0844 493 0787, 🖳 www.britishairways.com), and **KLM Royal Dutch Airlines** (☎ 0871 231 0000, 🖳 www.klm.com).

You might also want to consider getting a cheap ticket from a **charter airline**. The charter season generally runs from May to October, with some destinations served only in July and August. Fares are difficult to pin down but as a rule you can get from London to Toronto from around £320 in low season and from £420 in high season; and to Vancouver from £420 in low season and from £500 in high season. Charter flights to Halifax (often just in July and August) go from around £540, while flights to Edmonton and Calgary start at around £350 in low season, and from £550 in high season. The main charter airlines serving Canada are **Air Transat** (☎ 020-76169187, 🖥 www.airtransat.co.uk) and **Thomas Cook Airlines** (☎ 0844-8550515, 🖥 www.thomascookairlines.co.uk). Flights with both airlines can be booked through **Canadian Affair** (☎ 020-7616 9184, 🖥 www.canadianaffair.com), which also offers a range of add-ons and full package holidays. Another good flight and holiday agent is **Travelpack** (☎ 08705-747101, 🖥 www.travelpack.co.uk).

Getting to Canada from Eire and Northern Ireland

There are fewer options for flights to Canada from Eire and Northern Ireland, though between May and October **Air Transat** (🖥 www.airtransat.ie, from Eire ☎ 018 666700, from Northern Ireland ☎ 02890 312312) offers a very convenient service from Dublin and Shannon to Toronto and Montreal, from around €350 return in low season and from €600 return in high season. **Air Canada** (🖥 www.aircanada.com, from Eire ☎ 01 800 709900, from Northern Ireland ☎ 0871-220 1111) and **British Airways** (🖥 www.britishairways.com, from Eire ☎ 1890-626747, from Northern Ireland ☎ 0844 493 0787) both offer year-round scheduled flights to Toronto, Vancouver and other Canadian cities from Dublin and Belfast, via London; typical return fares to Toronto, for example, are around €520 in the winter and around €800 in summer.

Booking a package tour

If you're short of time and can't face the thought of planning all the details yourself, then package tours are a good solution. When choosing which company to go with, an important consideration – besides the itinerary and price – is whether you want an escorted tour or an unescorted one, as some companies offer only one or the other. Many tours combine a VIA rail trip with a ride on *The Rocky Mountaineer* (see p68); a common itinerary is Toronto to Jasper with VIA, Jasper to Banff by motor coach, then Banff to Vancouver on *The Rocky Mountaineer* (or the same in reverse). Also very popular are packages that concentrate on western Canada, which also combine VIA routes with *Rocky Mountaineer* routes and in some cases incorporate a ferry cruise down the spectacular Inside Passage from Prince Rupert to Vancouver Island too. Note that prices quoted below include flights and all accommodation.

● **1st Class Holidays** (☎ 0161-877 0433, 🖥 www.1stclassholidays.com). Besides serving as VIA Rail's UK sales agent, 1st Class Holidays also offers a wide choice of Canadian package holidays, including a couple that incorporate rail travel on the Rocky Mountaineer (from £2995).

● **Archers Direct** (☎ 08044-573 4806, 🖥 www.archersdirect.co.uk). Among this company's escorted rail tours is 'the Best of Western Canada', which combines the Inside Passage ferry trip from Port Hardy to Prince Rupert with a ride on the Skeena from Prince Rupert to Jasper (14 days, from £1714).

❏ **VIA RAIL INTERNATIONAL SALES AGENTS**
VIA Rail has a number of **sales agents** dotted around the world. These act as VIA's representatives: they answer rail enquiries, send out timetables and book tickets for you, which you buy in local currency. Most of them also act as agents for Rocky Mountaineer Vacations, who operate *The Rocky Mountaineer* (see p20).

Europe
● **Austria**: Canada Reisen ☎ 2243-25994, 🖥 www.canadareisen.at
● **Germany**: Canada Reise Dienst International ☎ 49-40-3000 6160, 🖥 www.crd.de
● **Netherlands**: Incento BV ☎ 035 69 55111; 🖥 www.incento.nl
● **UK**: 1st Class Holidays ☎ 0844-499 0771 or 0161-877 0432, 🖥 www.1stclass holidays.com (see p26)

Australia & New Zealand
● **Australia**: Asia Pacific ☎ 612-9319 6624, www.aptms.com.au
● **New Zealand**: Adventure World New Zealand ☎ 64 9 524 5118; 🖥 www.adventureworld.co.nz

Asia
● **Japan**: Japan Travel Bureau Inc ☎ 03-5366-1780, 🖥 jtb@jtb.com.uk
● **Hong Kong**: Japan Travel Bureau ☎ 2734 9288, 🖥 jtb@jtb.com.uk

● **Great Rail Journeys Ltd** (☎ 01904-521936, 🖥 www.greatrail.com). This excellent rail-holiday specialist offers a range of escorted rail holidays in Canada, including a 17-day 'Coast to Coast' trip from Vancouver to Halifax, starting at £2995 per person.
● **Travelpack** (☎ 0870-121 2020, 🖥 www.travelpack.com/Canada). This Canadian specialist offers a range of VIA and Rocky Mountaineer unescorted rail packages. Their 15-day Trans-Canada package starts from £1620 in low season and from £1965 in high season.

MAKING A BOOKING IN CANADA AND THE USA

Booking your rail tickets
Either book your **VIA Rail** tickets online, on VIA's easy-to-use website (🖥 www .viarail.ca), or call the booking line toll-free from anywhere in Canada or the USA on ☎ 1-888-842-7245 (or ☎ 514-989-2626 from Montreal).

Similarly, you can book tickets directly with **Rocky Mountaineer Vacations** on their website (🖥 www.rockymountaineer.com) or by phone (☎ 604-606-7245 or toll-free from Canada and USA ☎ 1-877-460-32000).

Getting to your starting point
The chances are you will need to get yourself to the starting point of your Trans-Canada rail journey either by plane, coach or train. Here are some contact details:

● **Amtrak** 🖥 www.amtrak.com, ☎ 1-800-872-7245 (toll-free). Direct rail connections with VIA: New York to Montreal or Toronto (via Niagara Falls); Chicago or Detroit to Toronto; Seattle to Vancouver.

● **Greyhound** 🖥 www.greyhound.com, ☎ 1-800-231-2222. North America's biggest coach company operates services throughout Canada and the USA, and between the two countries.

● **Air Canada** 🖥 www.aircanada.com, ☎ 1-888-247-2262 (toll-free). Numerous flights within Canada and between the USA and Canada.

● **West Jet** 🖥 www.westjet.com, ☎ 1-888-937-8538 (toll-free). Canadian airline offering low-cost flights within Canada and between the USA and Canada.

● **Travel Cuts** 🖥 www.travelcuts.com, ☎ 1-866-246-9762 (toll-free). Discount-flight specialist with branches throughout Canada.

● **STA Travel** 🖥 www.statravel.com, ☎ 1-800-781-4040 (toll-free) or ☎ 212-822-2700. Low-cost flight specialist, with many branches across the USA.

Booking a package tour

The following is a small selection of specialist operators offering package rail holidays in Canada. Note that **fares quoted below are in Canadian dollars**.

● **Rail Travel Tours** 🖥 www.railtraveltours.com, ☎ 1-866-704-3528 (toll-free) or 204-897-9551. A wide range of unescorted rail tours is offered by this small Winnipeg-based company run by Daryl Adair, the author of a railway guidebook (see p30), who puts together his programmes with much experience and enthusiasm. A great choice for rail enthusiasts. The 10-day 'Across Canada' package starts at $1995.

● **Discover Holidays** 🖥 www.discoverholidays.ca, ☎ 1-800-243-0129 (toll-free) or 604-639-9062). This Vancouver-based company offers a huge choice of unescorted rail holidays (usually combined with some coach travel) throughout Canada, including a 10-day Trans-Canada package from Toronto to Vancouver from $2587.

● **Fresh Tracks** 🖥 www.freshtracks.ca, ☎ 1-866-296-5877 (toll-free) or 604-737-8743. Operated by a British-American couple based in Vancouver, this excellent company offers a wide selection of unescorted rail tours in Canada, including a 19-day 'Coast to Coast' (from $6490), a 13-day 'Across Canada by Train' from Toronto to Vancouver (from $3311) and a five-day 'Best-Value Rockies by Train' (from $1246).

Visas and insurance

VISAS

Visitors from the UK and Ireland don't need a visa to get into Canada, just a full passport. Nor are visas required by citizens of Australia, Austria, Belgium, Chile, Denmark, Finland, France, Germany, Greece, Hungary, Iceland, Israel, Italy, Japan, Luxembourg, Malaysia, Malta, Mexico, Monaco, the Netherlands,

New Zealand, Norway, Saudi Arabia, Singapore, Slovenia, South Korea, Spain, Sweden, Switzerland, United States and Zimbabwe.

In addition, citizens of most Commonwealth countries or British dependent territories do not need a visa. Check with your nearest Canadian Embassy or High Commission.

If you do need a visa you should contact the Immigration section of a Canadian Embassy or High Commission and ask for a visa application form. This must then be submitted in English or French. You also have to pay a visa processing fee – $75 for single entry, $150 for multiple entry. Visas are valid for six months.

HEALTH AND TRAVEL INSURANCE

The only health precaution you need to worry about when planning a visit to Canada is medical insurance – and it is vital that you arrange this before your trip as medical treatment in Canada is extremely expensive. The best way to do this is through a general **travel insurance** policy, which should also include loss or theft of baggage and cash as well as transport delay or cancellation.

Popular travel insurance companies **in the UK** include **Columbus** (☎ 0870-033 9988, 🖥 www.columbusdirect.com), **Endsleigh** (☎ 0870-241 3070, 🖥 www.endsleigh.co.uk) and **STA Travel** (☎ 0871-230 0040, 🖥 www.statravel.co.uk).

In Canada and the US, well-known companies offering travel insurance include **Travel Guard** (☎ 1-800-826-4919, 🖥 www.travelguard.com), **Sun Life** (☎ 1-877-786-5433, 🖥 www.sunlife.ca) and **Seven Corners** (☎ 800-335-0611, 🖥 www.sevencorners.com).

What to take

CLOTHES

If you're going in winter, warm **clothing** is absolutely essential and should include a heavy coat (or a good down jacket), a hat, gloves and generous supplies of thermal underwear. You should also take a pair of warm, water-resistant boots ('moon boots' are perfect, though the fashion-conscious may draw the line here). The key thing to remember when dressing comfortably for a Canadian winter is to wear lots of layers which you can easily remove when inside heated buildings and then throw back on when you head outdoors again.

For the rest of the year the weather is more or less comparable to that in the UK, though if you're taking the train up to Prince Rupert in spring or autumn or to Churchill at any time of the year, be sure to pack the hat, gloves and thermals.

One of the most important things to get right is **footwear**. Sightseeing is a tiring business and shouldn't be attempted in anything other than a pair of very comfortable shoes. Special walking shoes may be your best bet as these can double up for walking in the Rockies if you plan to get off at Jasper.

MEDICAL SUPPLIES

You won't have any trouble at all getting hold of medical supplies in Canada, so only the most basic items need to be included in your luggage (paracetamol, antiseptic cream and plasters should be enough). When flying, remember to check current security restrictions about carrying liquids and creams in your hand luggage before you pack.

MONEY

The easiest way to obtain cash in Canada is to withdraw it from **ATMs/cashpoints** at banks, using your debit card (see pp48-9 for more on this). It would be unwise, however, to rely on the card as your sole means of obtaining money, just in case it's stolen. In this case, travellers' cheques are an handy backup; even if they're stolen you can claim back their value very easily, though be very careful to keep the numbers in a safe place.

BACKGROUND READING

Trees and lakes are all very well but they can get a bit tedious in large doses. Reading of some sort is essential on the train and is all the more interesting if it's relevant to your journey. Besides being good for passing the time en route, a bit of well-chosen pre-trip reading can be wonderful for getting you in the mood for your rail trip – and an evocative memento after you're back home.

Books about the railway
● ***The National Dream*** and ***The Last Spike*** by Pierre Berton. Eminently readable best-sellers on the trials, tribulations and dramas involved in building the first transcontinental railway across Canada (turned into a TV mini-series in the 1970s). They're also published together in an abridged version called ***The Great Railway***, widely available throughout Canada.

● ***Van Horne's Road*** by Omer Lavallée. Detailed and exhaustively researched book chronicling the construction of the Canadian Pacific Railway – by the man who set up the Canadian Pacific Archives. Lots of wonderful old black-and-white photos.

● ***Passing Trains*** by Greg McDonnell. This large-format hardcover book charts the recent history of Canada's railroads from the Atlantic to the Pacific. Beautifully illustrated with stunning colour photographs, this is the perfect pre-trip buy. Another great book by the same author is *Canadian Pacific: Stand Fast, Craigellachie!*, a tribute to the CPR, packed with evocative photos.

● ***The Kids' Book of Canada's Railway and How the CPR was Built*** by Deborah Hodge. If you're taking children on your rail trip, this is a good bet to whet their appetite. Suitable for ages 8–12.

● ***Canadian Rail Travel Guide*** by Daryl Adair. This thoroughly researched paperback guidebook is packed with information on Canada's trains and rail lines, including route descriptions and histories of the communities the lines pass through. The author, a life-long rail enthusiast, is the owner of Rail Travel Tours in Winnipeg (see p28).

● *Canadian Pacific Railway* by Tom Murray. Hard-cover large-format book offering a well-told overview of the history of the CPR illustrated with lovely colour photos throughout.

The following are out of print but should be available from second-hand book-sellers via Amazon, or in libraries.

● *Scenic Rail Guide to Western Canada* and *Scenic Rail Guide to Central & Atlantic Canada* by Bill Coo. Collectively the bible of Canadian rail guides, written by a man who worked on the lines for over 30 years. Used to be given away free on *The Canadian* but now out of print.

● *Ocean to Ocean* by Rev George M Grant. The author accompanied Sandford Fleming, head of the Canadian Pacific Survey, on his mammoth expedition across Canada in 1872. The book is a chronicle of the journey and a fascinating insight into Canada before the railway.

● *The Queen's Highway* by Stuart Cumberland. Lively account of the railway journey from Port Moody to Halifax by one of the CPR's first passengers.

History and general accounts

For a more general spread of background material, try some of the following:

● *A Short History of Canada* by Desmond Morton. Sensible and highly read-able history book by a renowned historian.

● *Penguin History of Canada* by Robert Bothwell. Lively, briskly paced account of Canadian history – an excellent overview, written by a University of Toronto history professor.

● *The Unknown Country: Canada and her People* by Bruce Hutchison. Awarded the Governor General Award for non-fiction, this fascinating narra-tive gives a mid-20th-century perspective on transcontinental travel in Canada. Inspired by a conversation with a New Yorker who wanted to know more about the unknown neighbour to the north, it took Hutchison only six weeks to write.

● *Canadians: A Portrait of its Country and its People* by Roy Macgregor. Inspired by Hutchinson's *Unknown Country* (see above), this engrossing and enlightening book seeks to give an up-to-date take on the country's national identity, taking in everything from hockey to immigration.

● *So, You Want to Be Canadian: All About the Most Fascinating People in the World and the Magical Place They Call Home* by Kerry Colburn and Rob Sonrensen. An entertaining, jokey celebration of Canada and its people. Light-hearted, but not short of insight.

● *The Battle for Room Service* by Mark Lawson. Reflections of a British jour-nalist as he travels through the 'world's safest places,' including Vancouver, Winnipeg, Toronto and Montreal. Cynical, scathing and hilarious.

● *The Great Lone Land* by Capt W F Butler. The evocative impressions of a young soldier as he journeys into the depths of Canada's North-West at the time of the Riel rebellion in 1870. The book was a bestseller when it was published in 1872 and is now back in print. Highly recommended.

● *Lost in the Backwoods* by Catherine Parr Traill. One of several books by Parr Traill offering a fascinating insight into the life of the early settlers building a new life in rural Ontario in the mid-19th century. The author moved to Canada from England in the 1830s with her sister, Susannah Moodie, who also chronicled her experiences with books such as *Roughing it in the Bush: Or, Life in Canada*.

Fiction

● *The Canadian Companion to Canadian Literature* by Eva-Mari Kroller (ed). The best introduction to Canadian literature, with themed chapters covering topics such as 'francophone writing', 'exploration and travel' and 'literature'.

● *The Edge* by Dick Francis. Dastardly doings on a private, luxury train as it crosses Canada, with some good landscape descriptions amongst the intrigue and suspense. Don't read it if you're travelling alone.

● *The Republic of Love* by Carol Shields. A superb comic romance by one of Canada's best contemporary novelists, set in the unlikely location of Winnipeg.

● *Cat's Eye* by Margaret Atwood. Excellent, sensitive novel about a painter who returns to Toronto to find it – and herself – indelibly changed.

● *Maria Chapdelaine* by Louis Hémon. Enduring bestseller written in 1913 about a young girl's life in the backwoods of northern Quebec. It veers towards sentimentality but nonetheless paints a vivid picture of the uncompromising harshness of frontier life.

● *The Shipping News* by E Annie Proulx. Pulitzer prize-winning novel set in a remote village on the Newfoundland coast. Apart from being a wonderful read it gives you an insight into the incredible regional diversity within Canada.

● *Barney's Version* by Mordecai Richler. Richler is one of Canada's best-loved living writers, and *Barney's Version* is one of his finest works – a fictional memoir of a middle-aged Montrealer, recounting his tragi-comical life. For a taste of the author's output, try *Mordecai Richler Was Here: Selected Writings*.

● *The Tenderness of Wolves* by Stef Penney. Set in the nineteenth-century Canada of trappers, settlers and the Hudson's Bay Company, this best-selling page-turner is a convincing evocation of Canada's frontier landscapes – despite the fact that the agoraphobic author has never set foot in Canada.

(**Opposite**) The image that has graced a million calendars, chocolate boxes and jigsaw puzzles – Lake Louise (see p228), in Banff National Park. (Photo © MG).

(**Overleaf**) Some Canadian wildlife.

WILDLIFE FROM THE TRAIN

You know it's out there but it's doing its damnedest to hide from you. Still, the vigilant observer should be rewarded with a few sightings – here's a rough guide to what to look out for and where. Note that changes to the timetables can mean that some of the places below are passed by in the dark; check : www.via.ca for the latest schedules.

● **Ocean** Tantramar Marshes near Amherst: Canada geese, marsh hawks, black ducks, blue-winged teal; Mont-Joli area (currently passed at night): moose and deer.

● **Canadian** Whiteshell Provincial Park (around Rice Lake): black bear, deer, moose, coyotes and beavers; near Viking: elk, coyote, ruffed grouse; Wabamun Lake (near Edmonton): moose, beaver, white-tailed deer; Rocky Mountains: grizzly and black bear, moose, elk, caribou; mountain goats, bighorn sheep; Coast Mountains: osprey, bald eagles, bears.

● **Skeena** Rocky Mountains: (see above); Endako to Smithers: moose; Pacific: bears; Skeena Valley: many bald eagles.

● **Hudson Bay** Wildcat Hills Wilderness Area near Hudson Bay (SK): bear, lynx, wolves, deer; Cormorant Lake, near The Pas: geese, teal, crow-ducks, other waterfowl; approaching Churchill: arctic ptarmigan, snow geese, arctic fox, caribou.

● **Rocky Mountaineer** Grizzly and black bear, moose, elk, caribou, mountain goats, bighorn sheep, osprey, bald eagles.

Above: Polar bear (© MT). **Opposite page**: (clockwise from top): Rocky Mountain goats (© TBC); Elk, Banff National Park (© JM); Mountain sheep (© TBC); Moose, near Jasper (© JM); Brown bear (© JM); Mountain sheep; Chipmunk (© MG).

CANADA

2

Facts about the country

BACKGROUND

Great stretches of wilderness, so that its frontier is a circumference rather than a boundary; a country with huge rivers and islands that most natives have never seen, a country that has made a nation out of the stops on two of the world's longest railway lines. **Northrop Frye**, *Sudia Varia*, 1957

Canada is the second largest country in the world (after Russia), covering a vast 9,970,610 sq km (almost four million square miles). It's flanked by the Atlantic on the east and the Pacific on the west, with some 6000km in between. Its southern boundary is the US border, which follows the 49th parallel from the Pacific to the Great Lakes, then loops all over the place between Lake Ontario and the Atlantic. To the north Canada stretches all the way up to Ellesmere Island in the Arctic Ocean, 4400km away from Toronto. In the north-west is the other US/Canada border, separating the Yukon and British Columbia from Alaska.

This colossal area is divided into ten provinces and three territories: Newfoundland, Nova Scotia, Prince Edward Island, New Brunswick, Quebec, Ontario, Manitoba, Saskatchewan, Alberta, British Columbia, North West Territories, Yukon Territory and the territory of Nunavut (see box p34). The capital of Canada is Ottawa; its largest city is Toronto.

CLIMATE

In 1881 a British periodical called *Truth* described Canada as 'frostbound for seven or eight months in the year....[and] as forbidding a country as any on the face of the Earth', a familiar but slightly unfair stereotype that persists to this day. Admittedly, it does get rather chilly in winter (everywhere except the west coast has average January temperatures well below freezing point and continuous snow cover) but the populated stretch along the south has very good springs and warm summers. A typical July on the prairies, for instance, is dry and hot (usually mid-20°sC/70°sF) while an average summer in Quebec and Ontario will be warm and humid. West coast summers tend to be temperate rather than hot but winters here are the mildest in the country,

---

(Opposite) Totem Pole (see p233), British Columbia. (Photo © MG).

CANADA

> ### Nunavut – the new territory
>
> On the somewhat inauspicious date of April Fool's Day 1999 a new territory was carved out of Canada's North West. Two million square kilometres in size, the place is one-fifth of Canada's total land mass and two-thirds of its coastline. It's the traditional home of the Inuit, once called Eskimos by Europeans. The name of the new land is **Nunavut**, which means 'Our Land'.
>
> For at least four thousand years the Inuit lived on the barren tundra of what's now northern Canada, developing a harmonious relationship with their harsh lands. Their first contact with Europeans was in the mid-1700s when whalers started visiting the Arctic seas. They remained pretty much untroubled by Europeans until the 1940s when the Canadian government began to establish itself in the area the Inuit were persuaded to abandon their traditional nomadic life and to base themselves in fixed settlements. Today there are 25,000 Inuit in Nunavut, living in 28 communities.
>
> The new territory faces a whole slew of problems. Not least is its sheer size: in Nunavut population density is just one person per 100 square km compared with 29 as the average for Canada as a whole. Other problems are economic: the average household in Nunavut earns only two-thirds of what a family in southern Canada earns, yet the cost of living is about twice as much. Traditional ways of life such as hunting and trapping are under threat, particularly from ecologically minded Westerners who object to fur trading. The Canadian government has attempted to foster alternatives, particularly (and imaginatively) a craft industry, and Inuit soapstone carvings can now be seen all over the country (look for the trademark Igloo stickers and tags to check for authenticity).
>
> Despite its problems, the Canadian government is optimistic about Nunavut's future and sees the establishment of the territory as an indication of the more sensitive way in which aboriginal people are treated in the country.
>
> One example is the government of Nunavut itself. It has been designed with an eye on the people it is to govern – it's highly decentralized, spread across 11 different communities and the traditional knowledge of the Inuit elders is built into the government systems.
>
> In 2002 Queen Elizabeth II, on her jubilee tour of Canada, acknowledged the new territory by visiting Nunavut's capital, Iqaluit, on Baffin Island, which is more than she did for the people of Quebec who were not included in her itinerary.

thanks to the influence of the warm Pacific Ocean (Vancouver's average January temperature is 3°C/37°F, compared to Winnipeg's –20°C/–4°F).

Moving further north, the 'frost-bound' label is rather more justified; indeed much of the upper two-thirds of the country is continuously affected by *permafrost* (ground remaining at or below 0°C/32°F for at least two years). The only train taking you into this frozen region is *The Hudson Bay* to Churchill, where winter temperatures regularly drop to –30°C (–22°F).

TRANSPORT AND COMMUNICATIONS

As might be expected in a country of this size and economic ranking, Canada's transport infrastructure is extensive and efficient. The majority of internal communications run east–west, such as the Trans-Canada Highway connecting St Johns (Newfoundland) to Vancouver – the longest national highway in the world at 7821km.

Rail remains an important means of transporting freight, principally bulk commodities like grain, lumber and coal, which are often carried in 'unit trains' of a hundred or more cars. It has been overtaken, however, by the car and the aeroplane as the chief transporters of people around the country. Shipping provides another important means of freight transportation, both from ocean ports like Vancouver and Halifax, and along the Great Lakes/St Lawrence Seaway system.

LANDSCAPE ZONES: FLORA AND FAUNA

The main landscape zones you'll travel through on your trans-Canada rail journey are as follows:

St Lawrence Lowlands

Spreading across the northern shores of the Great Lakes and east along the St Lawrence River towards the Atlantic Ocean, this is the most densely populated area of Canada. The high degree of urbanization and industrialization in this region is interrupted by large areas given over to agriculture and forestry, mainly mixed conifers such as red spruce and pines, and various deciduous trees, red and sugar maple in particular. In autumn their blazing red foliage is spectacular and draws thousands of tourists each year.

Canadian Shield

This is Canada's dominant geographic feature, stretching in a massive band from Hudson Bay down to the Great Lakes and east into Labrador. It spreads over 4.5 million sq km, much of it covered by Precambrian rock (570–1100 million years old). The erosive effects of glaciation over the last million years have scoured the Shield's surface, leaving a striking landscape of bare rock and countless lakes, rivers and streams. Much of the Shield is covered by coniferous **boreal forest** (millions of spruce, larch and pine, plus some poplar and aspen).

Tundra

As they approach Churchill, travellers aboard *The Hudson Bay* will find themselves in the most barren and inhospitable part of the country covered by rail track. Tundra is a region of permafrost and bitter cold where vegetation is stunted and sparse. The few trees that can survive here (mainly birch) rarely grow higher than a metre and most of the earth is covered by lichens, shrubs and mosses, though the most beautiful wild flowers spring up for a few weeks in summer. Wildlife, on the other hand, is plentiful, though most of it is well camouflaged: Arctic fox, Arctic ptarmigan, white squirrels and caribou are all local inhabitants.

The prairies

The vast expanse of land between the Shield and the Rockies is part of the Interior Plains spanning the whole length of Canada from the US border up to the Arctic coast. The famous part of the plains is the southern fertile belt, known universally as 'the prairies'. This is where Canada's wheat is produced, an average of 25 billion tonnes of it each year. It's known for its extreme flatness, especially in Saskatchewan; the Alberta prairies are a little more undulating. The

The Great Lakes
Lakes Superior, Michigan, Huron, Erie and Ontario are known collectively as the Great Lakes. Together they make up the largest body of freshwater in the world, with a total area of over 246,000 sq km. Apart from Lake Michigan, which lies entirely within the United States, they are located on the border between Canada and America. The largest is Lake Superior which is 563km long, 257km wide and reaches a depth of 406m. It is the largest freshwater lake in the world.

area was once home to enormous numbers of bison: an estimated 50–60 million roamed the plains in 1800 but had been hunted almost to extinction by 1885. These days you'll probably see little more than crops and grain elevators as you pass through.

Western Cordillera

The western mountains are part of the massive 14,000km-long chain that spans the length of the continent from Tierra del Fuego right up to Alaska. In Canada they're made up of several ranges, the most famous and most easterly being the **Rockies**. West of these is the Columbia system (the Purcell, Selkirk and Monashee ranges) followed by the Coast Mountains.

The Rockies are your best bet out of the entire route for spotting wildlife (see colour section pp64-5). In spring and summer you'll also be treated to a profusion of wild flowers with beautiful names like Indian Paintbrush and Glacier Lily. As you move into central British Columbia the terrain becomes arid and is sparsely covered by low shrubs such as sagebrush and prickly pear. Much of the coastal range, in contrast, is covered by luxuriant green fir trees, particularly towards Prince Rupert, with its dripping rainforest, cliffs, mosses and fjords. These mountains are home to numerous bald eagles; sightings are almost guaranteed.

HISTORICAL OUTLINE

First Nations

The first inhabitants of what we now call Canada arrived from Asia between 12,000 and 20,000 years ago, having crossed the land bridge connecting Siberia to North America. A second wave of migration from Asia occurred around 3000BC. These people spread themselves around the continent, adapting and developing according to the different environments they settled in. By the time the European explorers 'discovered' Canada, it was populated by a range of distinct peoples with differing languages, belief systems, lifestyles and traditions. The tribes scattered between the Yukon and the Atlantic led a hunting-gathering existence and fell into two language groups: Athapaskan and Algonquin. To the south were the agricultural-based communities of the Iroquois. Far north were the Innu who had adapted to life in the harsh conditions of the Arctic tundra. Tragically, all native peoples were rapidly depleted with the arrival of European diseases to which they had no immunity.

O Kanata!

It is ironic that the name of the second largest country in the world is derived from a word meaning 'village'. Cartier, in 1535, was directed to 'kanata' by a couple of Huron-Iroquois youths. They were referring to the village of Stadacona, where Quebec was later founded, but Cartier applied the word to the whole area subject to the rule of Donnacona, the chief of the village. The name somehow stuck and gradually came to be used for the region around the St Lawrence, and then for all of New France, but its boundaries were always vague and never officially delineated by the ruling French.

When the British took over New France they temporarily abandoned the name of Canada and called their new territory the Province of Quebec. The name was revived in 1791 when Quebec was divided into Upper Canada and Lower Canada, which were joined together again in 1841 as the single Province of Canada. Finally, when Nova Scotia, New Brunswick and Canada united in Confederation in 1867 they became 'One Dominion under the name of Canada'.

French colonization

Early visitors to Canada's Atlantic coast included the Vikings around 1000AD, John Cabot in 1497 and scores of European fishermen soon after. It wasn't until the beginning of the 17th century that a permanent European settlement got going when Samuel de Champlain, following the course down the St Lawrence River taken by Jacques Cartier 70 years earlier, set up a small colony in 1608 at what is now Quebec City. It was a great success and another settlement was founded at present-day Montreal in 1642. The French presence gradually spread throughout the region and in 1663 New France was officially declared a royal colony.

The Hudson's Bay Company

New France was the source of a vast supply of furs which fed the insatiable demands of European fashion and it wasn't long before France's arch rival, Britain, decided to muscle in on the action and corner a share of the profits of this new land for itself. In 1670 the Hudson's Bay Company (HBC) was set up to exploit the wealth of fur-trading possibilities around Hudson Bay. Charles II claimed thousands of miles of land around the bay and granted this to the Company; they named it Rupert's Land after the King's cousin, Prince Rupert, who was instrumental in creating the company. Trading posts were erected throughout the area and intense rivalry developed between the HBC and French traders which continued for the next century, often spilling over into violence.

New France becomes British

Meanwhile, Britain's involvement in Canada was not limited to the fur trade: renewed efforts were being made to drive the French out of their Atlantic settlements in Acadia (the name given by the French to their territories bordering the Atlantic, that once spread over eastern Quebec, the Maritime provinces and New England), which the British had renamed Nova Scotia. In 1713 the Treaty of Utrecht gave Britain what it wanted and the French were forced to hand over their mainland Atlantic territories. Still not satisfied, Britain pushed for control of the remaining French strongholds, notably Quebec with its prime position on the St Lawrence River. In 1759 the conflict came to a dramatic head when the British attacked Quebec City, scaling the Heights of Abraham in the night and defeating the French in the famous battle on the Plains of Abraham. By now France was ready to wash its hands of the troublesome North American colonies and in 1763 it officially ceded all of New France to Britain.

The division of Quebec

In contrast to the treatment meted out to the Acadians who were forcibly deported in the 1750s, the Quebec Act of 1774 safeguarded the rights of the French Canadians to speak their own language, practise Catholicism, hold civil appointments and keep their seigneurial land-owning system. However, they soon found themselves deluged with 10,000 Loyalist settlers (following the American War of Independence) who clearly did not expect to be governed according to the French system. In an attempt to get round this problem, the province of Quebec was divided into Upper Canada and Lower Canada in 1791. This way the French speakers, concentrated in Lower Canada, could remain separate from the English-speaking Protestants in Upper Canada with each side controlling their own local affairs.

The 1837 rebellions

In practice the French Canadians were increasingly discriminated against and the ensuing tide of resentment resulted in a violent but short-lived rebellion in 1837 led by Louis-Joseph Papineau. Upper Canadians had their own political grievances, too, expressed in a more scaled-down and equally abortive rebellion led by William Lyon Mackenzie in the same year. The British government's response was to reunite the two provinces in 1840, forming the single province of Canada which would be granted greater powers of self-government. It was hoped that this would bring the French Canadians into line and curb their demands for self-rule. As time would show, it was to do nothing of the sort.

Confederation

Britain's North American colonies got bigger and bigger as immigration stepped up in the 1840s. Many politicians recognized that the separate provinces would be economically and politically stronger if they were to unite – and strength was an all-important issue given the aggressive annexationist tendencies of the United States. At the same time, Britain was ready to give the colonies more autonomy: it was wearying of the huge cost of defending them for virtually no returns. So, after a big Confederation campaign and a few years of debate, the dominion of Canada came into existence on 1 July 1867 when the British North America Act became law. It consisted of the former colonies of New Brunswick, Nova Scotia and Canada (subsequently divided into Ontario and Quebec). These were shortly joined by Manitoba (1870), British Columbia (1871), and Prince Edward Island (1873).

Forging a nation

Canada's first Prime Minister was the Conservative leader, Sir John A Macdonald, a man blessed with both pragmatism and vision. Realizing that the links binding the provinces together were extremely tenuous, he set about strengthening the nation by expanding its territory and filling it with people. One of the major bedrocks of this policy was the creation of a transcontinental railroad which would physically join the provinces from east to west and transport a flow of goods, trade and immigrants across Canada. Accordingly, the first act of his government was to purchase from the Hudson's Bay Company the vast expanse of land between Ontario and British Columbia (still known as Rupert's Land) where settlers would be sent out to populate the southern, fertile stretch. This was not without its complications...

The first Riel rebellion

Rupert's Land had been almost but not completely unpopulated. At the meeting of the Red and Assiniboine Rivers (the site of present-day Winnipeg) was the small and isolated Red River Colony, made up principally of the Métis people (mixed French and Indian). When the government dispatched colonists and officials to 'settle' the area in 1870, the Métis, stirred up and organized by the passionate Louis Riel, staged a violent protest. Riel issued a series of demands to the Canadian government based on the creation of a French and English-speaking province with the provision of French-speaking schools. The government complied and the province of Manitoba was created but Riel was forced to flee to America following the execution of a Canadian by the Métis.

The second Riel rebellion

Fifteen years later, tensions between the Métis and the Canadian government broke out in a second rebellion. This time the Métis were supported by the Cree and Plains Natives whose lands had been encroached on by speculators and farmers. Louis Riel was whisked back from America (where he had been experiencing prolonged bouts of mental illness) to lead the rebellion, which he threw himself into with fervour. The uprising was crushed by Canadian troops, hastily transported to the scene by the almost completed railway, and Riel was captured and sentenced to death for high treason, even though he was clearly mentally unfit at the time. Riel was hanged in November, 1885 – immortalized for the French Canadians as a symbolic victim of brutal Protestant oppression.

Prosperity

It was prosperity, and not confrontation or drama, that characterized Canada's entry into the 20th century. Certainly the following decades were to bring their problems, such as the paralysing Depression of the '30s. On the whole, however, the nation followed a pattern of growth and success. New provinces were incorporated (Alberta and Saskatchewan in 1905); immigrants flooded in and the wheat empire of the prairies boomed. Meanwhile, successive Canadian governments, dominated first by the Conservatives and then by the Liberals after 1921, began to steer Canada along a more independent path, gradually severing all constitutional ties with Britain. In the mid decades of the 20th century, a series of prestigious projects such as the Trans-Canada Highway and the St Lawrence Seaway fostered a growing sense of nationhood, and in 1965 Canada finally adopted its own flag – the red maple leaf. This new-found national pride was further boosted by the hosting of major international events such as Expo '67 and the 1976 Olympic Games. However, national harmony was disrupted as French Canadian discontent took on a louder voice in the '60s and '70s.

THE QUEBEC ISSUE

Political awakening

French Canadians had been subjected to a multitude of social and economic injustices ever since the British had taken over New France in 1763. Incredibly, it wasn't until the 1960s that their grievances were given a coherent political voice by Quebec's provincial government, under the Liberal premier, Jean Lesage. In response, a Royal Commission was set up in 1963 to investigate the situation. It concluded that Francophones earned less, had a lower standard of living and were less likely to advance economically and socially than their Anglophone counterparts. It also warned that the situation was heading towards a national crisis.

The crisis duly exploded in 1970 when the militant separatist group, the Front de Libération du Québec (FLQ), embarked on a wave of terrorism culminating in the kidnapping and murder of a Quebec politician, leaving the country in a state of shock.

Parti Québecois in power

Meanwhile the nationalist wing of the Liberal Party in Quebec had broken away to form the Parti Québecois (PQ) under René Lévesque. In 1976 the PQ won provincial elections and Lévesque became Quebec's premier. The party turned Quebec into an officially monolingual province with a series of controversial language laws that triggered an exodus of thousands of Anglophones from Montreal. However, it failed to achieve its goal of independence when 60% of Quebec voters rejected the mild form of separation ('sovereignty-association') proposed by the 1980 referendum.

The 1995 referendum

In 1990 the Bloc Québecois was formed to represent Quebec's cause at a federal level. It was phenomenally successful, gaining the highest number of votes after the Liberal Party in the 1993 federal elections, making the Bloc Québecois the official government opposition. In 1995, fifteen years after the original referendum, a new sovereignty referendum was called in Quebec, considerably more radical than the first. Under the charismatic leadership of Lucien Bouchard, the separatist movement gained massive momentum and Quebec seemed to be spinning inexorably towards independence. In the event, the separatists were defeated by just one per cent of the vote, leaving the issue far from resolved. However, in 1998 the Supreme Court of Canada ruled that if Quebec were ever to separate it would have to negotiate with federal government and the provinces.

TWENTY-FIRST CENTURY CANADA

In February 2006 Stephen Harper led the Conservative Party to victory in the general election, ending 12 years of Liberal rule. With only a minority government,

Harper called a snap election in October 2008, in which his party was re-elected – but without the majority lead that Harper had hoped for. Nonetheless, despite a certain lack of charisma and popularity, the Prime Minister has been praised for his careful management of the country's economy, leaving it less vulnerable to the recent financial crisis that has dogged the USA and the UK. One of Harper's most publicized domestic strategies has been to assert Canada's sovereignty over its Arctic territory, amidst fears that Russia, Denmark and the US are interested in staking territorial claims there.

Meanwhile, the Quebec independence movement has become a less urgent domestic issue, with polls revealing a decline in support for separation. The Parti Québecois was defeated in the 2003 provincial elections, which were won by the Liberal Party. In late 2006 parliament decreed that the Quebec people should officially be considered a 'nation' within a united Canada – a largely symbolic gesture with no legal ramifications.

ECONOMY

Voltaire somewhat underestimated Canada's potential when he dismissed it as 'several acres of snow' in 1759. In fact, it boasts one of the world's richest bases of natural resources including huge mineral deposits (potash, zinc, nickel, iron, copper and gold), generous supplies of coal, oil, gas and phenomenal quantities of trees. Almost half the country is covered in forests, providing pulp for the paper industry, as well as timber for the construction industry. In addition, the western prairies are among the world's biggest grain producers and Canada's great provisions of water (what isn't covered by trees seems to be covered by lakes and rivers) is the source of a massive supply of hydroelectric power.

All this has been carefully and efficiently exploited to make Canada one of the richest countries in the world. It has developed a highly successful

Native settlement, Queen Charlotte Island, late 19th century.

industrial and manufacturing sector: major industries include vehicle manufacturing, logging, pulp and paper, and fish processing. Its most important trading partner is the US, which receives 75% of Canadian exports and provides 60% of Canada's imports, though Mexico looks set to play a larger role in Canada's economy now that NAFTA (North American Free Trade Agreement) is in operation. Most Canadians enjoy a very good standard of living but unemployment remains high at around 7%.

THE PEOPLE

Canada's population of 33.6 million people is concentrated in a thin east–west strip in the south of the country – indeed 90% of all Canadians live within 150km of the US border. This pattern of settlement follows the path taken by the transcontinental railways and, much later, by the Trans-Canada Highway. The climate is considerably milder here than in the more northerly parts of Canada and the land is more suitable for farming. The most densely populated provinces are Quebec and Ontario where about 62% of Canadians live. Even in the most populated areas of these provinces there are a mere 60 people to each square kilometre – compared to a miserable 230 per square kilometre in the UK.

The immigrants

Immigration has necessarily played a key role in boosting Canada's population and economy. Today, Canada's biggest ethnic group is of British origin (almost 50%) followed by that of French origin (about 27%). First the need to populate the prairies and then the shortage of a post-war workforce resulted in an influx of non French/British immigrants – mainly Germans, Italians, Finns, Ukrainians and Poles. Today, about 20% of Canadians are of European extraction other than French or British. Canada's immigration policies have often been characterized by racial discrimination; for example, Chinese and Japanese were virtually banned from settling in the country between 1885 and 1940. Since the 1970s, however, immigration policies have become increasingly liberal and Asians have constituted a high proportion of the annual 100,000 or so people settling in Canada over recent years.

The native peoples

At the time of early European contact, Canada had an indigenous population of up to two million people. The 2001 Canadian Census revealed that there are over 900,000 aboriginals in Canada and these consist of about 45,000 Inuit, until recently known as Eskimos, and around 600,000 descendants of the First Nations community (see p36). The remainder are 'non-status' Indians who have either abandoned their status rights or are of mixed blood, known as Métis.

The decline of these people is the saddest story of modern Canada. Initially, their numbers were ravaged by the arrival of Western diseases such as TB; then they were manoeuvred into a state of near-dependency on the fur traders and their European goods; finally they were forced off their land by British colonists and shunted into inadequate, isolated reservations where

> **Canada's a great place to live – it's official**
> Ever since the UN started to publish its annual Human Development Index in 1990, Canada has been at or very near the top. From 1994 to 2000 it was ranked in first place for seven years running – an achievement that's never been matched by any other country. The index looks at standards of living, measured by GDP per capita, life expectancy and achievements in education, including adult literacy.
> Canada has recently been nudged from the top spot by Norway but given that the index is composed of around 170 countries, it's unlikely anyone's too worried.

they witnessed a complete breakdown of the lifestyle that had served their people for thousands of years. For many native communities, the legacy of modern Canada has been high unemployment, alcoholism and depression.

On a more positive note, the Assembly of First Nations (AFN) has been formed to provide native peoples with political and legal representation. In 1992 the AFN scored a huge victory by negotiating a settlement for the Inuit land claim: in 1999 Nunavut (in the North West Territories) became a separate territory, governed by native Canadians. This is the first time in modern Canadian history that natives have been responsible for local government.

GOVERNMENT

Canada is a federal state with democratic parliamentary representation. It is also a constitutional monarchy (Queen Elizabeth II is still the official head of state). The way it works is that each of the provinces has its own government with its own premier and its own legislative body. They're in charge of things like taxes, social welfare, education, transport and general administration. Then there's the federal government in charge of everything else. Executive power is in the hands of the Prime Minister and his or her cabinet. Legislative power rests with the Canadian Parliament in Ottawa, consisting of the House of Commons (elected) and the Senate (appointed by the Prime Minister).

Since Confederation in 1867, central power has swung between the Conservatives and the Liberals with few major differences between the two. The other main party is the New Democratic Party (mildly socialist). The current Prime Minister is Stephen Harper of the Conservative Party.

EDUCATION AND SOCIAL WELFARE

Canada spends a higher percentage of its GDP on education (over 7%) than any other country in the world. It has a universal, free and compulsory school system: all children are required to attend elementary and secondary schools from the age of six to about sixteen.

Education is the responsibility of the provinces, not the federal government, which results in distinct differences across the country. Newfoundland, for example, has an exclusively denominational school system, whereas BC's is totally non-denominational. Controversial issues have included the provision of minority language teaching (eg for Francophones outside Quebec, for

Anglophones inside Quebec and for the children of immigrant groups) and the often ill-conceived programmes for the education of native children. There are 69 public universities in Canada and over 200 other post-secondary institutions.

Canadians are proud of their social welfare system, which provides free medical care, old age pensions, family allowance and unemployment insurance. The costs of these programmes are shared by the federal and provincial governments, and Canadians can generally take advantage of them whether they're in their own province or an outside province.

RELIGION

Religious mythology and ceremony were highly developed among the native peoples before the arrival of the Bible-brandishing Europeans. Beliefs and practices often differed from tribe to tribe but some were shared by many groups such as the myth of the Earth Diver in which the Transformer plunges into the ancient waters and gathers the mud from which he moulds the earth. Another common myth told of the mischievous Trickster who steals fire, light, water and food and sets them all lose to create a chaotic world.

Catholicism was, of course, imported by the French as soon as they arrived. Indeed, the Catholic Church provided the foundations for the society of New France and continued to be a dominant power in Quebec until recent decades. British settlers, on the other hand, were Protestant and set about populating the country with more of their ilk. The resulting pattern continues today: over 90% of Quebeckers are Catholic, while Protestantism (of various sects) dominates all the other provinces. All in all, about 90% of Canadians claim to be Christian. These include significant numbers of Orthodox Christians, particularly in the prairie provinces. The remaining 10% are made up principally of Jews, Muslims, Sikhs, Hindus and Buddhists, large numbers of whom are centred in or around Toronto.

Practical information for the visitor

DOCUMENTS

Americans aren't officially required to show a passport when crossing the border (just solid ID), though it's very much preferred. For everyone else, a full passport is mandatory. You must also be able to provide evidence that you will be leaving the country within three months (eg a return or onward air ticket).

A copy of your travel insurance policy should also be at the top of your document checklist and if you plan to rent a car remember, of course, to bring your driver's licence. Other useful ID includes student or senior citizen cards which will get you substantial reductions at most museums, tourist attractions and train tickets. Travellers' cheques are still widely accepted, though they are slowly falling out of use now.

❏ **Senior tip**
'It's worth mentioning the Senior Citizens' Discount. We always asked if it applied and in most places we were lucky and got a 10% discount.'
James and Joan Fundell (Cyprus)

ARRIVING IN CANADA

Before you touch down (or when you arrive at the border if you're coming over-land), travellers who don't need a visa (see pp28-9) will be given a waiver form to complete and hand in at passport control. If you do need a visa you'll have to line up in a separate queue at passport control and show your visa documen-tation. If you're travelling alone, and/or are staying for more than a few weeks and/or have a vaguely shifty look about you, be prepared to answer a long list of searching questions from a Port of Entry examining officer about your trav-el plans/job back home/childhood holidays in Brighton. If you're travelling as a couple or family, especially if you've got a couple of kids in tow, you should be spared the detective work.

Customs

Import allowances are: 200 cigarettes and 50 cigars, 200gm tobacco; 1.1 litres of spirits or 8.5 litres of beer (for persons aged 18 or over in Alberta, Manitoba and Quebec, aged 19 elsewhere in Canada) and gifts worth up to $60 each. Any food, plants and animals among your luggage must be declared to Customs.

HOTELS

Canada is well supplied with hotels and most of them are of a high standard. Many of the **upmarket hotels** are enormous and luxurious establishments, boasting grand lobbies, sumptuous dining rooms and state-of-the-art gym and pool facilities. Among the best – and certainly the most appropriate for the trans-Canada railway traveller – are the old Canadian Pacific Railway hotels (now owned by Fairmont), many of them built to accommodate wealthy tourists travelling across the country at the turn of the 20th century.

Mid-range hotels are usually clean, well-equipped and comfortable. They fall into two broad categories: the large and faceless (usually with good facili-

❏ **Online tourist information**
We list the relevant tourist office websites for individual cities and provinces at the start of each city guide in Part 4 of this book. In addition, the **Canadian Tourism Commission** has a very good website, customized for various countries, including the following:
Canada: 🖳 http://caen.canada.travel; **USA**: 🖳 http://uscw.canada.travel;
UK: 🖳 http://uk.canada.travel; **Australia**: 🖳 http://au.canada.travel;
France: 🖳 http://fr.canada.travel; **Germany**: 🖳 http://de.canada.travel

ties which nearly always include private bathroom, TV and phone) and the smaller inn or guest-house type of place, ranging from the very elegant to the distinctly shoddy. It is these smaller places that have the most character, particularly in the numerous converted Victorian or Georgian homes in eastern Canada, but some of them can be a little spartan. Mid-budget travellers might also consider the private en-suite rooms increasingly on offer in many hostels – see below.

The most popular base for **budget travellers** seems to be the Hostelling International youth hostels. On the whole their standards are excellent (small dorms, cafeterias, laundry rooms, plenty of hot showers and usually internet access), though this is reflected in their prices. Many HI hostels now offer private rooms with en-suite bathrooms in addition to their traditional dormitory accommodation – they're usually immaculate and make an attractive alternative to mid-range hotels.

Other popular budget accommodation is provided by university residences during the summer months – typically a small and rather basic private room with shared bathroom facilities. In addition, some YWCA and YMCA hostels offer accommodation to travellers (sometimes with free use of pool and gym), though some cater mainly for Canadians in need of temporary accommodation. Hostels in general are much cleaner and more pleasant than the really cheap 'hotels' you'll find adjoined to some of the less salubrious downtown bars, many of which are rowdy doss-houses left over from the days when alcohol could be served only in places that had rooms to let.

LOCAL TRANSPORT

Local transport in Canadian cities is exactly as you'd expect it to be: wide-ranging and frequent, clean, safe and efficient. In many remote areas, however, it is non-existent, so if jumping off the train at a trappers' flag stop in northern Ontario takes your fancy, don't expect to find a local bus network to transport you around.

Taxis

These are numerous in all cities and even small towns have their fair share of them. Fares are comparable to those in Europe. Note that it's customary to give cab drivers a tip of about 10-15%.

Subway

There are subway systems in Montreal and Toronto. Both are clean, safe and always busy but since there are relatively few lines it's often as quick to walk or take the bus if you just want to get around the downtown core.

Buses

Bus travel is far better than taking the subway as you can see where you're going and get a better idea of the city's geography. Buses are the mainstay of local transport in Canada with extensive routes in every city. You'll be able to get a route map at the local tourist office or you can ring the local transport information line – for the number, see the Transport section of the relevant city guide in this book.

One slightly irritating thing about buses is that to travel on them you need the exact change, which you deposit in a plastic box in front of the driver. There's usually a flat fare of about $2 or so.

Internal flights

Canada's cities are spaced out over thousands of miles, which makes flying the quickest and most convenient way of getting between them. Accordingly, the country's internal flight network is highly developed and heavily patronized. The main carrier is Air Canada (🖥 www.aircanada.com), serving hundreds of places in the country, including some of the most remote outposts such as Inuvik on the Arctic Coast. A smaller, low-cost competitor is WestJet (🖥 www .westjet.com).

Internal flights are cheaper if booked outside Canada (you don't have to pay tax); if you plan to take more than one flight, enquire about air passes.

Ferries

Canada has plenty of busy local ferry services such as those from Halifax to Dartmouth, Lévis to Quebec City, Vancouver to Victoria, and from Newfoundland, Prince Edward Island and Cape Breton Island to the mainland. New Brunswick operates toll-free ferries across the Saint John and Kennebecasis rivers as part of the highway system. The most popular ferry service among tourists is probably the spectacular 15-hour ride up the Inside Passage from Port Hardy on Vancouver Island to Prince Rupert, operated by BC Ferries (🖥 www.bcferries.com, ☎ 250-386-3431, or toll-free 1-888-223-3779). The Canadian Tourism Commission's website (see box p45) lists all ferry services operating in Canada (go to 'About Canada' and then 'Getting around').

Car rental

Renting a car in Canada is expensive (at least $500 a week). As well as your driver's licence it helps to have a major credit card, especially if you're under 25. People under the age of 21 aren't normally eligible to rent cars. If you're intending to hire a car in one city and drive to another part of Canada, it's usually possible to leave the car at the end of the journey – however, beware of 'drop-off fees' which can be fairly steep, and be sure to shop around to see who has the best offer. Note also that International Driving Permits aren't valid without a supporting national driver's licence.

ELECTRICITY

This is 110 volts AC. Sockets take two-pronged flat-pin plugs or adaptors. Be sure to buy the adaptor before you get to Canada because they're very difficult to obtain once you're there as, understandably, most stores sell the other type of adaptor, for Canadians travelling to Britain.

TIME

Canada has six standard time zones which are between $3^1/_2$ and 8 hours behind GMT as follows:

- Newfoundland Time   −3¹/₂ hrs
- Eastern Time   −5 hrs
- Mountain Time   −7 hrs
- Atlantic Time   −4 hrs
- Central Time   −6 hrs
- Pacific Time   −8 hrs

On the first Sunday in April the clocks are put forward an hour into Daylight Saving Time, which lasts until the last Sunday in October. This does not happen in most of Saskatchewan. Train timetables always show local time and indicate when the transition into a new time zone is made.

MONEY

Currency

Canada has a decimal currency system: 1 dollar is divided into 100 cents. Coins come in 1, 5, 10, 25 and 50 cent denominations, as well as the $1 coin (referred to by Canadians as a 'loonie' after the bird on one side) and the $2 coin (rather amusingly known as a 'toonie'). Notes come in $5, $10, $20, $50, $100, $500 and $1000 bills and unlike American currency, which is all the same colour, Canadian notes come in a number of different colours: $5 is blue, $10 is purple and $20 is green, which means there's less of a chance of handing over a $20 instead of a $5 once you've got used to the various colours.

❏ **Rates of exchange**

Can$1=US$0.94	US$1=Can$1.06
Can$1=€0.75	€1=Can$1.35
Can$1=UK£0.62	UK£1=Can$1.61
Can$1=Australia$1.11	Australia$1=Can$0.89
Can$1=NZ$1.37	NZ$1=Can$0.73
Can$1=Singapore$1.31	Singapore$1=Can$0.76

For up-to-the-minute rates of exchange visit:
🖳 www.xe.com.

The Canadian dollar has been very weak against the US dollar for the last few years, which is one of the reasons why American tourists are flocking to Canada.

Withdrawing cash

By far the easiest way to get your Canadian currency is to withdraw cash from an ATM/cashpoint at a bank, of which there are dozens in all Canadian cities, using your debit card. The amount you withdraw is then automatically debited from your account back home.

Most debit cards can be used worldwide at ATMs displaying either a Cirrus or a Maestro symbol. The advantages are obvious: most ATMs operate 24 hours a day, seven days a week, so you don't have to worry about bank closing times. Note, however, that many banks add a 1.5% handling fee to the amount you withdraw; check with your branch before you go. In addition, some apply a minimum charge per transaction, making it more cost-effective to withdraw relatively large amounts of cash at a time; check with your bank before travelling. Make sure, too, that your card actually carries a Cirrus or Maestro symbol before heading to Canada. If it doesn't, your card can still be used but acts as a credit card rather than a debit card which may make withdrawals more difficult or even limit the number of times you can take money out within a week (this applies to Barclays customers, so check with your branch before heading abroad).

From an ATM you can also get a cash advance on a credit card (Visa or MasterCard); all major Canadian banks accept one of these, eg the Royal Bank of Canada takes Visa and the National Bank of Canada takes MasterCard.

Travellers' cheques

The traditional way to get your dollars is, of course, to take travellers' cheques. Some banks don't change these (and if they do you usually have to pay a commission) but many restaurants, hotels and shops will accept small-denomination American Express or Visa cheques as cash.

Credit cards

All major cards – eg Visa, MasterCard, American Express, Diners – are accepted throughout Canada and are a very useful backup. They can also be used for payment in taxis across the country, though of course you should always check with individual drivers that credit cards are accepted before travelling, as certain places, such as Jasper, do not offer this service.

No extra charges are made when you use the card to pay for goods and services but if you use it to get a cash advance you are normally charged a 1.5% handling fee.

Banking hours

Standard banking hours are 9.30am–4pm, Monday to Friday (and often until 6pm on Fridays). Some banks stay open later during the week and on Saturday mornings as well.

Tipping

Tipping, usually around 15% of the bill, is practically obligatory in restaurants. It is also standard practice to tip bartenders, taxi drivers, porters and doormen.

POST, INTERNET AND PHONE CALLS

Post services

Post offices are open 8am–5pm or 9am–6pm Monday to Friday; some big offices also open on Saturday mornings.

Many drug stores have post office counters inside (look for the Canada Post sign on the window) and you can buy stamps from countless newsagents, general stores, hotels or stamp machines.

It currently costs 98 cents to send a postcard to the US, and $1.65 overseas. The service is very reliable and speedy: it takes about five days for a letter to get from Toronto to London (London, England, that is, not London, Ontario). Aside from the usual services, most post offices also now provide a free **internet** terminal.

Email and internet

You'll have no problem getting connected to the internet while in Canada. All cities have plenty of cybercafés, and many public libraries and post offices offer free internet access for a limited period of time. There are always a couple of internet terminals available for guests' use in hostels and hotels – on average expect to pay about $3–5 per hour in hostels, and $1 per fifteen minutes in hotels. In addition, all HI hostels (and some private hostels) offer free wi-fi, and most hotels offer pay-per-use wi-fi. There is also pay-per-use wi-fi on VIA trains between Montreal and Toronto, but not on *The Canadian*. The service costs $9 per day, or you can buy unlimited access for 30 days for $30.

Making phone calls in Canada

It is *extremely* cheap to make international phone calls from Canada if you use one of the more competitive **international calling cards** offered by companies such as Econo Call. These work on any phone; you simply dial the number on the back of the card, key in the card's pin (usually found by scratching away the foil strip) then dial the number you want to reach. Rates for calling Europe are often as low as 7 cents a minute with a $20 card (the higher value cards give the best rates). The best places to find the cheapest ones are newsagents or corner shops (known as 'dime stores' or 'loonie stores') in the bigger cities. Youth hostels usually stock them as well but not always those with the lowest rates. When you do find a good deal, it's best to stock up on a few cards if you intend to call home often.

Another option is the **standard pre-paid phone cards** that you insert directly into public phones. The problem with these is that the companies owning public phones differ across the country, which limits the transportability of your card. You'll find MTT phones in Halifax, Bell phones in Toronto, Montreal and Quebec, MTS in Winnipeg, Telus in Edmonton and Calgary, and BC Tel in Vancouver.

A final option is to use the phones which allow you to swipe your **credit card** through – a very convenient way of calling but you need to watch the time or you can clock up a huge bill. Public phones in most of the big cities offer this facility; if you can't find one on the street try the phones in the lobbies of the big hotels. Attempting to make an international call with **coins** is so frustrating it's not worth thinking about.

As a general rule, it's very costly to use **hotel phones**. However, a few do offer free local calls, which is actually a great deal if you have one of those cheap calling cards (eg 'Call Mama' etc) that you see for sale in many shops. As these cards are routed through a local number, you can thus call home from your hotel room without having to pay the exorbitant international hotel calling rates (just the cheap rates attached to the card itself). If you're staying in any Fairmont hotels, join their free-membership 'President's Club', which gives you free local calls from your hotel room, and free internet access in most of their hotels.

If you plan to use your **mobile phone** in Canada, check with your provider in advance whether you'll have coverage in Canada, and whether your phone needs to be enabled for use abroad. Note that it'll be expensive to phone the UK from Canada on your mobile (around 50p per minute), so try to find a phone card that gives good deals on international mobile phone calls. You will also be charged to receive text messages and phone calls on your mobile phone.

❑ TELEPHONE CODES

Phoning Canada from abroad
First dial your country's international access code (usually 00) followed by 1 for Canada, then the appropriate area code and finally the seven-digit local number you wish to call.

Phoning abroad from Canada
Dial 00 followed by the relevant country code, and then the number you wish to call, omitting the first 0 from the area code if there is one. **Australia** ☎ 00 61; **New Zealand** ☎ 00 64; **UK** ☎ 00 44; **Eire** ☎ 00 35; **USA** ☎ 00 1.

Making phone calls within Canada
When making a phone call within Canada, either local or long distance, you must include the three-digit **area code**, eg ☎ 416 for Toronto, or ☎ 604 for Vancouver. If the call is long-distance (outside the local area from which you're calling), you must first dial 1, followed by the area code.

Nova Scotia ☎ 902; **Manitoba** ☎ 204; **Quebec City** (and around) ☎ 418; **Saskatchewan** ☎ 306; **Montreal** (and around) ☎ 514; **Calgary** ☎ 403; **Toronto** (metro) ☎ 416; **Edmonton** ☎ 780; **Vancouver** (and around) ☎ 604; **Prince George** ☎ 250; **Prince Rupert** ☎ 250

Useful phone numbers
Operator assistance ☎ 0; Directory assistance ☎ 411; Emergency services ☎ 911.

NEWSPAPERS

The most widely read broadsheet is the *Globe and Mail*; it has good nationwide and some foreign news coverage and is the only paper circulated right across the country.

Many cities have their own quality newspaper (eg the *Toronto Star*, the *Vancouver Sun*) as well as a selection of tabloids. Canada's answer to *Time* magazine is *Maclean's* which is available throughout the country.

HOLIDAYS

As well as national holidays, which apply throughout Canada, there are a number of provincial holidays. In both cases banks, offices, schools and some shops are closed, though restaurants and tourist attractions usually remain open.

National holidays
New Year's Day; **Good Friday**; **Easter Monday**; **Victoria Day**: Monday before 25 May; **Canada Day**: 1 July; **Labour Day**: first Monday in September; **Thanksgiving**: second Monday in October; **Remembrance Day**: 11 November; **Christmas Day**; **Boxing Day**

Provincial holidays
Alberta – Heritage Day: first Monday in August; **British Columbia** – British Columbia Day: first Monday in August; **New Brunswick** – New Brunswick

Day: first Monday in August; **Newfoundland and Labrador** – St Patrick's Day: 17 March or Monday before; St George's Day: 23 April or Monday before; Discovery Day: Monday nearest to 25 June; Memorial Day: Monday nearest to 1 July; Orangeman's Day: Monday nearest to 10 July; **Manitoba, NWT, Ontario, Saskatchewan** – Civic Holiday: first Monday in August; **Quebec** – St-Jean Baptiste Day: Monday before 24 June; **Yukon** – Discovery Day: third Monday in August

FESTIVALS

The Canadians take their festivals very seriously and there are great numbers of these events throughout the year, right across the country. The great diversity and frequent bizarreness of their themes reflect the contrasts contained within Canada. Interesting examples include the Trappers' Festival in The Pas, Manitoba (February), the Indian Festival in Chilliwack, BC (June), the Potato Festival in Grand Falls, New Brunswick (July), the Trout Festival at Flin Flon, Manitoba (July), the National Ukrainian Festival in Dauphin, Manitoba (August) and the Whoop Up and Rodeo Festival in Lethbridge, Alberta (August).

The major festivals of interest to the trans-Canada rail traveller are the Montreal International Jazz Festival (June/July), the Carnival de Québec in Quebec City (February), the Festival d'été in Quebec City (July) and Caribana, the Caribbean carnival in Toronto (August). These and other festivals are listed in the relevant city guides in this book. Alternatively, find out more on the Canadian Tourism Commission's website (see box p45), listed under 'Events and Festivals'.

FOOD

At the lower end of the scale, Canada holds few gastronomic surprises. The most prolific food outlets you'll come across are the standard Western fast-food chains (McDonald's, Burger King, Kentucky Fried Chicken, Pizza Hut and the countless spin-offs) crammed into 'food halls' in shopping malls and lining main streets. Added to these are the typical North American diners and countless bagel stores.

If you can afford to give the cheapies a miss, however, you can eat very well in Canada, with most cities offering a range of good-quality upmarket restaurants. Many of these are of the same ilk: stylish, minimalist places serving Californian-derived or West Coast cuisine – sort of healthy Mediterranean, with lots of 'pan-seared' (never just 'fried'!) fish and meat fillets, imaginatively cooked with fresh local produce. In addition, there are also some notable regional specialities. The Maritime provinces (New Brunswick, Nova Scotia and Prince Edward Island) are famous for their excellent fish, particularly their lobster, salmon, oysters and scallops. Then there's the province of Quebec, where the generally superb food owes far more to Gallic than to North American influences. At the same time, the choice in most big cities is considerably enlivened by a wide range of ethnic restaurants, typically Italian, Greek, Vietnamese, Chinese and Japanese.

CANADA

DRINK

Non-alcoholic

The nation's favourite non-alcoholic drink is **coffee**, which is invariably the freshly ground variety, served with milk or cream. Canadians drink a lot of it and empty cups are nearly always refilled at no extra charge. Perhaps Canada's most popular coffee chain, and certainly one of its proudest establishments, is the delightful Tim Horton's which was created by, and named after, a successful ice hockey player who died tragically in a car accident in 1974, at the age of 44 – ten years after opening his first coffee and donut shop in Hamilton, Ontario. Today, you'll find Tim Horton's, or 'Timmy's' as the chain is affectionately known across Canada, dotted along highways and on street corners of towns throughout the country. Despite being part of an extensive chain network, the atmosphere is friendly, the coffee is really rather good and for a mere $2 you can fill up on coffee and a fresh muffin.

Tea, on the other hand, is not a Canadian speciality. British travellers may well be shocked by the manner in which this is prepared: instead of pouring the boiling water *over* the tea or tea bag (essential for a good brew), they simply fetch you a pot of vaguely hot water with a tea bag lying limply by the side. Their **milkshakes**, on the other hand, are a credit to the country.

Alcoholic

The most popular alcoholic drink is **beer**. Most of it is brewed by Labatt's or Molson and tends to be on the light and fizzy side.

Another favourite is **whisky** – as well as importing foreign labels, Canada distils its own stuff. A good and seriously strong Canadian malt whisky is Yukon Jack, while popular rye whiskies are Canadian Club and Seagram's. Believe it or not Canada also has its own wine, produced from grapes grown in southern Ontario and BC and developing steadily in quality.

WHAT TO DO IN THE EVENING

While many of Canada's smaller towns offer little more than a seedy, rough-edged bar by way of evening entertainment, there's usually no shortage of options in the big cities.

Drinking takes place in numerous establishments including English-style pubs, super-trendy bars, mellow 'lounges' (sit-around-chat-and-relax kind of places) and hundreds of bog-standard dimly lit taverns. A lot of these places serve food, too, and some have regular **live music** slots (lots of folk, rock and indie – with the quality ranging from good to dire – and jazz, usually the safest bet).

If **dancing** is what you're after, the best place for this is Montreal, which boasts hundreds of nightclubs catering to all ages and tastes. This activity is less widely pursued in the other cities, apart from in the prairies where the extraordinary country-and-western 'line dancing' is still enjoying its revival.

If this sounds a bit too energetic, there's always the **movies** – Canadian cities have plenty of cinemas showing all the mainstream American output, which is screened there ages before it reaches the UK. You'll usually find a couple of local art-house cinemas as well, or cinemas showing mainly Canadian releases.

Theatre is particularly well represented in Toronto, which claims to be the third-biggest theatre city in the English-speaking world after London and New York. Certainly there's lots to choose from, ranging from Andrew Lloyd-Webber to Shakespeare to new Canadian talent.

Ballet (from classical to contemporary) is widely performed not only in Montreal, Toronto and Vancouver but also in Winnipeg, whose Royal Winnipeg Ballet is internationally respected. **Classical music** and **opera** enthusiasts should find enough to keep them happy among companies such as the Montreal Symphony Orchestra, the Canadian Opera Company (Toronto) and Vancouver Opera. Moreover, all this high-brow cultural entertainment is very good value (much cheaper than in London) with tickets ranging from about $15 to $50.

Finally, if none of this takes your fancy you can always join the best part of Canada's youth and simply sit around with a bunch of mates in a shopping mall.

SHOPPING

Shopping in Canada is, on the whole, no different from shopping in the US. Most of it takes place in malls, of which there are thousands spread across the country. The advantage of these is that they protect shoppers from Canada's fierce winter weather. On the downside, they're often oppressively crowded and the absence of natural light makes them a bit depressing.

The big department stores are Eaton's and The Bay (part of the original Hudson's Bay Company), which you'll find in every city. Most shops are open 9am–6pm, or later in the bigger cities.

Souvenirs

Prints of Inuit paintings (originals are very expensive) and Inuit soapstone carvings are popular with tourists and Canadians alike. Indian crafts are also undergoing a revival; you'll find some beautiful and reasonably priced goodies for sale, such as beaded moccasins and handwoven sweaters. Look out for the cooperative stores owned and run by natives themselves so you can be sure that the profits are all going back to the people who produced the goods. Moving west, local specialities include stetson hats and cowboy boots (obligatory if you're thinking of taking up line dancing). Finally, wherever you go in Canada you'll come across zillions of bottles of maple syrup.

TAXES

When you first arrive in Canada you'll be amazed at how cheap everything seems until you go and buy something and watch the price shoot up by about 13% at the checkout. This is because most things you pay for including food, drink and accommodation are subject to a 5% **Goods and Services Tax** (GST). In addition, British Columbia, Saskatchewan, Manitoba, Ontario, Quebec and

Prince Edward Island levy a 5–8% **Provincial Sales Tax** (PST) on goods, restaurant bills and sometimes hotel bills.

To complicate things further, Nova Scotia, Newfoundland and Labrador and New Brunswick have a **Harmonized Sales Tax** (HST) of 13% combining GST and PST, levied on goods, services and accommodation.

You can claim a rebate for GST/HST paid for goods subsequently taken out of Canada and for some accommodation **but you must keep all your receipts** You can also reclaim PST on goods bought in Quebec and Manitoba.

Booklets containing a claim form and details on conditions and restrictions are available in tourist offices and many stores and hotels.

CRIME

Canada justifiably has a reputation for being one of the safest countries in the world in which to travel. That said, crime against tourists isn't unheard of. Use your common sense: don't stray into the rougher neighbourhoods waving a map about; don't wander around alone late at night, women in particular; keep your important tickets and documents in a money-belt, preferably with a belt-style strap rather than a quick release catch. Also, be careful about where you leave your luggage: if you're staying in a hostel leave valuables in a locker and remember that even the most expensive, security-conscious hotels aren't invulnerable to petty thieves.

CANADA

3 RAILWAY HISTORY

Building the first trans-Canada railway

What tempted the people of Canada to undertake so gigantic a work as the Canadian Pacific Railway? The difficulties in the way were great, unprecedented, unknown... We were under the inspiration of a national idea, and went forward. We were determined to be something more than a fortuitous collection of provinces. **The Century** (1885)

The story of Canada's first transcontinental railway has a plot as thick as a Hollywood movie novel. The only thing missing is sexual intrigue; everything else is there: corporate greed, political skulduggery, brave men, bankruptcy, war, danger, death, glory... It's a story that has gripped Canadians for more than a century spawning countless books, an epic poem and, of course, the inevitable TV mini-series.

Canada's ongoing preoccupation with the railway is due not only to the drama surrounding its construction but also to the crucial role it played in shaping Canadian history. For the CPR did more than build a railway: it built a nation. 'It can be argued,' reads a display in Winnipeg's Union Station, 'that November 7th 1885 – the day on which the last spike was driven on the CPR line at Craigellachie – is a more appropriate day from which to date the existence of Canada than July 1st, 1867.' Rather a tall claim for a railroad. But to understand this railroad's significance it is necessary to abandon one's concept of modern Canada and take a look at the young dominion of the 1860s and 70s.

CANADA BEFORE THE RAILWAY

The infant country

Canada officially became a country when Queen Victoria signed the British North America Act on 1 July 1867, but in no way did it resemble the country we know today. The new 'dominion' was basically a disparate collection of eastern colonial provinces with no real sense of unity or nationhood. It covered a relatively small chunk of a vast territory, for the most part uninhabited. British Columbia, which remained under the jurisdiction of Great Britain, lay 3000 miles west of Ottawa, beyond the Rocky Mountains. Stretching east from the Rockies were the immense prairies, still controlled by the Hudson's Bay Company – barren and empty save the little Red River settlement where Winnipeg now stands.

Fear of the Yankees

To make matters worse, Canada lay in the shadow of a large, intimidating neighbour. The United States boasted an ever-growing population of 40 million, an alarming number of people next to Canada's scanty three and a half million. Moreover, America had been pursuing an aggressive policy of expansion and annexation for a number of years.

'That the U.S. are bound finally to absorb all the world and the rest of mankind,' declared a San Francisco newspaper in 1869, 'every well-regulated American is prepared to admit. When the fever is on our people do not seem to know when and where to stop, but keep on swallowing, so long as there is anything in reach.' Canada understandably felt threatened.

Some twenty years earlier America had effortlessly absorbed Texas and California. Then, in 1867, it purchased Alaska from the Russians for $7.2 million. Any fool could see that the Americans now had their eye on British Columbia and the North West – natural extensions of California and Minnesota. Indeed, for these isolated communities, America was their closest link with the outside world; annexation would in many ways be logical and sensible. The future of Canada was by no means assured.

Macdonald reaches across the continent

Sir John A Macdonald, Canada's first Prime Minister, firmly believed that if Canada were to survive as a nation it would have to expand westwards and take control of British Columbia, the Pacific coast and the giant stretch of land in between. But this was easier said than done. How were these areas to be obtained and consolidated? How were settlers to be induced to move west with virtually no east–west transportation or communication? The answer came in the form of a demand put to the government by British Columbia as a condition of entering Confederation: a railway across Canada to the Pacific.

The railway is promised

The British Columbians got their way; the province joined Canada in 1871 and in return the government formally pledged to build the railway. The terms agreed were somewhat optimistic: it was guaranteed that construction of the line, which would take an all-Canadian route instead of cutting south of the Great Lakes through America, would begin within two years of union, and that the railway would be completed within ten!

Macdonald rightly saw in this enterprise the key to the creation of a transcontinental nation. As well as securing Canada its sixth province, the railway would encourage immigration, carry thousands of settlers out west and open up trade with the Orient. But it wasn't going to be easy. The distances to cover were enormous, the expense would be colossal and the physical challenges of laying track across the mountains and the Precambrian Shield would be back-breaking. It took a man of Macdonald's expansive vision not to baulk at these difficulties. Others did indeed: the leader of the opposition, Alexander Mackenzie, was almost apoplectic in his outrage at what he repeatedly denounced as 'an act of insane recklessness!'

The survey begins

The first gigantic step was to survey the land and determine the route. The government formed the Canadian Pacific Survey to do this work and placed it under the direction of Sandford Fleming. Thousands of miles of wild and inhospitable land had to be covered on foot, and the towering mountains had to be climbed again and again by men searching for passes the railway could go through.

Over the next six years Fleming's team was to complete 46,000 miles of survey and 38 men were to die in the process.

THE PACIFIC SCANDAL

Macdonald seeks a private company

Meanwhile Macdonald was searching for a suitable private company to build and operate the new railway. This way the government would avoid having to increase taxation to pay for it.

Two companies emerged in competition for the charter, one of them headed by the multi-millionaire, Sir Hugh Allan, backed by a group of Americans. Macdonald stipulated that the two companies should merge and insisted on Allan disassociating himself from his American backers; it was imperative that this should be a Canadian enterprise. Everyone complied and the charter was granted in March 1873, with Allan appointed as president of the new company.

Sir Hugh's double dealing

All the while, however, Allan had been engaged in a series of complicated secret agreements. In the first instance he and his American partners, owners of the Northern Pacific Railway lines in America, had plotted to delay completion of the all-Canadian route while they pushed on with a connection from the main line down to their own lines in the US. Later, Allan entered into clandestine talks with the government regarding his role in the new company. Then, when it became clear that he must disentangle himself from the Americans if he were to succeed in his plans, he proceeded to wriggle out of his previous US pact. The Americans were furious with him and decided to blow Allan's cover and reveal a few incriminating details to the Opposition...

Scandal erupts: the government collapses

The Liberals seized upon this gift horse with zeal. More investigations unearthed even better ammunition. Not only could the government be charged with handing over the railway to a bunch of American schemers disguised as a Canadian company: it also emerged that Allan had advanced large amounts of cash to fund Macdonald's 1872 election campaign – presumably in return for the promise of the presidency of the company.

Particularly indicting was a stolen telegram from Macdonald to Allan's lawyer: 'I must have another ten thousand; will be the last time of calling; do not fail me; answer today.' The Pacific Scandal, as it was known, filled all the newspapers and was on everyone's lips. Finally, charged with corruption in parliament, Macdonald resigned on 6 November 1873 and the government was dissolved.

RAILWAY HISTORY

THE RAILWAY UNDER THE LIBERALS

The dream gets watered down

The newly elected Liberal government found itself lumbered with a project it had never supported in the first place. Moreover, Canada was suddenly entering a continental depression. Private investment shrivelled up so the government was forced to undertake the railway as public works, handing out contracts for the construction of sections of track. The ambitious scheme was literally watered down as Mackenzie talked not of a single continuous track but of a land and water route. He planned to shorten the railway and use steamships to cross the Great Lakes.

Slowly on

To avoid corruption, Mackenzie ruled that contracts should always be awarded to the lowest bidder. These men, however, were not always the most qualified or competent builders.

The first section of track to be built was, in fact, a branch line going south from Winnipeg to the US border. Its construction was characterized by costly incompetence and blunder. Work progressed slowly – the Pacific Survey seemed to be dragging on forever – and it wasn't until June 1875 that construction began on the main line, the section linking Lake Superior and Winnipeg. It was becoming clear that the railway was languishing in the hands of the government.

OVER TO THE CPR

Macdonald back in power

It had been generally assumed that Macdonald's career had ended with the ruin and dishonour of the Pacific Scandal. But Canada was fed up with the Liberals and in the 1878 elections 'the Old Chief' was returned to power with a landslide victory. Once more he took up his old vision of transforming Canada into a strong transcontinental nation. This policy depended on completing the railway as quickly as possible.

More government contracts were awarded for the 125-mile section between Yale and Kamloops, west of the Rockies; but Macdonald was on the lookout for a group of private capitalists to take over the venture. This time their credentials would have to be flawless.

The CPR is formed

Such a group presented itself in the form of the CPR Syndicate. Its key members were leading directors of the Bank of Montreal. They came with an impeccable reputation, considerable financial backing and experience in running a railroad (they had recently transformed a bankrupt line into a resounding financial success). They were clearly perfect for the job and, following lengthy negotiations with the government, the Canadian Pacific Railway Company was incorporated in February 1881, a decade after British Columbia had been promised the transcontinental line.

RAILWAY HISTORY

Macdonald pledged a $25 million cash subsidy and 25 million acres of land to the new CPR, and agreed to turn over all the government contracted lines to the company once they were completed.

The task ahead

The CPR was faced with a mammoth task: a total of 1900 miles of track remained to be laid. In the east, there was the formidable challenge of carving a way through the Canadian Shield north of the Great Lakes. In the prairies they had to lay 900 miles of track west of Winnipeg to the Rockies. In the west they had to take that track over or through the Rockies and the Selkirks to meet the government contracted line at Kamloops.

The company hoped to forge ahead with this work as quickly as possible: the more rapidly the railway was completed, the sooner it could turn in a profit. The building season usually lasted only from April to November. The first season's work, however, was very disappointing – only 130 miles of track were laid. It became clear that some dynamic force was required to galvanize the operation and push it full steam ahead.

Enter Van Horne

This dynamic force was provided by William Cornelius Van Horne, a rising star in American railroad management. The appointment of Van Horne as General Manager of the CPR was possibly the most important decision the company ever made – he was soon to be ranked as one of the world's greatest railway men. He took the railway by the scruff of the neck, established control of the entire line himself and began work in February 1882 by declaring he'd have 500 miles of track laid by the end of the season.

Whirlwind construction across the prairies

The press and politicians openly scoffed at Van Horne's extravagant boast. But soon their jaws were hanging open at the breakneck speed of the track-laying west of Winnipeg. Men worked around the clock to push the track forward and construction gobbled up a mountain of supplies. In the end, Van Horne's goal was not reached; he was thwarted by spring flooding. But by the end of the building season no less than 418 miles of track had been laid.

The next season, 1883, was to see the fastest construction rate of the entire project, with the record set in the month of July when 92.3 miles were laid under scorching temperatures.

By November the prairie section was completed. However, the track had been racing towards the mountains all summer with one crucial question remaining to be answered: which route was it going to take across them?

Problems with the route

Based on the results of the exhaustive Pacific Survey, Sandford Fleming had concluded that the best route west of Winnipeg would be north to Fort Edmonton, then over the Rockies through the Yellowhead Pass. When the CPR took over they rejected this decision in favour of a southerly route – partly to shorten the line, and partly because they realized it would be easier to control and profit from an area as yet unpopulated. The problem was that a suitable pass through the Rockies had yet to be established, and a pass through the Selkirks had not even been discovered.

The company dispatched Major A B ('Hells Bells') Rogers. It took him a year and a half of scouring the mountains to discover a pass through the Selkirks (still known as Rogers Pass) that the railway could take after crossing the Rockies via the Kicking Horse pass. Rogers himself had some doubts about the feasibility of this route and alternative passes were still being explored as the track was approaching the mountains from Winnipeg in 1883. It wasn't until autumn that year that the CPR confirmed, to Rogers' great relief, that his route would be adopted after all.

Meanwhile, the planned route across the Shield was also proving controversial. Although the government had always stipulated that the railway should take an all-Canadian route north of Lake Superior, some of the directors had believed that this would never be enforced given how much cheaper and easier it would be to connect the line with existing American tracks south of the lakes. When George Stephen, the CPR president, made it clear that he was determined to follow the all-Canadian route, two of the directors resigned, convinced this plan was doomed to failure.

The track through the prairies had been straight and relatively easy to lay. Now the railway had to be forced across the two dreaded barriers: the Shield and the mountains. The challenges were to prove enormous.

DANGERS AND DIFFICULTIES

Muskeg, sinkholes and rock

Van Horne is said to have described the section north of Lake Superior as 'two hundred miles of engineering impossibilities'. Workmen had to blast their way through the granite of the Shield, often finding solid rock well below the level where earth had been expected. Track-layers also had to contend with the infamous muskeg and sinkholes, seemingly solid earth which would suddenly swallow up track under the weight of a train. One such sinkhole required fill to be dumped in it for three months before it could safely support trains.

Whisky peddlers

Life along the line in Ontario was frequently disrupted by the workmen's enthusiasm for liquor. A railway worker's life was particularly harsh and comfortless and for many, whisky was the only diversion. They were easy targets for the illegal whisky merchants, and results were often colourful.

The problem became chronic in the summer of 1884 as this construction supervisor's report testifies: 'These whisky peddlers would get off in the woods near the supply roads – get the teamsters drunk, racing teams, breaking wagons; destroying property and supplies would follow. They would waylay men, get them drunk, rob them of everything of value and threaten the life of anyone who opposes the traffic...' These events took place in areas so remote that few policemen were available to halt the lawlessness.

The weather

All along the line the workers had to cope with the paralysing effects of the weather. In 1884 there was no winter break on the Ontario line. Track had to be laid in snow that was sometimes up to five feet deep and in temperatures occasionally as low as minus fifty. Freezing weather conditions were also a problem in the mountains. Track was laid between Blaeberry Creek and Donald in temperatures of minus thirty; then, when the warmer weather came, the rails expanded and it was found that the track was out of gauge.

Construction in the Selkirks took place under the continual threat of avalanches. James Ross, head of construction in the mountain division, wrote to Van Horne of the dangers: 'I find that the snow-slides on the Selkirks are much more serious than I anticipated, and I think are quite beyond your ideas of their magnitude and of the danger to the line.... at one point, ten slips came down within six days, piling the snow 50 feet deep and 1800 feet in length along the located line..... The great trouble we are labouring under at present is that the men are frightened. Seven have already been buried in different slides, though fortunately only two were killed...'

The CPR built numerous snowsheds to protect the railway's passage through the Selkirks; nonetheless, avalanches were to cause the deaths of two hundred people between 1885 and 1909, prompting the construction of the remarkable Connaught Tunnel.

Mountains, tunnels and bridges

Of course the biggest challenge facing the railway builders was the physical barrier of the mountains. Trains had to cross three major summits – Kicking Horse Pass, Rogers Pass and Eagle Pass – each presenting an engineering nightmare. Tunnels had to be blasted through rock, bridges built over precipitous gorges, track laid close to vertical drops. It took thousands of workers to get the line through the gruelling mountain division; the Kicking Horse pass alone required 12,000 men. Typical of the kind of construction that had to be built was the Mountain Creek bridge on the eastern slopes of the Selkirks. This amazing feat of engineering was 164 feet high, 1086 feet long and contained two million board feet of timber.

On Andrew Onderdonk's section from Yale to Kamloops the difficulties of drilling tunnels through the Fraser Canyon were so great his men were able to advance the track no more than six feet a day. In some parts, the men had to be winched down to the track on ropes. Scores of men died on this treacherous route, some as a result of rockslides, many as a result of careless handling of explosives. The nearby hospital at Yale had to be enlarged to cope with all the injuries.

ON THE VERGE OF BANKRUPTCY

The money runs out

Despite these enormous difficulties, the track moved ever on. Then, in 1884, the CPR found itself in the midst of a severe financial crisis that threatened to throw the company into ruin even as completion of the line was in sight. The railway was swallowing up vast amounts of money. George Stephen, the CPR president, had been frantically trying to raise capital at home and in London but the funds he secured were not sufficient to keep the operation going. The CPR's debt in January 1884 ran to $15 million and time was running out. In desperation he begged the government for a loan of $22.5 million.

Temporary relief

Macdonald knew he'd have a tough time getting this through parliament but he also knew that if the CPR went under so would the government. He forced his party to support the relief bill by threatening to resign if it was rejected. As parliament dragged out the issue in endless debate, the CPR was sinking fast. Stephen wrote to Macdonald: 'I do not, at the moment, see how we are going to get the money to keep the work going... If I find we cannot go on I suppose the only thing to do will be to put in a Receiver. If that must be done the quicker it is done the better.'

At the end of February the bill was passed and the money was loaned to the company. By the end of the year it was gone. The CPR had reached its darkest hour. Stephen and his cousin Smith, a fellow CPR director, had sunk their entire personal fortune into the company. There was no more money to be had. Wages were months in arrears all along the line and men were striking or rioting. There was virtually no chance of persuading parliament to loan yet more money. The CPR was done for.

The North-west rebellion

Events suddenly took a dramatic turn in the spring of 1885 when the bloody North-west Rebellion broke out in Manitoba. Van Horne ingeniously seized on this opportunity to demonstrate the importance of the railway to the government: he immediately offered to move troops out by train to crush the rebellion. The line was not yet finished; there were four gaps, totalling 86 miles, but by shifting the men across the gaps by sled or on foot Van Horne was able to get them to Winnipeg in a week. Just 15 years earlier, during the first North-west Rebellion, that same journey had taken three months. By the time the troops returned, the gaps had been closed and the section was completed.

The final loan

As summer approached the CPR's credit could stretch no further. Disaster seemed imminent, as this telegram from Van Horne to George Stephen indicates: 'Have no means of paying wages, pay car can't be sent out, and unless we get immediate relief we must stop. Please inform Premier and Finance Minister. Do not be surprised, or blame me, if an immediate and most serious catastrophe happens.'

Once more a desperate Stephen begged Macdonald to bail out the company. He knew that they could quickly recoup the money once the line was completed and a through service was in operation; without a loan, however, the CPR faced bankruptcy even at this eleventh hour. Given the railway's crucial role in dealing with the recent rebellion, parliament could hardly fail to back the CPR. In July it passed another relief bill. This was the last time the CPR had to ask the government for a loan.

COMPLETION OF THE RAILWAY

The last spike

It took just a few more months to complete the line; all that was left to do was to close the gap between Onderdonk's tracks in the Gold Range and James Ross's in the Selkirks. The tracks met on 7 November 1885 in Eagle Pass at a spot named Craigellachie. The driving of the last spike was surely an emotional moment for all involved but it was a simple affair without pomp or ceremony. Van Horne declined to celebrate the occasion with the traditional golden last spike: 'The last spike will be just as good an iron one as there is between Montreal and Vancouver,' he said, 'and anyone who wants to see it driven will have to pay full fare.'

The spike was driven by Donald A Smith, the eldest member of the CPR Syndicate. His first blow bent the iron, the spike was quickly replaced with a new one, and Smith's second attempt was a success. The crowds cheered and demanded a speech of Van Horne. His response was typically succinct: 'All I can say is that the work has been done well in every way.'

EARLY RAILWAY SERVICE

Passenger service begins

The line had to be properly finished off and upgraded before a passenger service could be inaugurated. The CPR had extended the track to Montreal by taking over existing lines in eastern Canada and on 28 June 1886 the first regular passenger train, the 'Pacific Express', left Montreal at 20:00 hours. On 1 July it reached Winnipeg and on 4 July it reached Port Moody at 12:00 hours – exactly on time. This was the first scheduled trans-Canada rail trip and at the time the longest scheduled passenger train trip in the world. With the extension of the line from Port Moody to Vancouver in May 1887, the main line was 4675km long.

(**Opposite**) Most of the grand Canadian stations were built in the early part of the 20th century. Vancouver's Pacific Central Station (**top**) opened in 1919. (Photo © VRC).

The Gare du Palais (**middle, left**) serves Quebec City and was built in 1915. It was designed by Eugène-Etienne Taché in a style similar to that of the Château Frontenac. (Photo © VRC).

Jasper Station (**middle, right**) opened in 1911 but burnt down in 1925. The current building was constructed in 1926 and is now designated as a heritage railway station. (Photo © VRC).

Union Station (**bottom**) in Toronto dates from 1927. With over 200,000 people a day passing through its doors this is the busiest transportation facility in Canada. (Photo © MF).

The rear platform on an early CPR train

The first travellers

Until 1899, transcontinental trains ran on a daily basis; the westbound train was known as the Pacific Express and the eastbound train as the Atlantic Express.

The carriages were extremely luxurious with all sleeping cars boasting bathtubs, an unheard of novelty in North America at the time. The dining cars served fine international cuisine and vintage wines and were generally patronized by passengers travelling First Class. Coach passengers usually dined in the much cheaper Canadian Pacific restaurants located at division points along the line, while the train was being serviced or the locomotive was being changed. It was the popularity of these restaurants that gave birth to the famous Canadian Pacific hotels, still flourishing today.

As Macdonald had predicted, the railway carried droves of settlers out to the now accessible west. Special 'land seeker' tickets were offered at reduced rates to encourage people to go and investigate areas under development. By the end of the railway's first decade of operation it had changed the lives of thousands of Canadians and, in turn, had changed the face of Canada itself.

RAILWAY HISTORY

(Opposite) The Old Town Clock in Halifax (see p78) was a gift to the town from Prince Edward in 1803. (Photo © MG).

Into the 20th century: CNR and VIA Rail

Consult the annals of Canada for the past fifty years at random and whatever party may be in power, what do you find? The government is building a railway, buying a railway, selling a railway or blocking a railway. **Paul Lamarche**, Speech in Montreal, 1917

The CPR proved to be an enormous financial success. Not only did it operate a highly profitable railway service: it also established a national telegraph network, an express parcel service and it branched out into steamships, hotels and real estate. Entrepreneurs clamoured to emulate the company's achievements and the early 20th century saw a rapid and undisciplined growth in railway building, all of which finally led to the birth of the CPR's present-day competitor: the Canadian National Railways system.

TWO MORE TRANSCONTINENTAL LINES

The boom years of the first decade of the 20th century brought thousands of settlers flooding out west to make their fortunes. It was felt that the country needed a second transcontinental line and two companies eagerly put themselves forward for the task. Somewhat recklessly, the Liberal government, in power under Wilfrid Laurier, gave charters to both companies: the Canadian Northern Railway and the Grand Trunk Pacific.

The Canadian Northern Railway

This young company operated a series of railway lines along the northern prairies. The entrepreneurial owners planned to extend the prairie route to the Pacific via the Yellowhead pass in the Rockies, Sandford Fleming's original choice for the first transcontinental. The line would go down to Kamloops where it would meet the tracks of the CPR. From there it would follow the course of the CPR down the Fraser Canyon, always on the opposite bank since there was room for only one track on one side. Building proceeded and the last spike was driven on 23 January 1915.

The Grand Trunk Pacific

The Grand Trunk was one of Canada's oldest railway companies with a well established network in eastern Canada. The epitome of prudence and circumspection, the Grand Trunk wasn't ordinarily given to taking risks but its new general manager, Charles Hays, was convinced that the company needed to expand westwards to capture a share of the Pacific market. His new line would also follow a northern prairie route, taking the Yellowhead pass through the Rockies. From here, however, it would part company with the Canadian Northern and travel north-west up to the new coastal town of Prince Rupert. This was the closest Canadian port to Asia, and Hays envisioned it as the port of the future, the key to the Grand Trunk's success.

RAILWAY HISTORY

Sadly, Hays was never to see the line reach this terminus. Following a trip to London to raise more funds for the project, he returned in April 1912 aboard the ill-fated *SS Titanic* and drowned with the sinking ship. Two years later in April 1914 the last spike was driven in the Grand Trunk Pacific railway.

1920s poster advertising Canadian Pacific's Trans-Canada service
CANADIAN PACIFIC/GY KAUFFMAN (1924)

Failure

Canada had overstretched itself. There was nowhere near sufficient traffic to sustain three transcontinental lines. A world-wide depression was having dire effects on the economy, which grew steadily worse with the outbreak of World War I. The two new lines were dead losses. And they weren't the only ones. Canada's railways had by now got completely out of hand – there were about two hundred companies operating a chaotic network of profitless lines.

In 1916 a royal commission investigating the railway crisis concluded that the private companies should be taken over and reorganized by the government. This is exactly what happened in 1923 when all the railways, with the notable exception of the CPR, were combined to form the publicly owned Canadian National Railways (CNR) system.

THE CNR TAKES OVER

Railways overhauled

The CNR lost no time in trimming down, shaking up and integrating the sprawling rail lines it had inherited. As a result of innovative restructuring and tight management the chaos was eliminated and the CNR emerged as a highly efficient business. Like its competitor, the CPR, the new railway system carried both passengers and freight across its transcontinental lines. It also followed the CPR's example by building a series of grand railway hotels in major cities along the line.

Decline in passenger travel

As the railways advanced further into the 20th century the volume of passenger traffic steadily decreased, particularly after World War II. Motor cars were taking over as the primary mode of transport and highways were constructed right across the nation. Air travel, too, became increasingly affordable and cut travelling time down to a minimum. In an effort to win back passengers, both railways launched faster, spruced-up services in 1955: *The Canadian* was introduced by the CPR and 'the Super Transcontinental' by the CNR. Nonetheless, the volume of passenger traffic remained low and the CPR decided to concentrate on its freight operations, leaving the CNR to handle the bulk of Canada's passenger service.

RAILWAY HISTORY

Formation of VIA Rail

The completion of the Trans-Canada Highway in 1962 dealt a crippling blow to rail traffic. By the 1970s the situation had become dire and in 1976 a government report concluded that passenger traffic was set to decrease even further. In response, the government decided to discontinue non-essential rail services and place the remaining passenger lines in the hands of a new government-owned body: VIA Rail Canada. VIA would operate the passenger service, leasing CPR and CNR tracks while these companies focused on freight transportation.

Southern route abandoned

For some years VIA ran *The Canadian* across the southern and northern routes through the Rockies. In 1988 it introduced *The Rocky Mountaineer*, a daylight-only train ride through the mountains. However, the experiment proved a failure and a year after its launch the government decided to privatize this route. *The Rocky Mountaineer* was subsequently taken over by The Great Canadian Railtour Company Ltd, who have succeeded in turning the route into a highly profitable tourist attraction. Meanwhile the southern (and more historic) route via Calgary and Banff was abandoned by VIA Rail in 1989 leaving the northern route, via Edmonton and Jasper, as the only remaining transcontinental passenger line.

The future

Despite the acute financial pressures that squeeze the railway industry the world over, the Canadian government has continued to invest in rail travel in recent years, upgrading its locomotives and introducing on-board improvements such as the introduction of wi-fi on some services. The biggest investment came in 2001, when VIA Rail bought 139 modern railways cars that had been commissioned for a sleeper service through the Channel Tunnel, but never used. The new trains were modified and launched as VIA's 'Renaissance' fleet, used mainly on the Ocean and Corridor routes.

Nonetheless, a question mark hangs over the future of some of VIA's less profitable lines. You may hear rumours, for instance, about the supposedly imminent discontinuation of *The Hudson Bay* route to Churchill or *The Skeena* route to Prince Rupert. Even aboard *The Canadian*, fellow travellers may tell you they've heard the transcontinental line is soon to be terminated – and many people outside Canada think it's already stopped running! No one knows for sure what the future holds for passenger rail service in Canada. One can only hope that what is truly a first-class service through one of the most beautiful countries in the world will be able to withstand the onslaught of declining passenger traffic and cruise through the 21st century intact.

CITY GUIDES

Halifax

I am neither a prophet, nor the son of a prophet, yet...I believe that many in this room shall live to hear the whistle of the steam engine in the passes of the Rocky Mountains and to make the journey from Halifax to the Pacific in five or six days. **Joseph Howe**, speech in Halifax, 15 May 1851

Halifax, the hub of the Maritime Provinces (New Brunswick, Nova Scotia and Prince Edward Island), is exactly as you'd expect it to be: bustling, lively streets clustered around the waterfront; brightly painted clapboard houses; fish markets; quayside bars; the smell of salt in the air; old-fashioned charm. It's the capital of Nova Scotia and is located on the second-largest natural harbour in the world. The downtown core is extremely compact and all the interesting parts are within easy walking distance of each other.

Being one of the older Canadian cities, Halifax has taken enormous care to preserve its colonial heritage and you'll see some fine old buildings dotted around the place. It does tend to overdo the history thing though and just about every building over 80 years old seems to have a plaque on it. All the same, Halifax is an excellent starting point for a trip across Canada (it somehow feels like the proper place to begin) and is well worth a couple of days' visit.

HISTORY

The Micmacs
The first people to live here were the Micmac Indians who named the settlement 'Chebucto', meaning 'Great long harbour'. Their fishing and hunting communities proliferated throughout the region until contact with European fishermen in the early 16th century exposed them to new diseases which seriously depleted their numbers. These fishermen came over to take advantage of the area's prodigious supplies of cod, discovered by Italian sailor John Cabot in 1497.

Britain and France vie for power
The French staked the first European claim to the area in 1605 when they founded Port Royal on the Bay of Fundy. Britain was keen to get in on the act and attempted to establish its own colony nearby. In 1621 the area occupied by the French, known as Acadie, was claimed for the British Crown and renamed Nova Scotia ('New Scotland').

The rival claims dragged on until 1713 when the Treaty of Utrecht handed over the mainland Maritimes to Britain, forcing France to shift its power base to Louisbourg on Cape Breton Island.

Garrison town established

Britain continued to feel threatened by the French presence at Louisbourg, so in 1749 Edward Cornwallis was sent over with 2500 settlers to found a garrison town by the harbour to protect the New England colonies. They named it Halifax, after the second Earl of Halifax, and built a fort at the top of the town's hill.

The Royals in Halifax

For many years Halifax provided a home to the two wayward sons of King George III, who were practically kicked out of Britain by their frustrated father. The youngest, Edward (the future father of Queen Victoria), served as the commander of the Nova Scotia forces for six years. He was notorious for his obsession with discipline and punctuality. Modern-day Haligonians can still keep an eye on the time by the great clocktower standing on the hillside – a gift from Prince Edward to the city.

Halifax today

The city's importance as a military and naval base continued well into the 20th century. Halifax also emerged as the industrial, commercial and educational centre of the Maritime Provinces, boasting one of Canada's busiest ports (ice-free all year) and no fewer than five universities, giving the place a youthful, vibrant atmosphere. The current population of around 372,000 is made up of over a hundred different ethnic groups.

Halifax is also a very prosperous city, a fact reflected in the glittering high-rise blocks that have sprung up around town and the money poured into renovating its historic waterfront buildings. However, while Halifax has gone from strength to strength in recent decades, it suffered a horrific tragedy in the early part of the 20th century – for more details see p79.

ARRIVING IN HALIFAX

By air

Flights into or out of Halifax touch down at Halifax International Airport, about 35km out of town, where you'll find several ATMs and a well-stocked **tourist information** desk (open daily 9am–9pm).

❏ **Halifax online**

💻 **www.halifaxinfo.com** Halifax Regional Municipality's website, with details on city sights, accommodation and practical visitor information.

💻 **http://novascotia.com** 'Virtual Nova Scotia' site, put together by the Government of Nova Scotia, with travel information on the whole province.

💻 **www.where.ca/halifax** Another useful website providing information about the city. *Where* is also available from many hotels and tourism offices in magazine format.

CITY GUIDES

From the airport, the **Airbus** leaves for the town centre every hour (with a two-hour break between midnight and 2am), stopping at all the major hotels in Halifax. Tickets cost $21 and children under 10 travel free. A **taxi** into town costs $53. There are also several car-hire companies at the airport.

By rail
The train station is at the south end of Halifax, adjoined to the Westin Nova Scotian Hotel, about a 15-minute walk from downtown. The No 9 and 7 buses stop just outside the station about once every 30 minutes and will take you into the city centre (as will the No 35, less frequently). To get back to the station, the best place to catch a bus is on Barrington St.

GETTING AROUND

Halifax is a very manageable size and most places can be easily reached on **foot**. That said, if you're feeling footsore you might be interested in the free shuttle service, 'FRED' (Free Rides Everywhere Downtown), that runs from July to October. Buses serve specially marked stops on a downtown loop that includes Pier 21, Lower Water Street, Upper Water Street and Barrington Street, running every forty minutes between 10.30am and 5pm. Standard city buses charge a flat fare of $2.25 per journey which must be paid with the exact money; for more information on buses, including FRED, see 🖳 www.halifax.ca/metrotransit. Heading further afield, there's a regular **ferry** service (every 15 or 30 minutes; $2.25) across the harbour to the neighbouring town of Dartmouth, which makes a pleasant excursion and gives great views of Halifax's skyline.

Another good way of getting out of downtown, particularly for a jaunt to Point Pleasant Park, is by **bike**. These can be rented from Ideal Bikes (☎ 902-444-7433, 🖳 www.idealbikes.ca; $25 per day, $15 for a half-day). Freewheeling Adventures, based outside Halifax (☎ 902-857-3600 or 1-800-672-0775, 🖳 www.freewheeling.ca), offers organized bike tours around Nova Scotia – see their website for more details.

ORIENTATION

You can't get lost in Halifax. The city centre is situated on a hillside. At the top you've got the **citadel**, at the bottom you've got the **waterfront** and in between are about six streets running parallel to the water's edge. Right in the centre of all this is the **Grand Parade**, the city's main square, home to the City Hall and St Paul's Church.

SERVICES

Tourist Information
There are several tourist information centres around town. The most centrally located is the **Waterfront Visitor Centre** (☎ 902-424-4248) in a glass pavilion directly behind the Maritime Museum. Its opening hours are: June to September

daily 8.30am–8pm; October, November and May daily 8.30am–4.30pm; December to April Wednesday–Sunday 8.30am–4.30pm.

Money

There are ATMs all over the place, from hotel lobbies to shopping malls, with a big concentration on Spring Garden Rd. Most banks offer currency exchange facilities, including the Royal Bank at 5161 George St and the Bank of Nova Scotia at 1709 Hollis St. The Bank of Montreal at 5151 George St offers the same service but for lower denominations.

Consulates

Austria (☎ 902-429-8200) Suite 410, 1718 Argyle St; **Belgium** (☎ 902-468-1030) 90 Bluewater Rd, Bedford; **Denmark** (☎ 902-429-5680) 1525 Birmingham St; **Germany** (☎ 902-420-1599) Suite 1100, 1959 Upper Water St **Italy** (☎ 902-492-3934) 1959 Upper Water St; **Netherlands** (☎ 902-422-1485) 2000 Barrington St; **Norway** (☎ 902-468-1330) Suite 206, 11 Morris Dr, Dartmouth; **Sweden** (☎ 902-425-6500) 5151 George St; **USA** (☎ 902-429-2480) 1969 Upper Water St

Post, internet and laundry

Halifax's central **post office** is at 1680 Bedford Row. **Internet access** is available at a little café hidden away upstairs in Paperchase, a newsagent's store on Blowers St, just up from Barrington. The staff are helpful, the couches comfy and you can feast on home-baked treats and smoothies while you surf the net for $8 an hour.

The most central **laundries** in town are the Spin and Tumble Laundromat at 1022 Barrington St (☎ 902-422-8099), open Monday to Friday 8.30am–7pm and Saturday and Sunday 9am–7pm, and Kwik Wash Laundromat at 5506 Clyde St (☎ 902-429-2023), open Monday to Friday 9am–7.30pm, Saturday 9am–6pm and Sunday 11am–6pm.

WHERE TO STAY

There's a lot of accommodation in Halifax, the vast majority of it upmarket and of a high standard. Mid-range options are much thinner on the ground but there's a reasonable choice of budget rooms. Despite the large number of hotels it's not uncommon for the town to get booked out when events or big conferences are taking place so it might be worth booking in advance. That said, booking on or just before the day often gets you a big discount in the more expensive hotels.

Budget accommodation

Part of the Hostelling International (HI) network, the *Halifax Heritage House Hostel* (☎ 902-422-3863, 🖥 www.hihostels.ca), 1253 Barrington St, is a dream hostel. It's in the middle of town in a beautiful Georgian building, has a well-

---

❑ Accommodation prices quoted in this book are for **high season** (normally May or June to September). In low season many hotels offer substantial discounts.

Halifax

Where to stay
1 Marriott Halifax Harbourfront
10 Westin Nova Scotian
11 The Haliburton
12 Halifax Heritage House Hostel
13 Waverley Inn
21 The Garden South Park Inn
22 Lord Nelson
23 YMCA
24 Fountain View Guest House

Where to eat
2 Lower Deck
3 Upper Deck
4 Harbourside Market
5 Salty's
6 Split Crow
7 McKelvie's
8 Ryan Duffy's
9 Da Maurizio
14 Subway
15 The Pita Pit
16 Economy Shoe Shop Bar & Grill
17 The Five Fishermen
18 Maxwell's Plum
19 Susie's Shortbreads
20 Il Mercato

0   250   500m

Pier 21

Railway station

Laundry

Inglis St

South St

To Point Pleasant Park

To Risley Hall (Dalhousie University)

Lower Water St

11
12
13

Morris St

Queen St

South Park St

Robie St

Alexander Keith's Brewery

9

Paperchase

Tourist Info

14

Hollis St

Spring Garden Rd

20
Laundry
22
21

To Howe Hall (Dalhousie University)

Four Winds (Whale watching)

Tourist Information

Maritime Museum

Post Office

Bedford Row

7 8

Barrington St

Blowers St

19

23

Public Gardens

Art Gallery

Province House

Granville St

Argyle St

15

Grafton St

18

16

Sackville St

Old Town Clock

Ferry Terminal

HISTORIC PROPERTIES

City Hall

Grand Parade

6

Prince St

17

George St

Duke St

Brunswick St

Citadel

Summer St

5

1
2
4
3

Upper Water St

24

To Satisfaction Feast

To Halifax Backpackers Hostel

equipped kitchen, a big common room, a TV, laundry room and library, and is spotlessly clean throughout. What's more it's good value – dorm beds are $26 for members, $31 for non-members, with private rooms starting at $57. Note that sleeping bags are not allowed but bed linen and towels are included in the price. There are 75 beds but with standards like this they get snapped up quickly so book in advance.

Between mid-May and late August, *Dalhousie University Residency* (☎ 902-494-8840, 🖳 www.housing.dal.ca) offers small, neat rooms in two of its halls of residence on campus, a few blocks west of Robie St – Howe Hall, at 6230 Coburg Rd and Risley Hall at 1233 LeMarchant St. Rooms are $42 for a single ($27 for students) and $65 for a double ($49 for students), and include towels and bed linen.

Up near the citadel at 1565 South Park St, the *YMCA* (☎ 902-423-9622, 🖳 www.ymcahrm.ns.ca) has excellent facilities (café, fitness centre, pool) and 31 spartan but clean single rooms ($55). Available to tourists only between June and August, it provides mixed-sex accommodation with separate male and female bathrooms, plus a common room and kitchen.

About 15 minutes' walk north-west from downtown at 2193 Gottingen St is *Halifax Backpackers Hostel* (☎ 902-431-3170, 🖳 www.halifaxbackpackers .com), equipped with a small but pleasant café and library. The location is not great and those travelling alone may feel uncomfortable wandering around the area on foot but the hostel itself is friendly and cheap, with dorm beds from $20, private rooms for $57 and family rooms for $80; it also hosts regular social events.

The clean and comfortable *Fountain View Guest House* (☎ 902-422-4169, 🖳 www.angelfire.com/id/fountainview/) is on a busy road behind the citadel at 2138 Robie St. Doubles here (with separate bathrooms) cost from $40, single rooms from $30 and family rooms from $75.

Mid-range accommodation

The Garden South Park Inn (☎ 902-492-8577, 🖳 www.gardeninn.ns.ca) at 1263 South Park St is a pink clapboard house with 23 spotless en-suite rooms ($109–169, breakfast included) all with TV, phone, wi-fi and cheerful floral décor. Slightly more expensive, the charming *Waverley Inn* (☎ 902-423-9346, 🖳 www.waverleyinn.com) at 1266 Barrington St is crammed with antiques, gilt mirrors and fabulous old mahogany beds. The exquisite lobby and hallways boast as much character as the bedrooms themselves. Double rooms (all en suite) cost from $129 to $190 with breakfast included.

Upmarket hotels

Halifax is well endowed with top-range hotels, most of them of a very high standard. For rail travellers, the most obvious choice is the luxurious *Westin*

❏ **Room reservation service**
The Nova Scotia tourist board operates a room reservation hotline covering the whole province: ☎ 1-800-565-0000 from North America, or ☎ 902-425-5781 from elsewhere.

Nova Scotian (☎ 902-421-1000, 💻 www.westin.ns.ca), built in 1930 by Canadian National Railways, right next to the train station at 1181 Hollis St. The hotel originally contained a special section with living quarters for CNR staff and its vast kitchen prepared all the food for the trains as well as offering laundry facilities for the linen used on them. Today it's owned by the international Westin chain but remains a romantic and stylish symbol of the town's railway heritage. One of the highlights of a stay here are the so-called 'Heavenly Beds' in all 297 rooms, which amply deserve their name; the hotel also has a trendy cocktail bar and a good restaurant. Rates range from $179 up to $309.

More centrally located, right next to the Historic Properties at 1919 Upper Water St, the *Marriott Halifax Harbourfront* (☎ 902-421-1700, 💻 www.marriott.com) boasts fantastic harbour views and some nice art deco touches – and for those who fancy a flutter, links with Casino Nova Scotia through an indoor walkway. Rack rates here are anywhere from $199 to $399.

For a little more character try *The Halliburton* (☎ 902-420-0658, 💻 www.thehalliburton.com) at 5184 Morris St, which comes with immaculate, spacious rooms ($190–$249) and a central location. It's very charming and also has a pretty courtyard garden. Overlooking the Public Gardens at 1515 South Park St is the *Lord Nelson* (☎ 902-423-6331, 💻 www.lordnelsonhotel.com), built in 1928 and still preserving the original high ceilings, oak panelling and shining brass lifts of its entrance lobby. Room rates are from $199, with frequent special offers starting at $159.

WHERE TO EAT

There are dozens of places to eat in Halifax, many of them concentrated around the waterfront or along Spring Garden Rd.

The local speciality is, of course, fish and seafood, particularly Atlantic salmon, crab, scallops and lobster – the quality is generally excellent and the prices usually moderate, with main courses from around $15 in many places. Make the most of the ocean's delicacies while you can – you've got over 6000km to go before you'll get seafood this fresh again.

Where, a free weekly publication available in the tourist office and hotels, has a restaurant listings section with a rundown of each place's food and atmosphere.

Budget food

Perhaps the most atmospheric place to head for a cheap bite is *Harbourside Market* in the Historic Properties, which houses colourful fresh-produce market stalls alongside cafés, pizzerias and other snack outlets in a beautiful converted warehouse, with outdoor seating by the water's edge; *Loaf, Leaf and Ladle* is particularly good and offers delicious homemade sandwiches, soups and pastries. Also in the Historic Properties, the *Lower Deck Beer Market*, which sits upstairs from the very popular *Lower Deck pub*, has a nice selection of beers on tap, friendly staff and a good-value lunch menu, including soup and sandwiches – make the most of the fantastic harbour views by taking a table by the window.

On the corner of Argyle St and Blowers St, *Subway* is good for takeaway sandwiches and baguettes and offers well-priced meal deals. *The Pita Pit* at 1588 Argyle Street offers similar fare, offering a wide selection of good-value, healthy snacks. For a few dollars more you can get a cheap lunch (around the $10 mark) at many of the city's pubs, including the always-lively *Split Crow* on the corner of Granville and Duke, with a pleasant outdoor veranda and a selection of local beers on tap. Another pub renowned for its beer is the intriguingly named *Maxwell's Plum*, at 1600 Grafton St. It boasts 160 beers from around the world, including 60 on tap, and you can get a steak for under $10.

Halifax has a number of inexpensive vegetarian restaurants, including *Satisfaction Feast* at 3559 Robie Street, which offers nutritious wraps, hot sandwiches and great salads at very affordable prices (under $12). Finally, for an inexpensive sweet treat visit *Susie's Shortbreads* at 1589 Dresden Row, which offers over 100 types of cupcake and has cookies for under $2.

Mid-range and upmarket restaurants

Halifax has several excellent, moderately priced bistros including *Il Mercato* at 5650 Spring Garden Rd (☎ 902-422-2866), offering a contemporary fusion of Italian cuisine and seafood from the Maritimes. Charming by day, romantic by night, the eccentrically named *Economy Shoe Shop Bar & Grill* (☎ 902-423-7463), a pavement café at 1663 Argyle St, is a local treasure. The décor alone is worth a visit, with its three distinctly different dining areas which contrast candlelit nooks and twinkling fairy lights with funky artwork and indoor shrubbery. Soak up the ambience over mouthwatering snacks and meals, including their award-winning nachos.

For more traditional fish and seafood, try *McKelvie's* (☎ 902-421-6161) a large, busy restaurant housed in a former fire station at 1680 Lower Water St (the crab and leek bisque is excellent), or the popular, buzzing *Salty's* (☎ 902-423-6818) on the waterfront, offering first-rate lobster, an outdoor patio and harbour views. Close by, in Privateer's Warehouse, *The Upper Deck* (☎ 902-422-1289) is another perennial favourite, with starched linen tablecloths, candles at the table and a romantic atmosphere.

Over at 1740 Argyle St, the elegant *The Five Fishermen* (☎ 902-422-4421) is famous for its eat-as-much-as-you-can mussel bar and generally delicious seafood. If you aren't sure how to tackle a lobster this is the place to head: the friendly staff will provide you with a step-by-step guide, diagrams included.

If all this fish and seafood is proving a bit much, head for *Ryan Duffy's* at 1650 Bedford Row (☎ 902-421-1116) for the best steak in Halifax – wheeled out, cut and weighed in front of you, before being cooked to perfection.

Finally, if you fancy a splurge, the renovated old Brewery Market on Lower Water St contains one of the city's best (and most expensive) restaurants: *Da Maurizio* (☎ 902-423-0859), where superb homemade pasta is served to a background of Italian opera in a beautiful dining room crammed with Italian reproductions.

NIGHTLIFE

With more pubs per head than any other city in Canada and enormous numbers of students, Halifax boasts a lively nightlife scene. In summer the most enjoyable and popular of the pubs are those with rooftop decks, including *The Thirsty Duck* at 5472 Spring Garden Rd, near the corner of Queen, and *Your Father's Moustache*, a couple of blocks away at No 5686 on the same street, which hosts a blues set on Saturday afternoons, popular with an older crowd.

Many other pubs also offer live music slots, from jazz and blues through to fiddle tunes and rock; check out the free weekly listings paper, *The Coast*, for details (available at the tourist office or online at 🖥 www.thecoast.ca). Regular pub-venues include *The Split Crow*, on the corner of Granville and Duke, *The Lower Deck*, bottom floor of Privateer's Warehouse in the Historic Properties, and *Bearly's House of Blues & Ribs* at 1269 Barrington St, which hosts lively blues events at the weekend and a karaoke night on Wednesdays. For something quieter, try *The Henry House*, at 1222 Barrington St, where you'll find great ales in a handsome old granite building.

Halifax has opened its doors to many Irish immigrants over the years, so it's no surprise that there are a number of lively Irish pubs here, including *The Old Triangle* on the corner of Bedford Row and Prince Street, and *Pogue Fado Irish Public House* at 1581 Barrington St, featuring traditional Irish décor, live music and cheap chicken wings on weekday evenings.

For a spot of dancing, head for *The Liquor Dome*, or 'The Dome' as it's known locally, at 1726–1740 Argyle St, open Wednesday–Sunday until 3.30am. It's something of a Halifax institution and houses several bars under one roof, including *Cheers* (mainly an older crowd), *The Attic* (with live music) and *The Dome* itself, with a largish dancefloor.

WHAT TO SEE

Though it boasts a couple of good museums, Halifax is not really about 'sights' so much as strolling around and soaking up the atmosphere. If you're staying in the downtown core, try to fit in a walk out to the residential quarters south of town, towards Point Pleasant Park, where you can admire the fabulous clapboard townhouses and mansions from the early 20th century.

The Citadel

The star-shaped fortress atop the hill (with its entrance on Sackville St) is a good place to start exploring Halifax; there's a superb view from here over the harbour and city and you'll be able to get your bearings and take in the lie of the land. There have been four forts here since 1749; the current one dates from 1856.

From June to October there are 45-minute-long guided tours throughout the day featuring the changing of the guard (performed by students dressed up as members of the 78th Highlanders and the Royal Artillery), a visit to the barrack rooms (furnished as they were in the 1860s) and an audio-visual display. Tickets cost $11.70 for adults, with reduced rates for seniors, youths and families. Beware of the eardrum-splitting gun that's fired at the Citadel every day at noon.

Old Town Clock

This rather beautiful clocktower stands just below the Citadel. It was presented to Halifax as a gift by Prince Edward in 1803 – a fitting present, given his legendary obsession with punctuality.

St Paul's Church

You'll walk past this pretty, white-timbered church many a time while wandering around Halifax. It's right in the centre of town at the south end of the Grand Parade on Argyle St. Opened in 1750, it is the oldest building in Halifax and the oldest Anglican church in Canada.

It's open to visitors daily 9am–4.30pm year-round, with free guided tours from May to September. Walking-tour leaflets are available by the entrance, pointing out the church's most important features. Notice the Royal Pew, reserved specifically for Her Majesty the Queen or any representatives sent to Halifax on her behalf. Look out, too, for the piece of wood embedded in the north wall above the door; it's a bit of the *Mont Blanc* that exploded in Halifax harbour (over 3.5km away) in 1917; see box p79.

Halifax City Hall

Across from St Paul's Church at the other end of the Grand Parade is Halifax's Victorian City Hall, completed in 1890. Free guided tours can be booked in advance (☎ 902-490-4039).

Province House

Charles Dickens visited Province House in 1842 and said it was 'like looking at Westminster through the wrong end of the telescope'. Presumably he was referring to the business conducted inside and not the building, which is Georgian, sandstone and delicately understated. Built in 1819, it is Canada's oldest seat of government. It's a couple of blocks from the Grand Parade, on Bedford Row, and is open to the public Monday to Friday 9am–5pm and weekends 10am–4pm during July and August, and Monday to Friday 9am–4pm for the rest of the year. Guided tours of roughly 15 minutes are available and entrance is free.

Art Gallery of Nova Scotia

Opposite Province House at 1723 Hollis St, the Art Gallery of Nova Scotia (open daily 10am–5pm, with late opening on Thursday until 9pm; entrance $10 adults, $5 students) houses a substantial collection of Nova Scotian, Canadian and some international art, spread over eight floors in two adjacent buildings.

In the **north gallery**, the ground level contains some arresting works by **contemporary Canadian artists** including Tom Forrestall's *Island in the Ice*, showing enormous chunks of ice breaking up around a tiny island with a lighthouse and a fragile-looking home, and Jean Paul Lemieux's *The Explorer*, a menacing close-up of a man wearing a dark coat and sunglasses on a snowy plain. In contrast, William Kuralek's series of Eskimo scenes are light and celebratory, particularly those of children playing. One of the gallery's highlights is the **folk art** on level 2, displaying works by local, untrained artists including Francis Silver's delightful scenes painted on the wooden planks of a carriage house, and many life-size, brightly painted carvings by other Nova Scotian craftsmen. Other works in this gallery include numerous **landscapes** (level 3), from both Canadian and international artists.

Over in the **south gallery**, the main attraction is the tiny wooden house that belonged to **Maud Lewis**, the Nova Scotian folk artist who became a household name in Canada before her death in 1970. Transported in its entirety to the museum, every available surface has been painted with bright, cheerful flowers, making it look like an oversized doll's house. Many of Lewis's paintings – landscapes and country scenes – are on display alongside and there's some captivating footage of the artist herself which explores her background and passion for art. Free guided tours are held at 2.30pm daily, with an evening tour at 7pm on Thursdays (🖳 www.artgalleryofnovascotia.ca).

Historic Properties

Down by the waterfront is a collection of beautifully renovated wharves and warehouses known as the Historic Properties. The oldest is Privateers' Warehouse, built in local granite and ironstone in 1813 (the Privateers were the British Crown's licensed pirates). The area, which had been falling into a state of dereliction following years of disuse, has been successfully transformed into an attractive collection of shops, pubs, eating places and artists' studios. It's a lively location in which to linger on a sunny day or an excellent place for an evening stroll, after dinner, when the whole area is lit up.

Alexander Keith's Nova Scotia Brewery

In 1820, the young Scottish immigrant Alexander Keith established his humble brewery at 1496 Lower Water St. Little did he know that over 180 years later his name would be associated with the oldest working brewery in North America. The brewery offers fun, highly interactive tours led by actors in period costume who shed fascinating light not just on the beer-making process but also on life in 19th-century Halifax. The tour ends up at the Red Stag Tavern, within the brewery, where you can sample Keith's finest ales. From June to October it's open Monday to Saturday noon–8pm and Sundays noon–5pm, with

---

The Halifax explosion

On the morning of 6 December 1917 two ships collided in Halifax harbour. One of them, the French *Mont Blanc*, was carrying relief supplies for the war: 2300 tonnes of picric acid, 10 tonnes of gun cotton, 35 tonnes of benzol and 200 tonnes of TNT. The result was the biggest man-made explosion the world had ever seen.

Before she exploded the ship drifted to one of Halifax's piers and burned away for 20 minutes. This left plenty of time for crowds to gather round and watch the spectacle. When the big bang came more than 1900 people were killed instantly. Of the survivors, many were horrifically maimed – 25 limbs were later amputated and more than 250 eyes had to be removed. The force of the blast razed half the city to the ground, leaving thousands of Haligonians homeless. Incredibly, all but one of the men aboard the *Mont Blanc* survived the disaster, having rowed to shore in the right direction.

This tragic accident proved to be a precursor of atomic warfare; the physicist J Robert Oppenheimer studied the effects of the Halifax explosion while developing America's bombs for Hiroshima and Nagasaki.

CITY GUIDES

restricted opening hours for the rest of the year. Entrance is $16, with reduced rates for concessions; you'll find more details on ⌨ www.keiths.ca.

The Maritime Museum of the Atlantic

Down by the water's edge at 1675 Lower Water St, this museum has some good displays depicting the maritime history of the region. Particularly fascinating is the section on the *Titanic* featuring some salvaged items, recreated first-, second- and third-class cabins and a 3-D 'virtual tour' of the ship. When this unfortunate ship sank on 15 April 1912, a huge rescue operation got underway from Halifax. Two hundred and nine bodies were recovered and brought to the city and embalmers were enlisted from all over the Maritimes to cope with the work. About 55 bodies were claimed; the rest were buried in unnumbered graves. The privileges of first-class travel were upheld even in the face of death: the bodies of ordinary passengers were simply tagged before being brought into Halifax; the bodies of first-class passengers were immediately embalmed and laid in coffins. The museum's other highlights include a massive octagonal lens from an 18th-century lighthouse; a roomful of small wooden boats (including Queen Victoria's royal barge); casefuls of beautiful 19th-century sextants, clocks, figureheads and anchors – and a very vocal resident parrot named Merlin.

Summer opening hours (March–April) are daily 9.30am–5.30pm, with late opening until 8pm on Tuesdays; winter hours (November–April) are Tuesday to Saturday 9.30am–5pm, Sunday 1–5pm. Entrance is $8.75 in summer, $4.75 in winter and free on Tuesday evenings between 5.30pm and 8pm. The museum also gives free talks on Tuesday evenings at 7.30pm.

Pier 21

Directly behind the train station on the harbour front, Pier 21 is one of Halifax's most engaging attractions. Between 1928 and 1971, the pier was the entry point and immigration clearing post for over a million arrivals from Europe, most of whom boarded trains to other parts of Canada. Designated a national historic site, the building now provides a fascinating and often moving testimony to Canada's immigrants – whose numbers included thousands of refugees, war brides, wartime evacuees and 'home children' from orphanages – with a hall full of evocative black-and-white photographs, information panels, displays of passports, letters, telegrams and other personal effects, and a series of tape recordings of first-hand accounts reflecting the different experiences of immigration.

Rounding it all up is a highly entertaining holographic show depicting some of the typical people that passed through Pier 21, including a Ukrainian farm-

---

Whale-watching

There are a number of outfits on the waterfront near the Maritime Museum offering boat and, more specifically, whale-watching trips from June to October. One of the best deals is the Maritime Experience Tour with **Four Winds Charters** (☎ 902-492-0022 or toll-free on ☎ 1-877-274-8421, ⌨ www.fourwindscharters.com) who, for $25, offer 2½-hour trips in search of minke, humpback and blue whales with stories of shipwrecks and pirates to entertain along the way.

ing family, a Canadian soldier returning from World War II and a couple of hilarious British war brides (with rather dubious cockney accents).

Pier 21 (🖳 www.pier21.ca) is open daily 9.30am–5.30pm from May to October, and 9.30am–5pm in November. Between December and March the opening hours are Tuesday to Saturday 10am–5pm, while in April they are Monday to Saturday 10am–5pm. Entrance costs $8.50 year-round.

Point Pleasant Park

A few miles out of town is the splendid Point Pleasant Park, 186 acres of forest-land on the tip of the Halifax peninsula. The park has a good network of trails and footpaths (much more accessible than in the more famous Stanley Park in Vancouver) and the shoreline boasts a sandy beach from which you can bathe. Look out for the heather close to the southern shores; it grew from seeds accidentally brought over in the mattresses of the Scottish Highland Regiment and has flourished ever since. Incidentally, Halifax still rents this park from the British Government on a 999-year lease for the bargain rate of one shilling a year.

To get to Point Pleasant Park by public transport, take bus No 9 from Barrington St (around every 20–30 minutes on weekdays, hourly at 45 minutes past the hour on Saturdays and on the hour on Sundays).

MOVING ON

By rail

Trains leave Halifax for Montreal at 12.35pm daily except Tuesday. The journey takes 21 hours. The toll-free VIA information number is ☎ 1-888-842-7245.

To get to the rail station from downtown, take the No 9, 7 or 35 bus running south along Barrington St.

By air

The cheapest way of getting to the airport is on the Airbus (☎ 902-873-2091). Tickets are $21 and the bus picks passengers up at all the major downtown hotels. The phone number for Air Canada is ☎ 902-429-7111 or you can call toll free on ☎ 1-888-247-2262.

Quebec City

Nothing struck me as so beautiful and grand as the location of the town of Quebec, which could not be better situated even were it to become, in some future time, the capital of a great Empire. **Frontenac**, in a letter, 1672

Quebec City, spilling down Cap Diamant's slopes onto the banks of the St Lawrence, is surely one of the most picturesque cities in North America and amply deserves its status as UNESCO World Heritage Site. Inside the old quarter, Quebec's much-vaunted European flavour exceeds expectations: its narrow, cobblestoned streets are lined with 17th- and 18th-century houses; 95% of the population is of French ancestry and many inhabitants speak English with a strong French accent (and some not at all). It's all wonderfully exotic and more than a little disorientating.

It would be a great shame not to visit Quebec City while in Eastern Canada, but two or three days should be enough to savour its charms before moving on. This is, after all, a city that makes a living out of its history and after a while you can begin to feel that you're trapped in a little time bubble.

HISTORY

Cartier lands at Stadacona

Quebec City is the oldest European settlement in Canada though it was, of course, inhabited long before Jacques Cartier first landed on the site in 1535. When Cartier arrived it was the location of an Iroquois village named Stadacona, presided over by Chief Donnacona. After spending the winter there, Cartier and his men abducted Donnacona and some Iroquois and took them back to France. All of the natives except one girl died within a few years of arriving in Europe.

Permanent French base established

It wasn't until 1608 that a permanent European base was established, not by Cartier but by Samuel de Champlain, who founded a fur-trading post at the foot of Cap Diamant and named it Quebec. By this time the settlement at Stadacona had vanished and there was no trace of the Iroquois. Seven years later the first Récollet missionaries arrived, followed by the Jesuits in 1625. The new colony, however, provoked the jealousy and hostility of the British, who blockaded it until it surrendered in 1629. Britain held on to the settlement for just three years before the territory was returned to France in 1632.

Expansion

Back in the hands of the French, the settlement began to expand rapidly as more settlers came out and a church, a school and a hospital were built. It wasn't long before the economy, which revolved around the fur trade, began to diversify: leather manufacturing, shipbuilding and logging were all initiated in the latter half of the 17th century. Foreign aggression continued to disturb the city's peace, however, and in 1690 Quebec was unsuccessfully attacked by troops from New England. It was at this point that work began on the city's fortifications.

Battle on the Plains of Abraham

In 1759 the British were back to launch a massive assault on the city, with the aid of 76 warships, 9000 soldiers, 10,000 fire bombs and 40,000 cannon balls. Quebec, under the command of the Marquis de Montcalm, held out for three months before the British – under General Wolfe – managed to land on the western side of Cap Diamant during the night. Taken by surprise, Montcalm's forces were defeated in a battle lasting less than half an hour. Both Wolfe and Montcalm were killed and Quebec fell to the British. The battle marked the beginning of the end of New France, which was handed over to Britain in its entirety in 1763.

Quebec under the British

The city's French-speaking community of 8000 people suddenly found itself under the rule of an English governor. Despite fears of enforced Anglicization, the Quebec Act of 1774 guaranteed the protection of the Catholic religion and the French language. Apart from an unsuccessful attempt by the Americans to take the city in 1775, Quebec was allowed to develop undisturbed over the next century. The mainstays of its economy were logging and shipbuilding and it continued to be an important port right through to the 1950s when the St Lawrence was artificially widened to allow ships to reach Montreal.

Quebec today

Largely ignored in favour of Montreal by the immigrant Irish and Scottish merchants at the turn of the 20th century, Quebec City has remained almost completely Francophone. The city, which is the capital of the Province of Quebec, is an important administrative and educational centre and has spread out well beyond the confines of the old quarters. Today, the city of Quebec has a population of around 500,000.

For most visitors, however, the most visible face of Quebec is that of its narrow streets and old-world charm that draws millions of tourists here each year. Nonetheless, Quebec does not pander indiscriminately to tourists and its people often seem refreshingly detached from the predominantly English speaking, camera-clicking crowds wandering through their streets.

ARRIVING IN QUEBEC CITY

By train

Since the land where *The Ocean* used to pull in has been sold to property developers, trains from Halifax now arrive at **Charny**, a small town 26km outside Quebec City. From Charny, a small minibus takes passengers to the **Gare du Palais**, the beautiful old train station in Quebec's Basse-Ville (lower town). Minibus tickets should be booked in advance, from VIA Rail ticket counters. From the Gare, unless you're prepared to hike up the steep streets to the Haute-Ville where you'll probably be sleeping, the only way up is by taxi (roughly $6 to the top of the Haute-Ville); there are usually a few around the train station but if none appears, call one of the taxi companies listed on p84.

Alternatively, you can take a taxi from Charny to Quebec. It costs around $32 to get to the centre of town, which may be more cost effective if there are a number of passengers.

❏ **Quebec City online**

✉ **www.quebecregion.com** Put together by the Quebec City Tourism Board, this is a very useful website on the city. For more information, contact ✉ info@quebec region.com; ✉ **www.bonjourquebec.com** Tourisme Québec's site, with information on the whole province. Emails can be sent to ✉ info@tourisme.gouv.qc.ca.

CITY GUIDES

By air

Serving mainly domestic flights, Jean-Lesage Airport is 20km outside the city. It's connected to downtown by taxi (fixed rate of $32.50).

GETTING AROUND

Vieux-Québec is entirely navigable **on foot**. The only reason you might need to take a bus is to avoid the walk to the Musée du Québec or if you want to get out of town to the Montmorency Falls.

The **bus** service is run by the Réseau de Transport de la Capitale, otherwise known as RTC (☎ 418-627-2511, 🖳 www.rtcquebec.ca). The main point for catching buses is at Place d'Youville, near Porte Saint-Jean.

There are several **taxi** ranks dotted around town or you can call one from Taxi Co-op Québec (☎ 418-525-5191) or Taxi Québec (☎ 418-522-2001).

Finally, you can hire **bicycles** at Cyclo Services, 289 rue St Paul (☎ 418-692-4052, 🖳 www.cycloservices.net).

ORIENTATION

Quebec City is very small and you'll have no problem finding your way around. Most visitors are here to see Vieux Québec, which is divided between the **Basse-Ville** (lower town) at the foot of Cap Diamant and the **Haute-Ville** (upper town) perched on the top of Cap Diamant. There are steps leading from Place Royale in the Basse-Ville to the terrace beside Château Frontenac in the Haute-Ville. There's also a funicular to and from the same places. Haute-Ville is where you'll probably spend most of your time and it's where almost all the accommodation is located. Part of the Haute-Ville is surrounded by the old city walls. Quebec is, incidentally, the continent's only walled city north of Mexico.

SERVICES

Tourist information

There are two tourist information centres. The most centrally located is the large **Centre Infotouriste de Québec** at 12 rue Sainte-Anne, just across from the Château Frontenac, where you can pick up information about the whole province and book accommodation. It's open daily 9am–7pm between late June and mid August and 9am–5pm for the rest of the year. The other, focusing more on the city, is the **Bureau d'Information Touristique du Vieux-Québec** (☎ 418-641-6290) at 835 ave Wilfred-Laurier, just off Grande Allée Est and near the Drill Hall. It's open daily 8.30am–7.30pm from late June to early September; from September to October 12 it's open daily 8.30am–6.30pm and during the rest of the year from Monday to Saturday 9am–5pm, Sunday 10am–4pm.

Money

The conveniently located Caisse Populaire Desjardins du Vieux-Quebec, at 19 rue des Jardins, changes travellers' cheques between 9am and 3pm, closing at 2pm on weekends and at 6pm on Thursdays; it also has a 24-hour ATM. Other banks include the Royal Bank of Canada at 700 place d'Youville and the National Bank of Canada at 1199 rue Saint-Jean.

Consulates

Finland (☎ 418-683-3000) 500 Grande-Allée Est; **France** (☎ 418-266-2500) 25 rue St Louis; **Italy** (☎ 418-529-9801) 3876 Pollack St; **Netherlands** (☎ 418-525-8344)) 1040 avenue Belvédère; **Norway** (☎ 418-647-6633) 140 Grande Allée Est; **Switzerland** (☎ 418-527-3787) 2170 Boisjoli; **USA** (☎ 418-692-2095) 2 place Terrasse Dufferin

Post, internet and laundry

The main **post office** is at 5 rue du Fort. The city has a number of **internet cafés**: Tribune Café on place d'Youville has two terminals and charges $4.75 per hour; Centre Internet at 52 Côte du Palais charges $6 per hour, while just around the corner at 5 rue du Fort there's a free terminal in the post office.

The Lavoir St-Ursule at 17b rue St-Ursule, just off rue St Jean, is one of the most conveniently located **laundries**, though it's a little dated and all the signs and instructions are in French. Although the washing machines are fairly standard, the dryers appear to be a few decades old – you can actually catch a glimpse of flames as the gas heaters dry your clothing!

WHERE TO STAY

Surprisingly for such a popular tourist destination, accommodation in Quebec City is very reasonably priced and most of it is located right in the heart of the old town.

Budget accommodation

The best choice is the bright, attractive *Auberge de la Paix* (☎ 418-694-0735, 🖳 www.aubergedelapaix.com), 31 rue Couillard, in a beautiful old house with a garden; the beds are in small dormitories and the rate ($25, or $29 per person with bedding) includes breakfast. The hostel also offers a small number of rooms with beds for 2, 3 and 4 people at the same rate but, unlike dormitory beds in larger rooms, they cannot be booked in advance. The *HI Auberge Internationale de Québec* (☎ 418-694-0755, 🖳 www.aubergeinternationalede quebec.com) at 19 rue Sainte-Ursule is also very popular and tends to get packed out. Its dorm beds are $27.61 for members and $31.61 for non-members, while its private rooms start at $83.53. The staff are really friendly and there's a nice, bustling atmosphere. Both Auberge de la Paix and HI Auberge Internationale de Quebec are well located in the heart of the old town.

The *Université de Laval* (🖳 www.sres.ulaval.ca) has good private rooms with shared bath: singles cost $39.51 for students and $48.54 for non-students, with doubles at $58.70 and $66.60, respectively. The only downside is that it's

❑ Accommodation prices quoted in this book are for **high season** (normally May or June to September). In low season many hotels offer substantial discounts.

CITY GUIDES

CITY GUIDES

Quebec City

0 — 150 — 300m

Where to stay
2 Auberge de la Paix
4 Hôtel Manoir Victoria
8 HI Auberge Internationale de Québec
9 Manoir La Salle
10 Hôtel Maison Sainte-Ursule
11 Hôtel Acadia
12 Hôtel L'Ermitage
13 Hôtel le Clos Saint-Louis
14 Hôtel Louisbourg
16 Auberge Saint-Louis
19 Château Frontenac
21 Auberge St Antoine

Where to eat
1 Chez Temporel
3 Pub St Patrick
5 Le Casse-Crêpe Breton
6 Le Petit Coin Breton
7 Ristorante Il Teatro
15 L'Omelette & Café de Paris
17 La Cremaillere
18 Aux Anciens Canadiens
20 Café Buade
22 Panache
23 Le Petit Cochon Dingue

around a ten-minute bus ride from the centre (take bus No 13, 18, 87 or Métrobus 800 or 801 from place d'Youville).

Mid-range hotels

This is where the real bargains are to be found. Many of the city's old residences have been converted to small inns or guesthouses, usually containing about 10 to 15 rooms of varying sizes and prices. One of the cheapest options is friendly *Manoir La Salle* (☎ 418-692-9953) at 18 rue Sainte-Ursule, where you'll find a variety of simple, spacious rooms (some with shared bathrooms) from $45 for a single.

Another good choice, at No 40 on the same street, is *Hôtel Maison Sainte-Ursule* (☎ 418-694-9794), with 15 cheerful rooms, a friendly owner and an entertaining, bilingual cockatoo. Eight of the rooms are in the original old house, which in 1786 was only the second to be built on the rue Sainte-Ursule; the remaining newer rooms overlook a pleasant garden area. Rates here range from $49 to $119 depending on the type of room and bathroom facilities. Almost opposite, at No 43, *Hôtel Acadia* (☎ 418-694-0280, 🖳 www.hotelacadia.com) has 41 lovely rooms with period features; prices range from $89 to $295. It makes a relaxing place to stay, boasting massage facilities and an outdoor spa. Owned by the same company, the *Hôtel L'Ermitage* (☎ 418-694-0968, 🖳 www.hotellermitage.com) is further along rue St-Ursule, at number 60, and is a lot smaller than its sister hotel, with only ten rooms. It does, however, offer the same facilities as larger hotels, such as internet connection and cable TV; doubles range from $129 to $159.

Another street with a concentration of hotels is rue Saint-Louis, where at No 68 you'll find *Hôtel Louisbourg* (☎ 418-694-0656, 🖳 http://www.quebec web.com/hotel-louisbourg); the bare stone walls of the bedrooms here date back to 1814. Rooms cost from around $99 to $225; breakfast is available at an extra charge. *Auberge Saint-Louis* (☎ 418-692-2424, 🖳 www.aubergestlouis.ca) at No 48 has far less character but it's clean and fine, with doubles starting at $69 for two people with a full breakfast included.

Upmarket hotels

You can't get much more upmarket than the *Château Frontenac* (☎ 418-692-3861, 🖳 www.fairmont.com). If you feel like indulging your fantasy of staying in a glamorous hotel, this is the place to do it. Everything is swimming in luxury, from the vast entrance lobby with its shining brass elevators to the sumptuous marble bathrooms. Some of the guests, however, look rather out of place in their trainers and jeans: it's the kind of establishment where you'd expect everyone to wear 1930s evening dress at the very least. Breakfast is served in an elegant restaurant overlooking the Château grounds (and note that the Eggs Benedict are not to be missed). As you might expect, a night at the Château does not come cheap, with bed and breakfast packages starting at $287.

If there's no room at the Château, you could try the elegant *Hôtel Manoir Victoria* (☎ 418-692-1030, 🖳 www.manoir-victoria.com) at 44 côte du Palais. This 4-star hotel juxtaposes old with new, its handsome original architecture complemented by some impressive modern touches such as the water feature in the lobby. The hotel boasts the only pool within the walled area of Quebec City and offers a gorgeous spa. The spacious rooms are from $175 to $500 for a deluxe suite.

For something smaller and more intimate, head for the splendid **Hôtel le Clos Saint-Louis** (☎ 418-694-1311, 🖳 www.clossaintlouis.com) on 69 rue Saint Louis, where many of the 18 deluxe rooms boast antique beds, high ceilings and fireplaces. The lounge is a pleasure to relax in with its elegant décor and exquisite furniture and the staff are very friendly. Doubles are from $205 in high season.

Just outside the city walls, **Auberge Saint-Antoine**, 8 rue St Antoine (☎ 418-692-2211, 🖳 www.saint-antoine.com), offers an interesting alternative to other luxury hotels. The interior design incorporates both archaeological artefacts found on the site during the hotel's construction and modern pieces of furniture and art. Double rooms starts at $169.

WHERE TO EAT

The narrow streets of the old town are jam-packed with pavement cafés, bistros, crêperies and restaurants which, although directed mainly at tourists, are irresistibly appealing and atmospheric. As with the city's architecture, the food is disconcertingly French, with staples like *steak-frites*, *moules marinières* and *salade niçoise* featuring on many menus. Moreover, the quality is generally good and the prices fairly reasonable.

Budget food

An excellent choice for a cheap lunch is the always-packed **Le Casse-Crêpe Breton**, 1136 rue Saint-Jean, which features a huge selection of crêpes (including the option to design your own) at unbeatable prices cooked in front of you on a big hotplate. Another place to head for is **L'Omelette** at 66 rue Saint-Louis which, besides its 15 trademark omelettes, offers a wide variety of inexpensive breakfasts, salads, soups, lunches, pizzas and cakes in a cheerful, sunny dining room with polished wooden floors and high ceilings. The restaurant opens at 7am with some great breakfast specials, so get there early to grab a window seat and watch the world go by.

Pub St Patrick at 1200 rue St Jean has a lively atmosphere and a popular outdoor terrace where you can enjoy either traditional pub food or choose from a selection of French favourites, all at reasonable prices. The pub also hosts live music events several nights a week.

Le Petit Cochon Dingue, 24 boulevard Champlain, is a cosy café with a pleasant outdoor terrace overlooking the waterfront. Delicious croissants, quiches and *tartines* can be purchased for under $10.

Finally, if all this French fare is proving a bit too much head to **Café Buade** on rue de Buade, opposite the Basilica, with its comfy booths and American diner-style atmosphere, where you can fill up on tasty omelettes and a selection of hearty breakfast dishes.

Mid-range and upmarket restaurants

Tucked away at 25 rue Couillard, *Chez Temporel* (☎ 418-694-1813) is a mellow café-restaurant serving crisp salads, baguette sandwiches and light meals; it has a relaxed, friendly atmosphere and is the sort of place where locals read their newspapers over a long, leisurely coffee.

Le Petit Coin Breton (☎ 418-694-0758) at 1029 rue Saint-Jean, although unashamedly aimed at tourists (forcing its waiters to wear slightly ridiculous Breton costumes), serves a very decent range of sweet and savoury crêpes at affordable prices.

Next door to L'Omelette on rue Saint-Louis, *Café de Paris* (☎ 418-694-9626) provides a nice, candlelit environment in which to enjoy a variety of veal, fish and steak dishes. In a lively location at place d'Youville, *Ristorante Il Teatro* (☎ 418-694-9996) offers good Italian food (main courses between $19 and $25) and a sheltered outdoor patio where you can overlook the bustling square whatever the weather.

Outside the city walls at 203 rue St Joseph Est in the up-and-coming St Roch district, *Le Clocher Penché Bistrot* (☎ 418-640-0597) is a modern take on the French brasserie, with menus featuring fresh, seasonal ingredients and an affordable set menu at lunchtime.

Top end establishments include *La Cremaillere*, 73 rue Sainte-Anne (☎ 418-692-2216), with specialities such as milk-fed veal and a wine cellar stocked with fine Italian wines, and *Aux Anciens Canadiens* (☎ 418-692-1627), located at 34 rue Saint-Louis in one of the oldest buildings in Quebec. This old-fashioned restaurant specializes in traditional Québecois cuisine, such as game and rich meat, and has a reputation for excellent food. Distinctly more contemporary is award-winning *Panache* in the Auberge St-Antoine (☎ 418-692-1022), 10 rue St Antoine. Here, in a renovated old warehouse overlooking the river, you can enjoy excellent – if pricey – food such as poached lobster with lentils and crispy bacon, or spit-roasted duckling.

NIGHTLIFE

The city really comes alive at night and you'll find any number of pubs, bars and late-night cafés around town, with a concentration in rue Saint-Jean and Grande Allée Est, outside the city walls, where trendy young locals hang out after work and at weekends. A couple to look out for are *Le Pub St Alexandre* at 1087 rue St Jean, a slightly formulaic pseudo-English pub but with some good live folk music, and *Sacrilège* at 447 rue St Jean, a popular place for locals drawn here by some well-known local musicians. Down in the Quartier du Petit Champlain, *Le Pape Georges* at 8 rue Cul-de-sac is a dark and cosy little bar with live blues and folk.

Quebec City is famous for its **boîtes à chansons**, which should most definitely be sampled while you're here. They're basically intimate bars where earnest balladeers strum their guitars and sing their hearts out to an enthusiastic young crowd who seem to know all the words and delight in singing along. They're usually free and have a friendly, unthreatening atmosphere; they're

CITY GUIDES

liveliest on Friday and Saturday nights but don't really get going until around 11pm. One of the best boîtes à chansons is *Chez Son Père* at 24 rue Stanislas.

For a more energetic night out, visit *Maurice* nightclub at 575 Grande Allée Est, which houses several themed bars within one building and is one of Quebec's most popular night spots. *Dagobert*, opposite at No 600, is identifiable by its giant glitter ball that hangs outside, lighting up the street, and has a younger clientele.

WHAT TO SEE

Haute Ville

● **Château Frontenac** More than a hotel, the towering château has become the symbol of Quebec and is one of the most photographed buildings in Canada. Now part of the Fairmont group, it was commissioned for the CPR by Van Horne in 1893 and was designed by an eminent American architect, Bruce Price.

Château Frontenac
PHOTO © JIM MANTHORPE

Guided tours ($8.50; 🖳 www.tours chateau.ca) around the hotel's magnificent interior leave on the hour (daily 10am–6pm May to October, weekends 12–5pm November to April) and last around 50 minutes.

● **Terrasse Dufferin** Next to Château Frontenac is this long boardwalk skirting the edge of Cap Diamant. The views from here – over the St Lawrence, the Basse-Ville, the Laurentian mountains and even the foothills of the US Appalachians – are absolutely stunning, especially at sunset. The Terrasse extends into the **Promenade des Gouverneurs**, which climbs to the Citadelle and continues to the Plains of Abraham.

● **Citadelle** This massive star-shaped fortress was built over a 30-year period (1820–50) by the British. Contained within its wide dykes and thick, squat walls are 25 buildings, including the Governor-General's summer residence, the officers' mess and a military museum. Still used as the headquarters of the Royal 22nd Regiment, it is the oldest occupied North American fort and has its own mascot, a regimental goat named Batisse.

Entrance to the Citadelle costs $10 for adults; once inside you take a 45-minute guided tour, watch the Changing of the Guard (mid-June to August, 10am) or the Ceremony of the Retreat (July to August, 7pm on Friday nights). The grounds are open to the public on a daily basis (9am–5pm between May and June, 9am–6pm from July to early September); you'll find further details at 🖳 www.lacitadelle.qc.ca.

● **Plains of Abraham** It's hard to believe that this undulating parkland was the scene of the violent confrontation between Wolfe and Montcalm in 1759 (see p82), an episode that changed the course of Canadian history. Today it's a favourite area for picnickers and joggers and only a few monuments, plaques and information boards bear testimony to the famous battle played out on these fields.

● **Musée National des Beaux-Arts du Québec** Situated at the far end of the Plains of Abraham, this museum contains the biggest and best collection of Quebec art, covering a period of about three hundred years. Works range from 17th-century religious painting through to the latest movements in contemporary art and include sculpture, photography and decorative art. It also houses a compelling collection of Inuit art. The museum (🖳 www.mnba.qc.ca) opens daily 10am–6pm (Wednesdays until 9pm) from June to September, or Tuesday to Sunday 10am–5pm (Wednesdays until 9pm) for the rest of the year. Admission is $15.

● **Musée du Fort** This tiny museum (which hasn't changed much since it opened in 1965) is loads of fun. Visitors are seated in front of a huge plastic model of 18th-century Quebec City; the lights are dimmed and a rippling voice, accompanied by atmospheric music and flashing lights, relates the story of the six sieges of the city, including the famous battle in 1759. The show, alternating throughout the day in French and English, lasts about half an hour and costs $8; it's worth it just for retro-value and the entertaining interactive quiz which follows the story.

The museum (🖳 www.museedufort.com) is at 10 rue Sainte-Anne. It's open daily 10am–5pm between March and November and during the Christmas holidays, and Thursday to Sunday 11am–4pm for the rest of the year.

● **The Quebec Experience** A slightly dated 3-D hologram show depicts Quebec's history from the first explorers through to the last few decades. You don your 3-D specs and sit back to watch the show, with commentary provided by a hologram of Cartier. It's fairly entertaining and is especially good for kids. Shows alternate in French and English throughout the day at 30-minute intervals. It's at 8 rue du Trésor; admission is $7.50 and it's open daily 10am–10pm from mid-May to mid-October. The month of May tends to get packed with groups of enthusiastic schoolchildren, so check in advance as shows can get booked up quickly (🖳 www.quebecexperience.com).

● **Notre-Dame de Quebec Basilica Cathedral** Notre-Dame is the continent's oldest parish north of Mexico. Work began on the building in 1647 and the first Mass was celebrated in the cathedral in 1650. Sadly, it burnt to the ground in 1922 but has since been rebuilt to the original 17th-century plans. The interior is wonderfully light in tone, with its pale walls, shining gold-leaf altar and sky-blue ceiling.

● **Anglican Cathedral of the Holy Trinity** This church is supposed to be modelled on London (England)'s St Martin's in the Fields (though unfortunately they forgot to build a café in the crypt). There are some interesting features inside, such as the benches made of oak imported from the royal forest in Windsor and the rather under-used Royal Seat, reserved exclusively for the use of the British monarch.

● **Grande-Allée Est** Leaving the walled town via rue Saint-Louis, you'll find yourself on the Grand-Allée Est, a lively avenue lined with cafés, restaurants and shops. It has a very modern feel to it and lots of locals come here to enjoy an after-work drink in the bustling pavement cafés. Take a right onto avenue Cartier and you'll find an abundance of fresh fruit and vegetable stalls as well as fashionable boutiques.

● **L'Observatoire de la Capitale** If you've a head for heights and fancy looking down on Quebec from a different perspective, head for L'Observatoire (🖥 www.observatoirecapitale.org), an observation tower at 1037 rue de la Chevrotière. The lift takes you 221m up to the 31st floor where you can look out over the Laurentian mountains, the St Lawrence River and the whole of the city spread out below you. Entrance is $5; opening hours are daily 10am–5pm from February to mid-October and Tuesday to Sunday 10am–5pm for the rest of the year.

Basse-Ville
To get to the lower town you can walk down the steps starting at Terrasse Dufferin, or you can take the funicular running next to them ($1.75).

● **Quartier Petit Champlain** This little warren of winding streets full of craft shops and the like is wholly given over to tourism. It's Quebec at its cutest and quaintest.

At the centre of the quartier is **rue du Petit-Champlain**, the city's oldest street (dating from 1685) where you can walk down the charmingly named **Escalier Casse-Cou**, the 'break-your-neck staircase'. Look out too for the **Fresque des Québecois**, an enormous mural covering the entire side of a building in rue Notre Dame that details 400 years of Quebecois history.

● **Place Royale** This is where Quebec City was originally founded back in 1608. The square has been extensively restored over the past few decades and is another example of Quebec's carefully groomed prettiness.

Take a look inside the **Eglise Notre-Dame-des-Victoires** on the southern side of the square; note the curious high altar sculpted to look like a castle. At 1 place Royale is the **Maison des Vins** which was built in 1689. It is still operated by a vintage-wine specialist, with free wine tasting available.

● **Musée de la Civilisation** If you have time for just one museum in Quebec, make it the Musée de la Civilisation (🖥 www.mcq.org). The building alone won awards for its architectural excellence and the museum's exhibits are very innovative, particularly in this town that seems so firmly rooted in the past.

The exhibitions are mostly temporary and cover a diverse range of historical, sociological and scientific themes (and even a recent interactive Extra-Terrestrial exhibition). The clever use of space, light and technology makes the museum a pleasure to walk around. It's near to place Royale at 85 rue Dalhousie and is open daily from late June to early September 9.30am–6.30pm. September to early October it opens daily 10am-5pm, otherwise Tuesday to Sunday 10am–5pm. Entrance is $11, or free on Tuesdays between November and May.

Montmorency Falls

Some 12km east of the city are the spectacular Montmorency Falls. At 83m high, they are one and a half times the height of Niagara Falls. You can take a cable car ($10.50 per person) from the foot of the cliffs up to the beginning of the waterfall, which you can cross on a rather wobbly bridge. This is the third bridge to be built here; the second one collapsed five days after it was completed in 1855, causing three people to plunge down the falls to their deaths. Nearby is the Manoir Montmorency, a former residence of Edward, Duke of Kent, who was Queen Victoria's father.

You can get the No 50, 53 or 800 bus to the falls from the Haute-Ville at ave Dufferin. There's also a well-used cycle path from the city out to the falls, which can be reached in about half an hour by bike.

FESTIVALS

● **Carnival de Québec**, early February. Sixteen days of freezing madness featuring a mass roll in the snow wearing bathing suits, a canoe race across the frozen St Lawrence and the world's largest snow-sculpture exhibition.
● **Festival d'été**, early July. A ten-day whirl of street parties, concerts, singing, dancing and drinking. Excellent fun.
● **Saint-Jean-Baptiste Day**, 24 June. Provincial holiday – parades and celebrations.
● **Loto-Quebec International Fireworks Competition**, mid July to mid August. A spectacular event in which various nations present a fireworks display set to music over the Montmorency Falls. Not to be missed.
● **La Fête de la Nouvelle France**, mid-August. A five-day celebration of the Renaissance and Middle Ages. Lots of dressing-up in silly clothes.

MOVING ON

There's a frequent daily train service from Quebec's Gare du Palais to Montreal, just under three hours away. For information on trains from Quebec call ☎ 1-888-842-7245.

Montreal

This is the first time I was ever in a city where you couldn't throw a brick without breaking a church window.   **Mark Twain**, Speech in Montreal, 1881

Montreal is a delicious, feel-good city. Famous throughout Canada for its party atmosphere, it is positively spilling over with buskers, jazz cellars, wine bars, nightclubs and throngs of beautiful people. It's not an entirely frivolous place, however, and even casual visitors are aware of the complex balance of relationships contained within the city: between the English- and French-speaking inhabitants, for example; between the North American and European influences; and between the claims of Canada and Quebec.

You can see or feel Montreal's contrasts all around: in the architecture, the food, the newspapers, the snatches of conversation you hear on the streets. But far from producing a feeling of tension, it all adds up to a very rich and full-flavoured city that is one of the most appealing and intriguing in North America.

HISTORY

Early settlement

The site of present-day Montreal was first occupied by the Iroquois Indians who called their settlement 'Hochelaga' (meaning 'Place of the beaver'). The first European to arrive was Jacques Cartier who stopped off at the island in 1535 on his way to seek the North-West Passage. He climbed the mountain that rose out of the island's centre, named it Mont Réal and then promptly left. About 70 years passed before the French returned, only to discover that Hochelaga had mysteriously vanished. The site was subsequently chosen as a fur-trading base, erected by Samuel de Champlain in 1611.

French colonists arrive

It wasn't until 1642 that a permanent settlement was established outside the confines of the fur trade. This was created by Paul de Chomedey, the Sieur de Maisonneuve, who brought 53 French colonists out with the intention of converting the natives to Christianity. They built houses, a church and a hospital and named the new community Ville-Marie. By 1672 the population had reached 1200, a figure that began to multiply rapidly during the first half of the 18th century when land grants enticed French settlers out in their droves.

The British take over

In 1756 Europe became engulfed in the Seven Years' War. The fighting spread to the North American colonies and in 1760 the British took control of Montreal. When the war ended three years later all of New France was ceded to Britain under the Treaty of Paris. Scottish and Irish immigrants flocked to Montreal to make their fortunes and it wasn't long before the Brits started nudging the French out of their position in Montreal's business life. All this was briefly interrupted in 1755 when American troops marched in and occupied the city for several months. When they retreated, life in Montreal carried on in much the same way as before.

The French were feeling increasingly frustrated by the disappearance of their power and political representation and in 1837 Louis-Joseph Papineau led an uprising against the British. The rebellion was brutally crushed but resentment, of course, remained strong.

The economic hub of Canada

Following Confederation in 1867, Montreal emerged as the economic, financial and transportation centre of the new dominion. Expansion and rapid industrialization followed and as the city entered the 20th century it was firmly established as Canada's most important metropolis. Prosperity and success endured, culminating in a massive spate of architectural development in the 1960s in preparation for Expo '67 – a colossal affair that brought 50 million visitors into Montreal.

Unrest breaks out

Meanwhile, resentment within the Francophone community continued to bubble away. Despite being in the majority, they found themselves in a subordinate, disadvantaged position in most levels of society and the Anglophones appeared to remain indifferent to this injustice. While movements such as René Lévesque's Parti Québecois began to gather momentum, it was the dramatic action of the extremist FLQ that brought the crisis to a violent head in October 1970.

Following a wave of terrorism, they kidnapped and murdered a Quebec cabinet minister, Pierre Laporte. The assassins were captured and arrested but the shocked government realized that drastic measures would have to be taken to avoid similar explosions of violence. Laws were introduced to protect the French language and the general 'Frenchification' of Montreal got underway. Many Anglophones felt threatened by what was going on and over 100,000 left the city over the next few years.

Montreal today

The commercial and financial damage brought about by the Anglophone exodus was quickly repaired by a new wave of French-speaking entrepreneurs. Today they control about 60% of Montreal's economy, a balance more acceptable to most Francophones. Montreal is no longer Canada's biggest city, having been overtaken by Toronto in the late 1960s. Nevertheless it continues to be a thriving and affluent metropolis with a strong economy.

Secession continues to be a controversial issue in Quebec's politics but whereas in the 1995 sovereignty referendum almost half the province's population (49.4%) voted in favour of separation from Canada, recent polls indicate that support for separation has greatly declined in the intervening years.

ARRIVING IN MONTREAL

By air

Most international flights arrive at **Montreal-Trudeau Airport**, 22km southwest of the city. From here, L'Aerobus runs a shuttle service to the central bus station downtown (505 blvd de Maisonneuve Est) and several major hotels – it's a 20- to 30-minute ride and costs $16 one-way; buses run 24 hours a day, every 30 minutes to an hour. In addition, a rail shuttle between the airport and Montreal Central Station is available for $12 one-way. A taxi from the airport to downtown will cost around $35.

By train

The VIA Rail station is bang in the centre of town, in the large underground complex beneath the Queen Elizabeth Hotel.

GETTING AROUND

Montreal has a good public transport system, although wandering around on foot is probably the most pleasurable way of getting about the city. Its métro was designed by engineers from the Paris métro; stations are signalled by a white arrow on a big blue sign but they're so carefully hidden you may get half way to your destination before you find one. Once underground, it's all very clean, efficient and safe.

There's also an extensive **bus** network which uses the same fare system as the métro. A single ticket costs $2.75; if you ask for *une correspondance* (transfer) you can complete your bus journey by métro or vice versa. Alternatively, you can buy a book of six tickets for $12.75; a one-day pass for $9; or a three-day pass for $17; they're available at métro stations and at the Infotouriste Centre (see p97) and can be used on both buses and the métro. Public transport starts to wind down at 12.30am, though some buses operate all through the night. There are plenty of **taxis** around town which can be easily flagged down. To call one, try Co-op on ☎ 514-725-2667 or Diamond ☎ 514-273-6331.

An excellent way to get about town is by **bike**, easily done with the city's public-bike system, Bixi (☎ 515-789-2494, 🖳 www.montreal.bixi.com). Bixi bikes are available from May to November at numerous stations around the city, where you pick up or drop off the bikes. You'll need a credit card to swipe through the pay station; there's a basic fee of $5 for 24 hours, plus a sliding-scale usage fee (the first half-hour is free), working out at approximately $4.50 for the first 90 minutes, followed by a tariff of $6 per half-hour.

While Bixi bikes are great for short hops around town, if you want to hire a bike for longer than a couple of hours it makes sense to head to one of the bike rental outfits down by the port in Vieux Montréal, near the city's cycle paths. Try Ça Roule (☎ 514-866-0633, 🖳 www.caroulemontreal.com) at 27 rue de la Commune Est, near the corner with rue St-Gabriel, where bikes and **rollerblades** can be hired for $25 a day, and you can pick up a map of Montreal's cycle paths. Ça Roule also offers guided bike tours at around $49 per half-day tour – a great way to see the city and meet fellow travellers.

ORIENTATION

It comes as a surprise to many visitors to discover that Montreal sits on an island. The Ile de Montréal is 32km long and 16km wide and is the largest of 234 islands that make up the Hochelaga Archipelago in the St Lawrence River. To orientate yourself in the city forget about conventional directions and pay no attention to the sun's position in the sky: Montreal has its own definitions of north, south, east and west and they make navigation a lot easier. The old port is down in the south; Mont Royal, the extinct volcano known by everyone as 'the mountain', is a few kilometres north. So the streets between the mountain and the quays are deemed to run from north to south, and the streets crossing them at right angles east to west.

The city is divided into two main areas: downtown Montreal and Vieux Montréal. **Downtown** begins a few blocks south of the mountain and is basically everything within the square formed by rue Sherbrooke in the north, rue St Antoine in the south, blvd St Laurent in the east and ave Atwater in the west. This is the modern, high-rise, high-tech heart of the city. **Vieux Montréal**,

---

(Opposite) Top left: St Joseph's Oratory (see p108), Montreal. **Top right**: Quebec City Old Town. (Photos © HG). **Bottom**: The Biodôme (see p108), Montreal. (Photo © EK).

down by the port, is where the city's oldest streets were first laid out in 1672. Today it's Montreal's most picturesque, photogenic and tourist-packed quarter.

Finally, a word on **street numbers**. For east–west streets, 0 is at blvd St Laurent, with numbers increasing as they move east or west from this point. Addresses are suffixed with *est* (east) or *ouest* (west) to designate which side of the boulevard they're on. North–south street numbers start down by the St Lawrence and increase as the streets move north.

SERVICES

Tourist information
There's a large and very efficient **Infotouriste Centre** (☎ 514-873-2015 or 1-800-363-7777) at 1255 rue Peel, on the corner of Ste-Catherine and Peel streets (about a five-minute walk from the train station). It's open daily, 9am–7pm June to August and 9am–6pm for the rest of the year. It's stocked with masses of brochures and leaflets and there's an accommodation desk where the staff will ring around to find vacancies for you; it also offers internet access in the basement and a currency exchange desk.

A second, much smaller tourist office is located on the corner of the place Jacques Cartier in **Vieux Montréal**, open daily 9am–7pm June to August, 9am–5pm for the rest of the year.

❏ **Montreal online**
🖥 **www.tourisme-montreal.org**
Tourisme Montréal's very detailed website, focusing on the city.

🖥 **www.bonjourquebec.com**
Tourisme Québec's site is dedicated to the whole province but has some useful pages on Montreal.

🖥 **www.montrealinfo.com**
This handy listings-based website publishes a calendar of events, bar and restaurant recommendations and information about transport, among other things.

🖥 **www.martiniboys.com**
Reviews of restaurants, bars, hotels and more written by and for a young, hip crowd.

Money
There are numerous banks downtown including several by the train station. The following charge no commission for foreign exchange: Banque Nationale du Canada at 801 rue Sainte-Catherine Est and Banque Nationale du Canada at 500 place d'Armes. There is also a Bureau de Change at 660 Sainte-Catherine Est.

Consulates
Belgium (☎ 514-849-7394) 999 blvd de Maisonneuve Ouest, suite 850; **Britain** (☎ 514-866-5863) 1000 rue de la Gauchèterie Ouest, suite 4200; **Denmark** (☎ 514-877-3060) 1 place-Ville-Marie, 35th floor; **France** (☎ 514-878-4385) 1501 McGill College, Bureau 1000; **Germany** (☎ 514-931-2277) 1250 blvd René Lévesque Ouest, suite 4315; **Italy** (☎ 514-849-8351) 3489 rue Drummond; **Japan** (☎ 514-866-3429) 600 rue de la Gauchèterie Ouest, suite 2120; **Netherlands** (☎ 514-849-4247) 1002 rue Sherbrooke Ouest, suite 2201; **Spain** (☎ 514-935-5235) 1 Westmount Sq, suite 1456; **Sweden** (☎ 514-397-

(Opposite) Quebec City – Dating from 1893 this magnificent CPR hotel, the Château Frontenac (see p90), is a symbol of the city. (Photo © MG).

4444) 100 rue de la Gaucheterie Ouest; **Switzerland** (☎ 514-932-7181) 1572
ave Dr Penfield; **USA** (☎ 514-398-9695) 1155 rue St-Alexandre.

Post, internet and laundry

Post offices are dotted about the city, with one of the most central at 1500
Sainte-Catherine Ouest. There are several **cyber-cafés** in town; one of the hand-
iest is inside the Infotouriste Centre on Square Dorchester where it costs $5 to
go online for an hour. In the old town, at 40 rue Notre Dame, you'll find three
terminals in the Wilson & Lafleur bookshop.

A reasonably central **laundry** is Buaderie du Parc, 3486 ave du Parc;
besides this, most hostels offer laundry facilities.

WHERE TO STAY

There are plenty of places to stay in Montreal and you can generally get some
good deals, particularly in the mid-priced range. Be warned, though, that the best
places get snapped up very quickly in July and August and if you're planning on
coming during the Jazz Festival (beginning of July) you should book well ahead.

Budget accommodation

The excellent Hostelling International's *Auberge de la Jeunesse* (☎ 514-843-
3317, 🖳 www.hihostels.ca) is in a beautifully renovated old house on the southern corner of rues Mackay and René Lévesque (1030 rue Mackay). Rooms con-
tain three to ten beds and each one has its own private bathroom; rates are
$26.90 a night for members and $32.25 for non-members. There are also private doubles which cost $76 for members or $86 for non-members. The facilities here are fantastic with a small café and bar, hairdryers available to borrow
and free towels provided. The staff are extremely friendly and run weekly pub
crawls on Tuesdays and Thursdays as well as tours of the city – a great way to
meet other travellers and experience Montreal's nightlife.

Also very central, and a short walk from the train station, is the **YWCA**'s
mixed-sex *Montreal Y Hotel* (☎ 514-866-9942, 🖳 www.ydesfemmesmtl.org),
1355 blvd René-Lévesque, where fresh, neat rooms with en-suite bathroom cost
$75 for a single and $85 per double ($60 per single / $70 per double with shared
bathroom). As the name suggests, rooms are more typical of a hotel than a youth
hostel and the area is remarkably peaceful considering its central location. Gym
and laundry facilities are also available and there's a great little café in the lobby.

McGill University Residence (🖳 www.mcgill.ca/residences/summer)
offers spartan but clean singles from mid-May to mid-August for around $51
($46 for students): they're available on the quiet campus of Bishop Mountain
Residence at 3935 University (☎ 514-398-6367) and at Royal Victoria College
at 3425 University, on the corner with Sherbrooke (☎ 514-398-6378).

❑ Accommodation prices quoted in this book are for **high season** (normally May or
June to September). In low season many hotels offer substantial discounts.

CITY GUIDES

Downtown Montreal

Where to stay
1 Hôtel Château Versailles
2 Le Manoir Ambroise
3 Ritz Hotel
4 Le Nouvel Hôtel
5 Auberge de la Jeunesse
6 Mont'real Y Hotel
7 Le Crystal
8 Novotel
13 Fairmont Queen Elizabeth
16 L'Abri du Voyageur
17 McGill University Residence:
   Royal Victoria College
19 Hôtel du Manoir St-Denis
20 Castel St-Denis

Where to eat
9 Mr Steer
10 Reubens
11 La Ferreira
12 Au Pain Doré
14 Toqué
15 Cristal No.1
18 Chez Gauthier
21 Mañana
22 La Bohème

0   0.5   1km

CITY GUIDES

Mid-range hotels

At the lower end of the scale, the city's best-value hotel is without doubt *Hôtel L'Abri du Voyageur* (☎ 514-849-2922, 🖳 www.abri-voyageur.ca) at 9 Ste-Catherine Ouest. The rooms are spotless, with scrubbed pine floors, exposed brick walls and high ceilings, and the owners are very welcoming. Double rooms, all with shared bath, cost from $70; advance reservations are highly recommended.

Another great-value choice is *Castel St-Denis* (☎ 514-842-9719, 🖳 www .castelsaintdenis.qc.ca) at 2099 rue St-Denis, run by delightful Mr Imam. The rooms are simple, clean and well priced, starting at $60 for a single and $70 for a double; the Castel is handy for the cafés and restaurants lining this part of St-Denis. A bit further down, on the opposite side at No 2006, *Hôtel du Manoir St-Denis* (☎ 514-843-3670, 🖳 www.manoirdenis.com) has 22 small but comfort-able double rooms (with fridges) from $49, with continental breakfast included.

For something with a bit more character, try *Le Manoir Ambroise* (☎ 514-288-6922, 🖳 www.manoirambrose.com), a lovely Victorian house converted into a small hotel. The rooms are big and attractively decorated and the guest book is full of enthusiastic comments such as 'C'est fantastique!'. It's situated on a tree-lined avenue at the quiet end of rue Stanley (No 3422, at the foot of Mt Royal) and is just a stone's throw from the centre of town. Doubles with a private bathroom start at $110 including breakfast.

Moving up a couple of notches, at 1740 blvd René Lévesque, *Le Nouvel Hôtel and Spa* (☎ 514-931-8841, 🖳 www.lenouvelhotel.com) is a fairly smart hotel; singles start at $149 but there are often offers available, so do check the website in advance. The rooms are well-lit, spacious and neat and come with phone, TV and room service. A similar establishment, though more expensive, with doubles from $179, is the *Novotel* (☎ 514-861-6000, 🖳 www.novotel .com), 1180 rue de la Montagne, which has a gym, café and a smart, fresh feel.

For something more intimate, the charming *Hôtel Château Versailles* (☎ 514-933-3611, 🖳 www.versailleshotels.com) stands at 1659 rue Sherbrooke Ouest. A converted Victorian mansion, it combines elegant décor with lovely old peri-od features and is run to a very high standard. Rooms start at around $179, with discounts available when demand is low. Another appealing option is *Hotel Nelligan* (☎ 514-788-2040), at 106 rue St-Paul Ouest (see map p104), a stylish hotel in Vieux Montreal with a delightful rooftop terrace overlooking the old port. Double rooms here are from $179.

Upmarket hotels

The classiest joint in town is the *Ritz Hotel* (☎ 514-842-4212, 🖳 www.ritzmon treal.com) at 1228 rue Sherbrooke Ouest. The height of hotel luxury since it opened in 1912, it's currently in the throes of a multi-million-dollar renovation project and is scheduled to reopen some time in 2011. An added touch of glam-our: it was here that Elizabeth Taylor married Richard Burton in 1964. If its prices are beyond your reach (around $325 in high season, from $158 in low season), it's worth going in for a drink at the piano bar, or splashing out on din-ner in its beautiful garden restaurant. If old-world luxury isn't your cup of tea, try one of the city's newest 5-star hotels, *Le Crystal*, at 1100 rue de la Montagne

(☎ 514-861-5550, www.hotel lecrystal.com). The hotel has 131 spacious suites, each with a separate sitting room area, and some with kitchenettes. It also has a top-floor pool and a rooftop deck with a plunge-pool. Rooms start at $229.

If you like the idea of stepping off the train right into your hotel you can do just that at the *Fairmont Queen Elizabeth* (☎ 514-861-3511, 🖳 www.fairmont .com) which is literally right on top of the station. It's a large, stylish hotel and is always busy with a high-powered international crowd. The hotel's guest list from previous years includes Her Majesty Queen Elizabeth II, Princess Grace of Monaco and Indira Gandhi. John Lennon fans should also note that it was in a suite on the 17th floor that he and Yoko Ono recorded their famous song, *Give Peace a Chance*, in 1969. A standard room here costs from $189.

WHERE TO EAT

Montreal is blessed with a wealth of eating establishments ranging from gourmet restaurants to dirt-cheap delis. While it shares the North American obsession with bagels, and although European immigrants have imported interesting specialities (notably smoked meat), the majority of Montreal's restaurants are firmly rooted in the city's French heritage. Many restaurants have a fixed-price *table d'hôte* menu that's considerably cheaper than ordering *à la carte*.

Budget food
One of the best places to sample Montreal smoked meat is at *Reubens*, 1116 Sainte-Catherine Ouest – ask for the 'special', which consists of a giant smoked beef sandwich on sourdough bread, with salad and relish. A couple of blocks east at No 1198, *Mr Steer* has been a local institution since 1958, serving good-quality burgers, chicken and steak and daily set lunches at unbeatable prices. It's a great place to escape the hustle and bustle of rue St-Catherine's busy shops.

One area where you're guaranteed to find a cheap meal is Chinatown, packed with tiny restaurants that fill with the local Chinese population. One of the best is *Cristal No. 1*, hidden away at 1068 blvd St-Laurent, which offers a vast choice of soups and delicious spring rolls among other delights.

There's another concentration of cheap restaurants at the northern end of St-Denis: *Mañana*, at No 3605 (☎ 514-847-1050), is a small, friendly Mexican restaurant serving inexpensive nachos, burritos and ceviche. The dining area is strewn with large sombreros and other cheerful accessories which add to the fun atmosphere of the restaurant. Meanwhile, *La Bohème* (☎ 514-286-6659), a few doors up at No 3625, is a charming little bistro where you can eat tasty Moroccan and French food for around $10 to $20 a head. You'll find plenty more bistros and cafés on St-Denis, particularly between Sherbrooke and Maisonneuve.

Also worth a try is *Gallianos* (☎ 514-861-5039), on rue St-Vincent in the old town (see map p104), where you can get great Italian dishes for under $25. Alternatively, if you fancy some pub food, head to the corner of rue de Vaudreuil and rue St-Paul in Vieux Montréal, where *Les 3 Brasseurs* (see map p104), or 'The 3 Brewers', serves tasty burgers, wraps and a traditional pizza-type dish from Alsace called 'Flamms'. The bar has a lively atmosphere and the restaurant is part of a chain with other locations in Montreal.

CITY GUIDES

Finally, for a fine selection of panini, croissants and mugs of rich coffee, take a seat in *Au Pain Doré*, situated above an excellent little bakery at 1451 rue Peel, where you can watch the world go by from its large windows overlooking the street.

Mid-range and upmarket restaurants

Downtown, *La Ferreira* (☎ 514-848-0988), at 1446 Peel, has a stylish, colourful interior and an outdoor terrace where you can feast on first-rate Portuguese dishes like seafood broth and fresh sardines from around $35 per person. Arguably the city's best restaurant, *Toqué!* (☎ 514-499-2084), 900 Place Jean-Paul-Riopelle, boasts a buzzing atmosphere, great service and outstanding food (the duck foie gras is amazing), with main courses around $40–45 and a fantastic gourmet menu starting at $101 per person, duck foie gras included. If your budget won't stretch to it, try *Chez Gauthier* at 3487 ave du Parc (☎ 514-845-2992), where you can feast on decent bistro food for around $25 in a pretty, wood-panelled room, or head there in the morning for delicious breakfast dishes priced around $9.

A good choice in Vieux Montréal is *Le Club Chasse et Pêche* (☎ 514 861 1112) at 423 rue St Claude, which specializes in upmarket French cuisine. The surroundings are low-key but the menu features lots of luxurious ingredients with dishes such as 'scallops served with grapefruit mousse and fennel', and there's an extensive wine list – bank on around $60 per head for a couple of courses with a glass of wine.

Also in old Montreal, *Le Jardin Nelson* (☎ 514-861-5731), 407 place Jacques Cartier, puts on live jazz at lunch and dinner, which are both served in an atmospheric outdoor patio area filled with luxuriant tropical plants. Main dishes – mainly crêpes, pizzas, pasta dishes and salads – are around $20.

❏ BYOBs

Quebec was until fairly recently the only province in Canada that allowed customers to bring their own wine (but not beer or spirits) to certain restaurants, namely those that have been granted a special licence. These restaurants are popularly known as BYOBs (bring your own bottle) in English and '*les apportez votre vin*' in French and are immensely popular. We've listed a handful of the best below, which all serve typical French bistro food. Most BYOBs are not in the downtown core but in the neighbourhoods just out of the centre.

● *L'Entrepont* (☎ 514-845-1369, 🖳 www.lentrepont.com) 4622 ave de l'Hôtel de Ville (Mont-Royal métro). Elegant décor and an imaginative menu make this an excellent choice. Reservations are advised.

● *Le P'tit Plateau* (☎ 514-282-6342) 330 rue Marie-Anne Est (Mont-Royal métro). Simple, friendly restaurant with generous portions, an emphasis on fresh produce and many vegetarian options.

● *Les Héritiers* (☎ 514-528-4953, 🖳 www.lesheritiers.com) 5091 rue de Lanaudière (Laurier métro). Delicious salads, meat dishes and lots of rustic style, tucked away in a tiny street between Laurier and St-Joseph.

● *Yoyo* (☎ 514-524-4187) 4720 rue Marquette (Laurier métro). Lively bistro with attractive décor and great food including not-to-be-missed crême brulées.

> ❑ **La Vitrine and Le Quartier des Spectacles**
> *La Vitrine* is a not-for-profit organization selling last-minute discounted tickets for theatre, music, dance, concerts, comedy and other events taking place throughout the city. It's part of the new '*Quartier des Spectacles*' initiative (🖥 www.quartierdes spectacles.com), a huge renovation project aimed at promoting the area around rue Ste-Catherine Ouest as a cultural and entertainment district. You can buy tickets from La Vitrine either online or in person at 145 rue Ste-Catherine Ouest.

NIGHTLIFE

Montreal's dazzling nightlife scene is concentrated in several different areas, each with its own character and crowd.

Rue Crescent (between Sainte Catherine and Maisonneuve) is an out-and-out party street. Traditionally regarded as the preserve of the Anglos, it's packed with pubs, nightclubs and a dolled-up crowd whose main pursuits seem to be drinking, dancing and attempting to pull. Favourite spots include the *Sir Winston Churchill* at No 1459 and *Thursday's* at No 1449.

The **boulevard Saint-Laurent** is considerably more sophisticated (and Francophone) and has some of the most interesting nightspots in town. *Le Balattou* (No 4372) is a steamy, immensely popular African nightclub, established over 20 years ago, while further down at No 3556 is *Orchid*, where a fashionable, lively clientèle come to dance to hip hop and R&B music. Rue Saint-Denis has a more studenty, bohemian feel to it. There are some excellent jazz bars here, including *Les Beaux Esprits* at No 2073.

There's also a thriving gay scene in Montreal, most of it centred in what's known as the **Gay Village**. The core of the village runs along Sainte-Catherine between Saint-Denis and Papineau. One of its most lively clubs is *Caberet Mado* at 1115 Ste Catherine Est, which attracts a mixed crowd. Decorated in a 1920s décor, it has its own resident drag queen, Mado Lamothe.

If you just want a cheap beer and great nachos head to *Carlos and Pepe's*, tucked away at 1420 rue Peel (☎ 514-288-3090) – don't miss the $8 pitcher specials on Sunday and Monday nights, and the gigantic great-value cocktails during happy hour and beyond.

WHAT TO SEE

Vieux Montréal

Old Montreal, with its cobblestone streets, immaculately restored buildings, churches, boutiques, cafés and restaurants is a magnet for tourists. It contains some of the best examples of 18th-century architecture in North America and, despite the crowds, is completely irresistible.

The Infotouriste Centre at the corner of place Jacques Cartier hands out free walking-tour booklets which give a detailed account of the district's main historic and architectural features. The highlights of Old Montreal are as follows:

● **Notre-Dame Basilica** This Gothic Revival extravaganza (🖳 www. basilique nddm.org) at 110 Notre-Dame Ouest was the biggest religious building in North America when it was completed in 1829. It was designed by James O'Donnell, a New York-Irish architect who was so proud of his work he converted to Catholicism so he could be buried in it. The interior is a dazzling spectacle of gold leaf and stained glass and the main altar is breathtaking. Note also the beautiful vaulted ceiling and the huge 5772-pipe Casavant organ (remember St-Hyacinthe? See p195). Entrance is $5 which includes an optional 20-minute guided tour.

● **Château Ramezay** More a large house than a château, this is nonetheless a fine old residence. It was built in 1705 for the Governor of Montreal and has since been used as a furs and spices store for the French West India Company and a base for American revolutionaries trying to get Montreal to join forces with the US. It's now a museum featuring mainly 18th- and 19th-century furniture and costumes and houses historically themed temporary exhibitions throughout the year. It's located at 280 Notre Dame Est and is open daily 10am–6pm June to September and Tuesday to Sunday 10am–4.30pm for the rest of the year. Entrance is $9; you'll find more information at 🖳 www. chateauramezay.qc.ca.

● **Bank of Montreal** At 119 rue Saint-Jacques stands Canada's oldest banking institution. This is where George Stephen and Donald Smith were directors before leaving to form the CPR Syndicate; the bank continued to be an important source of funds throughout the railway's construction. This domed, neo-classical building, modelled on the Pantheon in Rome, is particularly grand inside with its marble counters, massive columns and bronze trimmings everywhere.

❏ **Cruises down the St-Lawrence**
A memorable way to see Montreal is to take a cruise down the St Lawrence River, which will reward you with spectacular views of the city. Croisières AML (☎ 1-800-563-4643, 🖳 www.croisieresaml.com) offer short river cruises both during the day and by night from $23 per person, as well as a range of longer options including a 9hr cruise from Montreal to Quebec City ($159).

● **Marché Bonsecours** Montrealers clearly delighted in these neo-classical, temple-style buildings. The old market hall at 350 rue Saint-Paul Est is a very striking example with its doric columns and silver dome. The line of Georgian sash windows is something of a leap in period but the overall effect is lovely. Inside you can find lots of artisan jewellery and ceramics.

● **Notre-Dame-de-Bonsecours Chapel** There's none of the grandeur here of the Notre-Dame Basilica but this pretty little church at 400 Saint-Paul Est is well worth a visit. It was a favourite of Montreal's sailors who would pray here for a safe voyage and then bring votive offerings on their return. Many of these are still here, such as the carved model ships hanging from the roof of the nave.

The church also houses the **Marguerite Bourgeoys Museum** (🖳 www.marguerite-bourgeoys.com), named after a French woman who came to Montreal in 1653 to open a school and teach the children of native people and settlers. It was thanks to her efforts that Montreal's first pilgrimage chapel was built in 1675, on the site of the current Notre-Dame-de-Bonsecours Chapel. Marguerite was canonized in 1982 by Pope John Paul II; the museum commemorates her life and work with a variety of religious artefacts. It's open Tuesday to Sunday 10am–5.30pm from May to October and 11am–3.30pm November to mid-January and mid-March to April; entrance costs $8.

● **Old Port** No longer used commercially, the old port has recently been landscaped and redeveloped with gardens, cycling paths, exhibition halls and an IMAX cinema. The views along the river are splendid and a lookout tower gives excellent views over the city. You can also see one of the old grain silos – a huge, grey block that apparently sent the visiting Le Corbusier into raptures.

Downtown
The pace of life shifts up a few gears as you move into the hustle and bustle of downtown Montreal. While many streets are dominated by skyscrapers, there are more than enough department stores, bars, museums, restaurants and even churches to give Montreal a softer edge. The proliferation of young people here makes it as lively by night as it is by day.

● **Le Musée des Beaux Arts** Many of the paintings in this wonderful museum (🖳 www.mbam.qc.ca) were acquired from the private collections of Montreal's early 20th-century business magnates. The European collection, in particular, is excellent and includes works by El Greco, Canaletto, Renoir, Sisley, Monet, Giacometti, Dali and Picasso. The museum is at 1380 rue Sherbrooke

Ouest and is open Tuesday 11am–5pm, Wednesday, Thursday and Friday 11am–9pm, Saturday and Sunday 10am–5pm. Entrance to the permanent collection is free but entrance to temporary exhibitions is a steep $15 (children under 12 go free), with half-price entry every Wednesday between 5pm and 9pm.

● **Centre Canadien d'Architecture (CCA)** Housed in a landmark, award-winning (if slightly brutal) building, skilfully adjoined to a grand 19th-century townhouse, the centre's vast galleries house a changing collection of drawings, models, photographs, prints and documents relating to a very diverse range of architectural themes. The adjoining house, known as the Shaughnessy Mansion, was once the home of the great WC Van Horne, the man who saw the building of the Trans-Canada railway to completion; you can visit its beautiful reception rooms and conservatory. The centre occupies a whole block at 1920 rue Baile, on the corner with Atwater. From June to September opening hours are Wednesday to Sunday 10am–6pm and Thursday 11am–9pm. Entrance is $10, with free admission on Thursdays after 5.30pm; find out more at 🖳 www.cca.qc.ca.

● **McCord Museum of Canadian History** This enjoyable museum (🖳 www .mccord-museum.qc.ca) was founded in 1919 when David Ross McCord donated his collection of Canadiana to McGill University so that it might form the basis of a history museum. The exhibits, which include old photographs, native and immigrant clothing, paintings, china, toys and jewellery, are captivating and very well displayed, particularly in the First Nations gallery where textiles, beadwork, furs and carvings are shown to stunning effect. Located at 690 rue Sherbrooke Ouest, the museum is open Monday to Friday 10am–6pm, and Saturday and Sunday 10am–5pm during the summer, and is closed on Monday during the winter (September-May). Entrance is $13 for adults with free admission on the first Saturday of each month between 10am and noon.

● **McGill University** Just over the road from the McCord Museum, this is one of Canada's most prestigious universities. The campus, with its limestone buildings and well-tended gardens, extends to the foot of the mountain and is a very pleasant place to stroll around.

● **Christ Church Cathedral** This Anglican cathedral, on the corner of Sainte-Catherine and University, quietly sums up some of the remarkable contrasts of Montreal: the graceful old building, containing some beautiful William Morris stained-glass windows, is set on top of a shopping mall. This connects it to a towering glass skyscraper next door, where the cathedral's offices are located!

● **Rue Ste-Catherine** This is the main shopping street in Montreal and offers some of the best shopping in Canada. It's always incredibly busy but has a vibrant rather than stressful atmosphere to it. There are two modern shopping centres on the street: Complexe Les Ailes and the Eaton shopping centre, which both have food courts and plenty of good clothes shops.

● **Place-Ville-Marie** Designed by the architects who went on to create the pyramid in the Louvre, Paris, Place-Ville-Marie is a complex of towers built over the railway tracks. The most arresting one is the famous cruciform skyscraper, supposedly a symbol of the city's roots in Catholicism. It also provides a handy landmark. The tower houses hundreds of offices, including the headquarters of VIA Rail.

● **Sun Life Building** Right next door to Place-Ville-Marie is the former headquarters of the massive Sun Life insurance company, who objected so strongly to Montreal's language laws that they moved their head offices to Toronto in the 1970s. This was the biggest building in the British Empire when it was erected in 1917 and, despite being dwarfed by surrounding skyscrapers today, it remains an impressive sight. It is also where the crown jewels were hidden during World War II.

● **Cathédrale Marie-Reine-du-Monde** Opposite the Sun Life Building is the green-roofed scale model of St Peter's in Rome; it's exactly one third of the original's size and is the third-largest church in Quebec. It was built in the late 19th century in a flagrant attempt to overshadow the Notre-Dame Basilica in Old Montreal. Note the 13 copper statues above the entrance: these are of the patron saints of Montreal's parishes.

● **Gare Windsor** When Van Horne decided that Montreal needed a new railway station to house the terminus of the transcontinental line, he got Bruce Price to draw up the plans. (Price was a leading American architect who went on to design the Château Frontenac and other CPR hotels.) The result was Gare Windsor, a huge Romanesque building whose grandness reflected Montreal's importance as the railway centre of Canada. Although inter-city trains moved over to Central Station after World War II, it continues to be used by local commuter trains.

The station is open seven days a week (but is closed Sunday mornings) to visitors. A downstairs office at the station (Room G-1) houses the Canadian Pacific Archives, a massive collection of photographs and documents pertaining to CPR history. Members of the public aren't encouraged to come wandering in off the street but if you're interested you can always phone them at the station's information desk on ☎ 514-395-7686 and see if it's possible to visit.

Underground City

Each year more than 40 million tonnes of snow are ploughed up from Montreal's streets. Hardly surprising, then, that most Montrealers take to their incredible Underground City (also known as the Indoor City) during these winter months. This 18-mile system of shops, cinemas, restaurants, hotels and banks has even become something of a tourist attraction but be warned: it's notoriously difficult to find your way around, so be sure to equip yourself with a map (available at the tourist office and at most metro stations) before venturing down.

Most downtown métro stations connect to the Underground City; good retail sections of the network can be reached via Peel and McGill stations on the green line, and Bonaventure station on the orange line.

CITY GUIDES

CITY GUIDES

Mont Royal

You can't come to Montreal without going up its little mountain which, at just 232m, is not a taxing climb. You will be rewarded with superb views over the city, a little like those over Paris from the Sacré Coeur. Besides the views, the expanse of parkland at the top of the hill is a fine place to wander about. You can also take in **St Joseph's Oratory**, a magnificent basilica built at the request of one Brother André, who is reputed to have performed miraculous healings. He was beatified by Pope John Paul II in 1982 and the site has since become an important pilgrimage destination for North Americans. The footpath up the hill starts at the northern end of rue Peel.

Maisonneuve

A few kilometres east of downtown is the Maisonneuve area, the site of three major attractions: the Olympic Stadium, the Biodôme and the Botanical Gardens. All three can be visited on a one-day 'Get an Eyeful' package, which costs around $32 for adults and $16.50 for children under 17. The best way to get out there is by taking the métro to Pie IX; everything is well signposted from the métro exit.

● **Olympic Stadium** Mention the stadium to most Montrealers and you'll get a raising of the eyebrows and shrug of exasperation. The giant complex, with its 175-metre inclined tower supporting a supposedly retractable roof, was built at colossal expense for the 1976 Olympic Games. Not only did it leave the city with an enormous debt but it didn't even work very well – the controversial roof was replaced in 1998 by a permanent roof costing a further $26 million. Still, the tower is an impressive construction and the shuttle ride up to the observation desk at the top is good fun, even if it does set you back $15. It's open daily 9am–7pm in summer and 9am–5pm in winter (closed mid-Jan to mid-Feb), with regular tours in French and English costing $8. For more information contact ☎ 514-252-4141 or 🖳 www.rio.gouv.qc.ca.

● **Botanical Gardens** Among the largest in the world, these thirty outdoor gardens include the beautiful replica of the old Ming Gardens of Shanghai, Montreal's twin city, designed by experts brought over from China.

The gardens also house the **Insectarium**, a fun museum devoted to creepy-crawlies. The botanical gardens are open Tuesday–Sunday year-round, 9am–5pm (until 9pm from early September to late October). Entrance is $16 in summer and $13.50 in winter.

● **Biodôme** This amazing environment museum (🖳 www.biodome.qc.ca) contains four different ecosystems from the Americas under one roof: Tropical Forest, Laurentian Forest, St Lawrence Marine Ecosystem and (most interesting) Polar World. The habitats are home to thousands of plants and animals, living as though in their natural environment. Helpful staff, easily recognized by their safari-style hats, are on hand throughout the Biodôme to answer any questions you might have or to point out animals hidden from view.

Opening times are 9am–5pm daily, year-round (until 6pm in summer); entrance is $16. During the winter it is closed on Mondays.

FESTIVALS

● **International Fireworks Competition**, around June and July. Spectacular displays in the beautiful setting of the Parc des Iles.

● **Montreal International Jazz Festival**, late June to early July (11 days). Outstanding, world-class cultural event attracting well over a million tourists annually. Two thousand international musicians (including lots of big names) and over 300 shows, many of them free.

● **Just for Laughs Festival**, mid-July. The world's largest comedy festival, a fascinating insight into the contrasts of Anglo and Franco humour.

● **Montreal World Film Festival**, late August to early September. New films screened practically around the clock. At the end of the festival prizes are awarded, the top one being the Grand Prix des Amériques.

Montreal International
Jazz Festival
PHOTO © JIM MANTHORPE

CITY GUIDES

MOVING ON

By rail

The service between Montreal and Toronto is the busiest in Canada. A good number of trains run daily between the two cities. Several trains a day also leave Montreal for Ottawa and for Quebec City and there's a daily (except Tuesday) service to Halifax via Charny (close to Quebec City). For more information call VIA on ☎ 514-989-2626 (or ☎ 1-888-842-7245 when calling from outside Montreal).

Note that there is also an Amtrak rail service from Montreal to New York and Washington – call Amtrak toll-free on ☎ 1-800-872-7245, or see 🖳 www .amtrak.com.

By air

Montreal's international airport serves hundreds of internal and world-wide destinations. L'Aerobus run a shuttle bus to the airport, picking up passengers at the central bus station (505 blvd de Maisonneuve Est) as well as several major hotels for $16 one-way.

Other useful phone numbers include Montreal-Trudeau Airport information: ☎ 514-394-7377; Air Canada: ☎ 514-422-5000; American Airlines: ☎ 514-397-9635; and British Airways: ☎ 514 394 7377.

Toronto

The country round this town, being very flat, is bare of scenic interest; but the town itself is full of life and motion, bustle, business and improvement.

Charles Dickens, *American Notes*

Toronto's had a considerable amount of bad press over the years and many people have agreed with Peter Ustinov's unflattering conclusion that it is 'a kind of New York run by the Swiss'. Yet the city is nowhere near as boring or sanitized as the cliché suggests.

On the contrary you'll see beggars on the street and eccentrics on the subway, you'll hear lots of loud music pumping out of ghetto blasters and you'll see any number of hip young things gracing the town's sidewalks. Toronto, you'll quickly realize, is a crowded, noisy and very exciting place to be and fulfils European expectations of a big North American metropolis more than any other city in Canada.

One of the most refreshing things about Toronto is that it doesn't keep going on about its history – possibly because it has very little to go on about – but the welcome result is a moving, dynamic and forward-looking environment where new theatre, art and music flourish. It also boasts some outstanding museums, architecture and other attractions, from the CN Tower to the Royal Ontario Museum (ROM). There really is plenty to do and see here, the only drawback being the vast amounts of money required to do it and see it.

HISTORY

Early settlement
The site was first occupied by the Huron Indians who named it Toronto, meaning 'Meeting place'. Lying on a sheltered harbour on the north shore of Lake Ontario, it was part of the connecting land route to Lake Huron.

In 1750 the French set up a fur-trading post here and built a stockade to protect their trading operations but the British ejected them in 1759 and destroyed the fort. They proceeded to ignore the place for several decades. However, when Loyalists to the British Crown started fleeing America after the War of Independence, many came and settled in the area.

Bought from the natives
In 1788 the Governor-in-Chief of Canada officially bought the site of Toronto from the Mississauga Indians. What was to become the nation's biggest city was a bargain at £1700, a few bales of cloth and some axes. The new purchase was renamed York and a few years later became the capital of Upper Canada. The first of the city's grid-patterned streets was laid out and the community slowly began to take shape.

America invades

When war broke out between England and America in 1812, York was invaded by 1700 US troops who pillaged the town and burnt down the Parliament Building. In revenge, British troops tried to burn down the building occupied by the US President in Washington. They didn't succeed but the damaged walls had to be white-washed, which is how it came to be known as the White House.

After the war ended in 1814, colonists began to come over in greater numbers: the city's population grew from 700 in 1816 to over 9000 in 1834. In this year the city was incorporated and given back its old name of Toronto.

Industrial and economic boom

With the arrival of the Grand Trunk and Great Western railways in the 1850s, Toronto entered a period of rapid economic expansion. It quickly emerged as an important agricultural, manufacturing and distribution centre and as its population and industrial clout boomed, expensive new buildings were erected at a similar pace. Following the difficult years of the 1930s' Depression, Toronto's economic strength was reaffirmed when the St Lawrence Seaway was opened in 1959, bringing with it a mass of trade and investment. The next few decades saw the construction of a multitude of gleaming skyscrapers and Toronto's business world was further enlarged by the arrival of many firms from Montreal, in flight from Quebec's language laws.

Toronto today

Toronto is Canada's biggest city with some 2.5 million inhabitants. Its population is astoundingly multicultural as a result of Toronto's policy of welcoming immigrants from around the globe, and the city has been identified by the United Nations as the most ethnically diverse in the world. Racial relations are exemplary, giving weight to Toronto's claim that it is 'a city that works'. It is the financial, industrial and commercial capital of Canada and is also the most expensive city in the country.

ARRIVING IN TORONTO

By air

Most flights to Toronto arrive at the massive Lester B Pearson International Airport, 25km north-west of the city centre.

Pacific Western Airport Express buses (🖳 www.torontoairportexpress.com) will bring you into town for $19.95 one-way, stopping at a handful of major hotels from where free transfers are available to a further 32 hotels and hostels. Buses leave the airport every 20 minutes from 5am to 1am and every 30 minutes outside these times; during rush-hour traffic expect the journey to take from one hour thirty minutes to two hours. You can also, of course, take the quicker 40-minute option and use a taxi, which costs around $50.

Commuter flights from Ontario and Quebec arrive at the Toronto Island Airport, also known as Toronto City Centre Airport, from where a ferry and shuttle bus take travellers to the railway station.

By rail

Trains arrive at Union Station on Front St, near the CN Tower. It's right at the southern end of town but, if you need to go north, you can catch the subway here. This huge, imposing building was opened by the then Prince of Wales (the future King Edward VIII) in 1927 and is still the grandest railway station in Canada.

GETTING AROUND

Toronto's public transport system – a network of **buses**, **streetcars** and the **subway** – is arguably the best in Canada. It's operated by the Toronto Transit Commission (TTC); their website shows all schedules and route maps and has an excellent trip-planner (🖥 www.ttc.ca), or you can call for information on ☎ 416-393-4636. Single tickets cost $2.75 or you can get a day pass for $9. Note that you need the exact fare, or a ticket or token (available at subway stations). The subway is open 6am–1.30am and when the subway is closed there are regular Blue Night Network buses running through the night along the main streets of Bloor-Danforth and Yonge. **Taxis** are plentiful and can be flagged down on the street; alternatively call Co-op Cabs (☎ 416-504-2667) or Diamond Taxicab (☎ 416-366-6868). **Cycles** and **roller-blades** can be rented for $30 a day at Wheel Excitement, 249 Queen's Quay W, south of Radisson Plaza (☎ 416-260-9000, 🖥 www.wheelexcitement.ca).

ORIENTATION

Toronto's downtown layout is very uncomplicated: it's contained within a rectangle formed by Front St in the south, Bloor St in the north, Jarvis St in the east and Spadina Ave in the west. A couple of blocks south of Front St is the harbourfront. The biggest and busiest north–south street is Yonge St; the streets running across it at right angles are divided into East and West at this point. The distance between Bloor and Front is about 2.5km, while Jarvis to Spadina is just under 2km.

SERVICES

Tourist information

The most centrally located tourist information office is **Ontario Tourism's Travel Centre** (☎ 416-314-5899) adjoining the Atrium on Bay Mall at 20 Dundas St West, opposite the Eaton Centre; opening hours are Monday to

---

❏ **Toronto online**

🖥 **www.toronto.com** and 🖥 **www.seetorontonow.com** Both sites are produced by Tourism Toronto and both include plenty of information on the city's sights, accommodation, attractions and more. The latter is particularly strong on current events in Toronto; 🖥 **www.ontariotravel.net** Information about the whole province from Ontario Tourism; 🖥 **www.martiniboys.com** Get the lowdown on the city's most happening bars, restaurants, shops and more at this popular website.

(Opposite) The CN Tower (see p119) seen from the Rogers Centre. (Photo © EK).

Friday 10am–9pm, Saturday 10am–6pm and Sunday 11am–5pm in summer. In winter, it's open 10am–6pm Monday to Saturday and noon–5pm on Sunday.

Tourism Toronto's **Visitor Information Centre** (☎ 416-599-1548) is inside the Metro Toronto Convention Centre at 255 Front St West, a few blocks west of the train station, near the CN Tower. Besides stocking maps, leaflets and so on, staff can assist with booking theatre tickets and tours of the area and can also make hotel bookings; the centre is open Monday to Friday 9am–5pm. Tourism Toronto also operates a visitor information phone line on ☎ 416-203-2600, or ☎ 1-800-363-1990 from within North America.

Money

There is no shortage of **banks** in Toronto; whichever part of town you're in you'll find one nearby. Thomas Cook has numerous foreign exchange branches in the city, including 100 Yonge St (15th Floor), 123 Queen St West and 9 Bloor St West. There's also a currency exchange within Ontario Tourism's Travel Centre.

Consulates

Australia (☎ 416-323-1155) 314-175 Bloor St East; **Austria** (☎ 416-967-3348) 2 Bloor St East; **Belgium** (☎ 416-944-1422) 2006-2 Bloor St West; **Britain** (☎ 416-593-1290) 777 Bay St; **Denmark** (☎ 416-962-5661) 2 Bloor St West; **Finland** (☎ 416-964-0066) 1200 Bay St; **France** (☎ 416-925-8041) 2 Bloor St East; **Germany** (☎ 416-925-2813) 77 Bloor St East; **Italy** (☎ 416-977-1566) 136 Beverley St; **Japan** (☎ 416-363-7038) 77 King St West; **Netherlands** (☎ 416-598-2520) 2106-1 Dundas St West; **Republic of Ireland** (☎ 416-366-9300) 100 First Canadian Place; **South Africa** (☎ 416-944-8825) 110 Shepherd St East; **Spain** (☎ 416-977-1661) 2 Bloor St East; **Sweden** (☎ 416-963-8768) 1504-2 Bloor St West; **Switzerland** (☎ 416-593-5371) 154 University Ave; **USA** (☎ 416-595-1700) 360 University Ave

Post, internet and laundry

Downtown **post office** branches include those at 31 Adelaide East and 69 Yonge, near the corner with King; there's also a handy branch inside the Atrium on Bay mall, next door to Ontario Tourism's Travel Centre at 20 Dundas West. **Internet access** is available at various places around town for an average of $3 per hour. Webfusion has branches at 614 Yonge St (a block north of Wellesley) and 545 Sherbourne St (also a block north of Wellesley); there's also the Internet Centre at 324 Yonge St (at Dundas St). Free internet can be found in post offices and, if you buy a coffee, at The Croissant Tree at 1033 Bay St. Downtown **laundries** include St Lawrence Super Coin Laundry at 222 The Esplanade (a block west of Sherbourne St) and The Laundry Lounge at 527 Yonge St (at Wellesley).

(**Opposite**) **Winnipeg** – **Top**: Saint-Boniface Cathedral (see p137) was all but destroyed in a disastrous fire in 1968. A new cathedral was built behind the façade in 1972. (Photo © EK). **Bottom left**: Winnipeg Railway Museum (see p134) is well worth a visit and usually open when *The Canadian* takes its long break here. (Photo © MG). **Bottom right**: Grain elevators tower over the rail track all the way across the prairies. It has been said that they are the only indigenous form of Canadian architecture. (Photo © MG).

CITY GUIDES

WHERE TO STAY

Budget accommodation

Toronto has some excellent downtown hostels. At 76 Church St, the *HI Hostel* (☎ 416-971-4440, 🖳 www.hihostels.ca) has a friendly atmosphere and offers plenty of activities plus free entry to some club and comedy nights. Most dorms have three to four beds (from $29 for members, slightly more for non-members), and come with a private shower room and lockers. There are also a few private en-suite doubles which cost $89 per room including breakfast ($99 for non-members). It's extremely popular, so reserve well in advance.

Global Village Backpackers Hostel (☎ 416-703-8540, 🖳 www.global backpackers.com) at 460 King St West is a large, brightly painted old house with dorm beds at $27 (six to ten beds per room) and $30 (four beds per room), as well as private doubles at $80. Global Village has its own bar on the premises and offers free wi-fi facilities to guests. Like the HI Hostel, the Global Village Backpackers Hostel has kitchen facilities and a patio area.

Just around the corner at 42 Widmer St is *Canadiana Backpackers* (☎ 416-598-9090, 🖳 www.canadianalodging.com), a renovated Victorian townhouse with dorm beds from $27 and double rooms from $75. There's lots on offer here such as pancake breakfasts and weekly BBQs; the hostel even has its own TV room complete with reclining 'aeroplane style' seats and a selection of films for those looking for a quiet night in.

From May to August, *Neill Wycik College* (☎ 416-977-2320, 🖳 www.neill-wycik.com), at 96 Gerrard East, offers single rooms for $50 (or $43 for students, seniors and hostel members) and doubles for $88 ($75 with discount). Rooms are private but they do share a kitchen/common room and washrooms with four or five other rooms. Some of the rooms are a bit spartan, as you might expect from a university residence, but the location is fantastic, the staff are very friendly and there are fine views from the pleasant rooftop sun deck. Rates include continental breakfast and daily housekeeping.

Finally, the most recent addition to Toronto's hostel scene is the *Clarence Castle Hostel* (☎ 416-260-1221, 🖳 www.clarencecastle.com) at 8 Clarence Square, just off Spadina Ave – a brand-new, beautifully decorated and well organized establishment. Dorms ($28 per person) are typically for six people and come with an en-suite bathroom, and private rooms are also available at $80 per double. Free breakfast and free internet access are included and there are two spacious TV rooms, a fully equipped kitchen and a rooftop terrace.

Mid-range accommodation

Toronto has an ever-increasing number of **B&Bs**, many of them in handsomely renovated Victorian houses. A good one to try, at 3 Selby St, is *Au Petit Paris* (☎ 416-928-1348, 🖳 www.bbtoronto.com/aupetitparis), run by a very friendly couple, Paul-Antoine and Michelle. Its lovely guest rooms with en-suite baths (from $130 a double) are decorated with artwork and photographs shipped over from Paris; vegetarian breakfast is served in a bright, cheerful breakfast room but the real gem is the rooftop terrace which seems a world away from the busy

CITY GUIDES

Toronto

0   0.5   1km

Where to stay
2 Four Seasons Hotel
5 Au Petit Paris
6 Isabella Hotel & Suites
7 Les Amis Bed & Breakfast
8 Neill Wycik College
10 Delta Chelsea
13 Alexandra Apartment Hotel
14 Canadiana Backpackers
16 Global Village Hostel
19 Clarence Castle Hotel
20 Strathcona
22 Royal York Hotel
25 Novotel
26 HI Youth Hostel

Where to eat
1 Bellini's
3 The Croissant Tree
4 Fran's
9 Z-Teca Gourmet Burritos
11 The Pickle Barrel
12 Oro
15 Ravi Soups
17 Z-Teca Gourmet Burritos
18 The Red Tomato
21 Canoe
22 Epic
23 Richtree Market Restaurant
24 Old Spaghetti Factory
27 The Boiler House

streets of Toronto. The Parisian hosts own another B&B, too, at 31 Granby St: *Les Amis Bed & Breakfast* (☎ 416-591-0635, 🖳 www.bbtoronto.com) has attractive rooms, most with shared bathrooms (from $110). Wireless internet access is available at both places.

Just round the corner from Au Petit Paris, at 556 Sherbourne Street, the *Isabella Hotel and Suites* (☎ 416-922-2203, 🖳 www.isabellahotel.com) occupies an 1891 mansion, officially designated a historic landmark. The hotel's 39 rooms and suites are nicely decorated in neutral tones and come with cable TV, internet access and phones with free local calls; standard rooms are great value at $109, while the suites start at $159.

Over at the west end of downtown, the *Alexandra Apartment Hotel* (☎ 416-504-2121, 🖳 www.alexandrahotel.com), at 77 Ryerson Ave, is a block of 60 small studios with kitchenette, cable TV, phone and private bathroom (with bath-tub and shower) from $95 for doubles. Handy for the train station at 60 York St, the recently refurbished *Strathcona* (☎ 416-363-3321, 🖳 www.thestrathconahotel.com) is another good deal, offering smart but small doubles from $125; the hotel also has a café, a pub and offers wi-fi.

Upmarket hotels

If you want to do things in true style there's only one place to stay: the *Royal York Hotel* (☎ 416-368-2511, 🖳 www.fairmont.com), opposite the railway station. Built by Canadian Pacific Railways in 1929, the one-time tallest building in the British Empire is splendidly luxurious inside. Everything here is on a grand scale: it has 1365 rooms, boasts the largest hotel kitchens in Canada and no less than 72km of carpeting cover its vast halls and corridors. This is where the rich and famous stay when they're in town. Guests have included the Queen, Bob Hope, Ronald Reagan, Dolly Parton and the Dalai Lama. It has also been the location of a number of big movies, with the express lift recently starring alongside John Cusack in *Serendipity*. A night at the hotel is surprisingly affordable, with doubles starting from $189 for a standard room; if you do book a room, ask to be on the lake side as there's no difference in price.

Other upmarket hotels include the swanky *Four Seasons Hotel* (☎ 416-964-0411, 🖳 www.fourseasons.com/toronto) whose beds are so comfortable that guests have asked to buy them. It's located in the trendy Yorkville district at 21 Avenue Rd; standard doubles cost from around $365 during the week with discounts at weekends.

At 33 Gerrard West, the massive *Delta Chelsea* (☎ 416-595-1975 🖳 www.deltahotels.com) has lots of special facilities for children and doubles from $139, while the *Novotel* (☎ 416-367-8900, 🖳 www.novoteltorontocentre.com), in an elegant landmark building at 45 The Esplanade, close to the train station, has smart doubles from around $184. Many of its spacious, elegant rooms feature

❏ Accommodation prices quoted in this book are for **high season** (normally May or June to September). In low season many hotels offer substantial discounts.

powerful 'rainforest showers' which are wonderfully invigorating – especially after a long day of sightseeing.

WHERE TO EAT

The highlight of Toronto's restaurant scene is its sheer diversity, owing to the multiculturalism of the city: from Korean to Greek, Italian to Chinese, there's something to suit all tastes and at very agreeable prices. Equally, at the top end of the market there are some fantastic places to go for a splurge, most of them sporting stylish décor, excellent food and a lively crowd.

Budget food

Get your day off to a good start at the delightful *The Croissant Tree*, 1033 Bay St, where you can breakfast on delicious croissants and toasted bagels (with sandwiches, salads and other snacks available too). It also offers free wi-fi. A few blocks south at 20 College St, *Fran's* (☎ 416-923-9867) is a Toronto institution, going strong for forty years. This authentic diner serves up a selection of reasonably priced meals including breakfasts, burgers and sandwiches, and an array of delicious cakes and milkshakes 24 hours a day. Continuing south, at 312 Yonge St, the *Pickle Barrel* is best known for its jumbo sandwiches; it also serves cheap hot meals like pastas and noodles and has a pleasant patio area.

There's a clutch of good places to eat in the western area of downtown, around King and Spadina. Among them is excellent-value *The Red Tomato*, in a dark basement at 321 King St West (☎ 416-971-6626), which serves pizzas, pastas, stir-fries and salads, with all main courses around $10 to $12. There's plenty of choice nearby as well, as the whole block is taken up by pavement cafés and restaurants. Virtually opposite the Red Tomato, *Z-Teca Gourmet Burritos* at 327 King St West (☎ 647-346-5035), specializes in filling, affordable and very tasty burritos; there's another branch at 66 Gerrard St East. One block north of the King St West branch at 322 Adelaide St West, *Ravi Soups* (☎ 647-435-8365) serves up wraps and soups inside around a giant wooden table or on a pleasant outdoor patio area with bright murals and tropical plants. Meals are priced around $9.

Down near the train station inside a former blacksmith's workshop at 54 The Esplanade, *The Old Spaghetti Factory* (☎ 416-864-9761) is an always-reliable bet, offering excellent-value homemade pastas and good service.

Mid-range and upmarket restaurants

Very popular with tourists, the *Richtree Market Restaurant* at 42 Yonge St (☎ 416-366- 8986) is a kind of mock market where you wander from stall to stall, pile your plate high with goodies like rösti potatoes and spit-roasted chicken, then pay for it all at the check-out (count on around $30 per head). For something more sophisticated, head to *The Boiler House* at 55 Mill St in the Distillery District (☎ 416-203-2121). The large, bare-brick open-plan dining area is in keeping with the industrial heritage of the district but the menu is ultra-modern with mains (such as glazed confit of Quebec duck leg) starting at around $23.

One of Toronto's most enduringly popular eating spots is *Bellini's* at 101 Yorkville Ave (☎ 416-929-9111), a small, intimate and rather old-fashioned Italian restaurant whose clientele has included Elton John and Mick Jagger. The restaurant serves first-class pastas and risottos, with main courses ranging from $14 to $40, and a choice of three set dinner menus ($50, $60 or $78) in a refined setting, complete with crisp white tablecloths and attentive waiters.

Another beautiful interior can be found at the excellent *Oro* (☎ 416-597-0155), 45 Elm St, where Italian, Portuguese and Oriental influences make up an adventurous menu featuring such items as 'Australian rack of lamb with maple-Dijon pistachio crust'; most main courses are between $20 and $40. For a buzzing, glamorous atmosphere and sensational views, head to *Canoe* (☎ 416-364-0054) on the top (54th) floor of the Toronto Dominion building, 66 Wellington St. The food's excellent, too, with some fine Canadian specialities like roasted Alberta springbank elk tenderloin. The six-course taster menu costs $100 per person, or $145 with wine. Another fine place for a splurge is the luxurious and intimate *Epic* at the Royal York Hotel (see p116), where chef Ryan Gustafson serves up mouthwatering treats like seared sea scallops and Quebec foie gras. A three-course menu including wine will cost around $85 per person, and is worth every cent. The service and attention to detail are second to none.

NIGHTLIFE AND ENTERTAINMENT

One of the liveliest stretches of town after dark is **Queen St West** (see p120) between University and Spadina. Places to look out for are the *Black Bull* at No 298 (live bands); the *Horseshoe Tavern* at No 370 (more live bands); *Rivoli* at No 332 (lounge bar); and the *Big Bop* at No 651 (nightclub). The city's trendy **gay village** runs down Church St.

More relaxed in tone is the **Yorkville** area, where you'll find a cluster of bars sporting rooftop patios, including *Remy's*, 115 Yorkville Ave, and *Hemmingways*, 142 Cumberland St, which is very popular with the young professional crowd and has a heated patio.

Another area with a concentration of nightspots is **College St**, west of Bathurst St; if you're heading this way, try *Mod Club* at No. 722, where the mixture of British underground classics, soul and Top 40 hits attracts a hip crowd. If live jazz and blues is more your cup of tea, head for the *Grossman's Tavern*, a laid-back, unassuming venue just south of College St at 379 Spadina Ave, attracting excellent musicians.

A couple of blocks north of the Rogers Centre (see p120), above Gretsky's restaurant at 99 Blue Jays Way, the *Oasis* bar attracts a trendy crowd who come to enjoy after-work cocktails on its relaxing rooftop deck, complete with tropical plants and a fountain.

One of the most memorable places to sip a cocktail is the glitzy bar at *Canoe* on the top floor of the Toronto Dominion building, 66 Wellington St, where the views out to the islands are magical. Another swanky bar with top-of-the-world views onto Toronto's skyline is *Atlantis*, 955 Lakeshore West at

Ontario Place (take a taxi or bus No 121A or B from opposite the train station). Mention should also be made of the luxurious *Avenue Bar and Lounge* at the Four Seasons Hotel (see p116) – a hotspot for celebrities during the Toronto International Film Festival and a luxuriously elegant spot for a cocktail at any time of year.

There's a thriving **comedy** scene in the city with one of the best comedy clubs, *Yuk Yuks* (☎ 416-967-6425) to be found at 224 Richmond St West. A number of big Hollywood names such as Jim Carrey started their careers here. Cover charges start from $12.

Toronto claims to be 'the third-largest **theatre** centre in the English-speaking world' after London and New York. There's certainly an enormous variety of shows being put on, from glitzy musicals (*Phantom* et al) to the best of contemporary theatre (particularly from the Canadian Stage Company; ☎ 416-368-3110). Check the local papers for listings. There's a half-price ticket outlet *T.O.Tix* (☎ 416-536-6468) opposite the Eaton Centre for same-day performances (open Tuesday to Saturday from noon to 6.30pm), or you can buy full-price tickets for most shows online with Ticketmaster at 🖳 www.ticketmaster.ca.

WHAT TO SEE

CN Tower

Never mind the five-mile queues, never mind the exorbitant entrance fee, the CN Tower is something that has to be done while in Toronto.

This long, spindly telecommunications tower that looks as if it might snap in two in a high wind is still the tallest free-standing structure in the world at 553m high. When your turn finally comes you ascend the first 442m to the **Observation Level** in a glass elevator on the outside of the tower. Once you're up you can enjoy the staggering views over the toy-town city from either an indoor or outdoor viewing deck. The particularly brave can also take a stroll across the gut-churning glass floor.

CN Tower
PHOTO © JIM MANTHORPE

Serious height enthusiasts can go up an extra 100m to the **Skypod**, enclosed by a curved floor-to-ceiling glass wall, from where, on clear days, you can see as far as Niagara Falls, 137km away.

The entrance to the CN Tower (🖳 www.cntower.ca) is on Front St, about five minutes' walk west of the railway station. It costs $21.99 (children aged 4–12 $14.99, seniors $19.99) to get to the Observation Level and a further $5 to get to the Skypod; Hostelling International members receive a 15% discount. The Tower and Observation Deck are open daily year-round, excluding 25 December, between 9am and 11pm.

Rogers Centre (SkyDome)

Right next door to the CN Tower is Toronto's answer to Montreal's Olympic Stadium: the Rogers Centre (still popularly known by its old name of SkyDome), also with a fully retractable roof. The huge arena is home territory for the Toronto Blue Jays (baseball) and the Toronto Argonauts (football) and is the venue for numerous concerts and shows. It's certainly an impressive building but it's debatable whether it's worth parting with $13.75 for the behind-the-scenes hour-long 'Rogers Centre Tour Experience' in the arena (daily, on the hour, 10am–6pm in the summer; 💻 www.rogerscentre.com).

Hockey Hall of Fame

Continuing the sporting theme is this shrine to ice hockey – arguably Canada's national sport – on the corner of Front and Yonge. It's filled with a dazzling display of memorabilia (trophies, photos, movies, etc) which Canadians and Americans seem to love with a passion. Opening hours during summer are Monday to Saturday 9.30am–6pm, Sunday 10am–6pm, and during winter Monday to Friday 10am–5pm, Saturday 9.30am–6pm, Sunday 10.30am–5pm. Entrance costs $15; for more information see 💻 www.hhof.com.

City Hall

Unlike many daring edifices erected in the 1960s, this one continues to be raved about today. It comprises two tall, thin buildings curving towards each other with a short, dome-covered building in between them. City Hall is at Nathan Phillips Square (on Queen St West), which turns into a skating rink in winter. The city hall still stands at the east side of the square (on the corner of Bay and Queen), its Romanesque grandeur somewhat diminished by its towering neighbours.

Queen West

Starting a few blocks west of the City Hall, Queen St West suddenly goes all young and trendy – a change in tone due mainly to the close proximity of Canada's biggest art school, the Ontario College of Art. Cafés, nightclubs, bookshops and restaurants are interspersed with art studios and fashion design workshops. This very lively and slightly downbeat area stretches between University and Spadina and is known simply as 'Queen West'.

Art Gallery of Ontario

This wonderful museum is a pleasure to visit and not to be missed. Good use of space and light makes it an airy and stress-free environment – especially following the recent addition of a new four-storey titanium and glass wing, designed by celebrated Toronto-born architect Frank Gehry, who also gave the museum a stunning new timber and glass façade on Dundas St.

The first rooms you reach on Level 1 house the 19th- and early 20th-century European collection, including works by Renoir, Degas, Sisley, Matisse, Monet and Picasso. Monet's gorgeous *Vétheuil in Summer* seems to light up in increasingly golden hues the further back you stand from it. Note also his *Charing Cross Bridge: Fog* which depicts a dreamy London fog of pinks, greens and blues. In the same gallery look out for Otto Dix's startling *Portrait of Dr Heinrich Stadlemann*.

Up on Level 2 there's a very good collection of paintings by the Group of Seven (see box below). Their work powerfully evokes the vast wilderness of northern Ontario, which you pass through on the train journey between Toronto and Winnipeg. On the same level is the Henry Moore Sculpture Centre, which houses the world's largest public collection of Moore's work. The sculptor insisted on natural, overhead lighting and the effect is beautiful; his mammoth bronze women bathed in sunlight make an arresting sight. On Level 4 you'll find Andy Warhol's gun-slinging *Elvis* alongside other 20th-century works from iconic artists.

The museum is at 317 Dundas St, on the edge of Chinatown, with an entrance on McCaul St, and is open 10am–5.30pm Tuesday to Sunday, with late opening on Wednesdays until 8.30pm. Entry is $18 (youths aged 6–17 and students $10, seniors $15) and is free on Wednesdays from 6pm to 8.30pm. For more details see 🖥 www.ago.net.

Royal Ontario Museum

A few blocks north of Chinatown is the fabulous Royal Ontario Museum (usually referred to as 'the ROM'). Like the Art Gallery of Ontario, this, too, boasts a dazzling new extension, in this case the startling Michael Lee Chin Crystal, a huge glass and aluminium crystalline structure thrusting dramatically skywards behind the original, rather sedate, Victorian building.

The Group of Seven

If you plan to spend any length of time in Canadian art galleries you had better get to grips with the Group of Seven, still Canada's artistic pride and joy. The movement was initiated by the commercial artist, Tom Thomson, in 1912, following a trip to the Mississagi Forest Reserve in Northern Ontario. Thomson developed a bold new approach to painting Canada's wilderness, characterized by heavy colours, expressive patterns and a move away from similitude. His style was embraced by several of his friends who shared his frustration with the conservative nature of Canadian art, which had barely moved on from the 19th century. Together the artists began painting the wild and rugged terrain of Ontario's northern interior, where they honed their hallmark style of vibrant colours and stark, swirling landscapes.

In 1920, three years after Thomson's tragic death in a boating accident, his fellow artists – Frank Carmichael, Lawren Harris, AY Jackson, Franz Johnston, Arthur Lismer, JEH Macdonald and FH Varley – formed the Group of Seven and staged their first exhibition. They were wildly successful and their influence grew rapidly over the following years. Talent and innovation were helped by clever self-promotion and influential friends, which provoked resentment among Canada's established artists. The public, on the other hand, adored them, perhaps responding to their romantic evocation of the lonely, wild frontier.

The Group's work was to dominate Canadian art for the next thirty years. The irony of their success is that whilst they had set out to liberate Canadian art from the constraints of naturalism, their influence was so great that it stifled the development of alternative styles and became as restrictive as the artistic establishment they had replaced. Nonetheless, they engendered an important sense of national pride and showed that Canadian painters didn't have to look to Europe for the way forward.

This enormous museum contains both arts- and science-based collections, including dinosaur skeletons (most of them from the Alberta Badlands), a display of luminous minerals that glow in the dark and exhibitions on the ancient civilizations of Greece, Rome and Egypt (including some amazing mummy cases). Best of all are the internationally famous Chinese Galleries, whose highlights are the magnificent Ming tomb and a series of 14 towering Buddhist sculptures dating from the 12th to 16th centuries.

Other must-sees are the Dynamic Earth Gallery, which explains phenomena such as earthquakes and volcanic eruptions with state-of-the-art displays, including a massive plastic volcano, and the Hands-on Biodiversity Gallery, looking at the interdependence of plants, animals and humans and featuring a real beehive among other displays.

The easiest way to get to the ROM is to take the subway to Museum then follow the signs to the main entrance on Bloor at University. Opening hours are 10am–5.30pm daily, with late closing on Friday at 9.30pm. Entrance is a costly $22 for adults and $19 for students and seniors, and $15 for children aged 4–14; admission is half price after 4.30pm on Fridays, and free for the last hour on Wednesdays. For more information, see 💻 www.rom.on.ca

---

❏ Toronto's ethnic neighbourhoods

Officially deemed by the UN to be the most ethnically diverse city in the world, Toronto is made up of an exotic patchwork of cultural neighbourhoods. The largest ones are as follows:

● **Corso Italia**: Torontonians of Italian origin are outnumbered only by those of British extract. The Latin culture has been kept very much alive in 'Little Italy', centred along St Clair between Bathurst and Bloom.

● **Chinatown**: Toronto's Chinese population is the second biggest in North America, the biggest being in San Francisco. Starting with Sam Ching, a laundry shop owner who was Toronto's first Chinese immigrant at the turn of the 20th century, the community has grown to 350,000 people – equal to almost the entire population of Halifax. It's an exhilarating place to wander around, especially at the weekend when the street markets are in full swing and the shoppers are out in their thousands – walk along Spadina to Dundas and marvel at all the stalls filled with Chinese produce. All signs and prices are in Chinese and there's barely a Westerner in sight.

● **The Danforth**: East along Danforth Ave (between Pape and Woodbine) is the heart of 'Little Athens', where you'll find white-walled restaurants, little Greek bars and the National Bank of Greece.

● **The Jewish Community**: Centred mainly in the suburb of North York, Toronto's thriving Jewish community has no fewer than 60 synagogues and a fabulous supply of kosher delis.

● **Little Poland**: Along Roncesvalles Ave, west of downtown, the shops are stocked with Polish pastries and other delicacies. There is also a statue of the first Polish pope and a monument in honour of the 20,000 Poles who died in the Katyn massacre in World War II.

● **West Indies in Toronto**: Spreading around the suburbs north of Highway 401 is the 300,000-strong Caribbean community. Over a million visitors a year come to see the community's Caribana Carnival in July.

Bata Shoe Museum

One block west of the ROM, at 327 Bloor West, you'll find the Bata Shoe Museum, which houses a monumental and fascinating collection of footwear, taking in everything from Victorian wedding slippers and outrageous platform boots through to ancient Japanese sandals.

All the shoes are placed in their historical, functional and social context and are beautifully displayed. Among the highlights is a roomful of fine beaded moccasins produced by the Apaches of the American south-west, as well as a selection of shoes owned by the rich and famous, including Madonna, Elton John, Marilyn Monroe and Elvis Presley.

The museum's opening hours are Monday to Saturday 10am–5pm (until 8pm on Thursday), and noon–5pm on Sunday; entrance is $12. For a taste of the collection, see 🖳 www.batashoemuseum.ca.

Casa Loma

One of Toronto's quirkiest and most fascinating attractions is this grandiose mansion standing on a hillside. It was built in 1911 for Sir Henry Pellat, a self-made multimillionaire, and his wife, Lady Mary, who was the first Chief Commissioner of the Canadian Baden-Powell Girl Guide movement. Sir Henry lavished enormous quantities of his fortune on his 98-room castle in an effort to make it as ornate and opulent as it could possibly be. The palatial interior is fabulously over the top with a mixture of mediaeval-style banquet halls, secret passageways, marble bathrooms and fluffy boudoirs. Poor Sir Henry was able to enjoy these comforts for just ten years before bankruptcy forced him and his wife to move out and sell up.

These days the house is owned by the City of Toronto. It's a really fun place to visit and its beautiful grounds are a delight with their fountains, rhododendrons and 'secret garden'.

Casa Loma (🖳 www.casaloma.org) is a short walk uphill from Dupont subway. It's open daily 9.30am–5pm, with last admittance at 4pm; entrance is $18.

St Lawrence Market

Just outside the downtown core, on Front St between Church and Jarvis, the indoor St Lawrence Market (🖳 www.stlawrencemarket.com) is packed with a

---

The longest street in the world
The biggest and brashest thoroughfare in Toronto, **Yonge** (pronounced 'Young') **Street** is packed with skyscrapers, hotels, theatres, upmarket boutiques, scruffy discount stores, exclusive restaurants, greasy diners, thousands of people and much, much more. It's also the location (at Dundas) of the main entrance to the Eaton Centre, a veritable mega-mall that swallows up a million shoppers each week. Originally the street was built as a military pathway to link Lake Ontario to the Great Lakes in the north, which explains why it is so remarkably straight and long.

Not only is Yonge St one of Toronto's oldest and longest streets; it is also the world's longest street. Starting near Toronto's harbourfront you could drive north along Yonge (petrol supplies permitting) all the way to Rainy River, Ontario – a distance of 1900km. If you were to drive that distance from London you'd end up in Morocco!

fabulous array of fresh fruits, vegetables, meats, cheeses, flowers and numerous craft stalls. It's made up of two historic market buildings: the Farmers' Market (also known as the North Market) and the South Market, which incorporates Toronto's original City Hall building. Selling everything from home-grown produce to Asian specialities, it's a food-lover's paradise and has a bustling, lively atmosphere. The Farmers' Market is open on Saturdays 5am–5pm, and the South Market is open Tuesdays and Thursdays 8am–6pm, Fridays 8am–7pm and Saturdays 5am–5pm. It's a short walk from downtown (three blocks east of the Hockey Hall of Fame), or you can take a streetcar east along King St (get off at the St Lawrence Hall stop, a couple of minutes' walk from the market buildings).

The Distillery district

Some five blocks further east of the St Lawrence Market, the Distillery district (referred to by locals as simply the Distillery) is one of Toronto's up-and-coming areas. It's centred around a block of recently renovated 19th-century warehouses on Mill St, at the intersection with Parliament St, which were originally

Daytrip to Niagara Falls

A visit to Toronto would be incomplete without making the two-hour journey south of the city to one of the world's most famous sights, **Niagara Falls**. No amount of hype can prepare you for the sound and view of the falls thundering down the wide, horseshoe cliff with almost unimaginable force. Some 790,000 gallons pour over the edge each second, partly obscured by a thick curtain of spray that frequently drenches onlookers when blown across by the wind. Inevitably the surrounding streets are overflowing with gift shops, themed restaurants and arcades filled with slot machines and cheesy rides – but not even this unbridled commercialism can spoil things; indeed, some of the attractions are even rather fun.

The most rewarding are the **Journey Behind the Falls** ($12.50), in which you travel along tunnels carved through the rock behind the waterfalls, with several viewing holes just a couple of metres from the water; and the famous *Maid of the Mist* boat ride (30 minutes; $14.50) towards the base of the falls.

It's also worth considering paying the $11 to go up the **Skylon Tower**, which gives excellent views over the falls. Check online at 🖳 www.skylon.com for a list of dates and times when the falls are lit up at night.

Getting here

VIA Rail **trains** to Niagara Falls leave Toronto's Union Station daily at 8.30am, arrive just before 10.30am and return to Toronto at 5.45pm, getting back into Union Station at 7.37pm. Tickets should ideally be bought at least a day in advance or earlier if you want to get discounted train tickets (return ticket $76 regular fare/$42 special fare).

part of the Gooderham and Worts Distillery – at one time the biggest whisky distillery in the British Empire. Today, the cobbled streets are lined with a variety of stores, restaurants, cafés and charming boutiques, popular with tourists and locals alike. Chocoholics should head straight to the Soma Chocolatemaker, where the shelves and cabinets are laden with chocolate delights: a mug of Mayan hot chocolate here is highly recommended. Another place worth visiting is the Mill Street Brewery, which produces local ales and offers free tours around the brewery every day at 3pm. To get to the Distillery from downtown, either take bus No 172 eastbound from Front St or Bay St, or take the streetcar east along King St and get off at King and Parliament. For more information on the Distillery check out 🖳 www.thedistillerydistrict.com, which includes a map showing the location and opening hours of all of the stores.

The Islands

Having expended vast amounts of energy and money cramming in Toronto's many attractions, most visitors find a trip to the islands a well-deserved break. For just $6.50 for a return ticket, you can take a 15-minute ferry ride to one of

The Niagara Falls train station is about 4km from the falls themselves, which can be reached either by taxi (about $10) or on the 'People Mover' shuttle bus (all-day ticket $7.50) plying up and down Niagara Parkway, alongside the river. For the 'People Mover', from the train station cross over the road to the small bus station directly opposite where you can buy your day pass and catch the bus.

Alternatively, you could try one of the many **organized bus trips** from Toronto. One of the best outfits is the small and informal Chariots of Fire (☎ 1-866-833-0460, 🖳 www.chariots-of-fire.com) with day trips to the falls for $60 in summer, giving you two hours' free time at Niagara and one hour at Niagara-on-the-Lake (see below), along with some wine-tasting at one of the vineyards on the return journey.

Niagara-on-the-Lake and the wineries

A short drive from the falls through an idyllic stretch of vineyards is **Niagara-on-the-Lake**, a quaint little town full of pretty clapboard buildings and neat gardens. It's a lovely place for a wander and has the added attraction of being close to an abundance of fantastic **wineries** scattered around this part of southern Ontario, which thrive on the region's climate, soil conditions and latitudinal position. A good one to aim for, within walking distance of town, is the family-owned Peller Estates (☎ 905-468 4678, 🖳 www.peller.com), which boasts a beautiful setting with gorgeous views of the Niagara Escarpment. Once there, you can take a tour (from $10) around the winery and taste a variety of wines, including a local speciality, ice wine, a very sweet dessert wine made from frozen grapes. Other samples at the Tasting Bar range from $1 to $5, depending on the wine.

The easiest way to get to Niagara-on-the-Lake from Niagara Falls is on the Niagara Shuttle bus (☎ 1-800-268-7429; May–Oct, three daily, rest of year one daily), leaving from the bus station opposite the train station, with other pick-up points around town. Alternatively, a taxi will cost you around $30 each way. A fun way to explore the vineyards near Niagara-on-the-Lake is by **bicycle**, which can be hired from Zoom, 280 Hunter Rd (☎ 905-468-2366).

three interconnecting islands – Ward's Island, Centre Island, or Hanlan's Point – where you can wander around the parkland, take a picnic, stroll along the beach and generally relax. It's worth it for the view alone: Toronto's downtown skyline is breathtaking from the ferry.

The Island Ferry Docks are right at the bottom of Bay St on the lakeshore; you can walk from Union subway or go one stop from there on the connecting Harbourfront LRT line; note that the ferry goes only to Ward's Island in winter. You're allowed to take bikes on the ferries, or you can hire bikes on Centre Island at Island Bicycle Rental (☎ 416-203-0009) – the islands are virtually traffic-free, making cycling a lovely way to explore.

FESTIVALS

● **Toronto Downtown Jazz Festival**, late June to early July. Canadian and international jazz musicians. 🖳 www.torontojazz.com.
● **International Dragon Boat Race Festival**, late June. Boat races and lots of hoopla on Centre Island.
● **Caribana Parade**, late July to early August. Massive Caribbean festival of music and dance, with a fabulous parade.
● **Toronto International Film Festival**, mid-September. High-profile film festival showing new films from around the world. 🖳 www.tiffg.ca.

MOVING ON

By rail

The *Canadian* leaves Toronto for Vancouver on Tuesdays, Thursdays and Saturdays. The journey takes four days (three nights). There are frequent daily services to Montreal (four hours on the express) and Ottawa (just over four hours). In addition, Amtrak connections provide a service to New York and Chicago.

The VIA information number is ☎ 416-366-8411 (or ☎ 1-888-842-7245 when calling from outside Toronto). The Amtrak number is ☎ 1-800-872-7245.

By air

To get to Pearson International Airport take the Airport Express bus (☎ 905-564-3232). It picks up passengers from several major hotels, including the Royal York, opposite the train station. To arrange a free transfer from your hotel to the bus pick-up point, call ☎ 416-861-1234.

Useful airline numbers include Air Canada (☎ 416-925-2311) and American Airlines (☎ 1-800-433-7300).

Winnipeg

The manners of Winnipeg, of the West, impress the stranger as better than those of the East, more friendly, more hearty, more certain to achieve graciousness, if not grace.
Rupert Brooke, in a letter from 1913, as published in *Letters from America* (1916)

Winnipeg is a convenient place to take a break, being right in the middle of the country: it lies midway between the Atlantic and the Pacific, just 20km from the longitudinal centre of Canada. Its short but hot summers coax the crowds out of the malls and onto the streets and Winnipeg in July is a lively city, boasting some enjoyable attractions, such as the Exchange District, the Forks and the Winnipeg Museum. Out of season, however, it's a drab and chilly place. Winters here are long and bitterly cold and the intersection of Winnipeg's two main streets – Main and Portage – has the unenviable reputation of being the windiest spot in the world. The area around the intersection is also, particularly along Portage, something of a gathering place for the city's down-and-outs, whose presence, along with some run-down corners of downtown, can give Winnipeg an unsettling atmosphere.

The city is described in Carol Shields' *The Republic of Love* as 'a place with a short tough history and a pug-faced name' and receives less than flattering treatment at the hands of the English writer, Mark Lawson, in *The Battle for Room Service*: '... it was somehow just one of those places that sounded as if it might be Indian for shit-hole.' The people of Winnipeg, however, are known for their warmth and friendliness – perhaps in an effort to live up to the provincial slogan, 'Friendly Manitoba'. In the end, many visitors might be inclined to agree with one of Shields' characters who declares: 'I love Winnipeg because the people here are the salt of the earth. You walk down Portage and you get smiles from everyone, even the cops.'

HISTORY

The fur trade
Winnipeg is situated where the Red and Assiniboine rivers meet. This junction, known as The Forks, was an important centre of the fur trade: in 1738 Sieur de la Vérendrye erected a post here, which was later taken over by the French-owned North West Company (known as 'the Nor'westers'). It soon became a playing field for the bitter antagonism between the Nor'westers and their rivals, the Hudson's Bay Company (or 'the HBC').

The Red River Colony
In 1812 the Earl of Selkirk of the HBC set about creating a settlement near The Forks, which he named the Red River Colony. The life of the new settlers, most of whom had come from Scotland, was not an easy one. The Nor'Westers felt

threatened by their presence and systematically attempted to destroy the colony. The aggression reached a head in 1816 when the Seven Oaks Massacre left 21 of the settlers dead. The problems were in a large part resolved when the North West Company and the Hudson's Bay Company amalgamated in 1821 (keeping the HBC name). The Red River Colony began to grow in size, this time populated mainly by local Métis (of French and Indian extraction).

The Riel rebellions

After Canada became a dominion in 1867, the new government purchased the land occupied by the Red River Colony from the Hudson's Bay Company. They somewhat insensitively began to reorganize the settlement without consulting its inhabitants. The Métis staged a rebellion (see p39) organized by Louis Riel, which resulted in the creation of the province of Manitoba but also in the exile of Riel.

When a second Métis rebellion broke out 15 years later, Riel was summoned back to lead his people once more. This time the results were less successful and Riel was hanged for high treason.

The boom years

When it became clear that Winnipeg was going to be an important stop on the new transcontinental railway, it became in 1881 the site of a feverish and undisciplined land boom. Thousands of speculators rushed in to buy and sell lots and as the value of land rocketed, vast fortunes were made overnight.

Over the following years a steady flow of immigrants arrived to settle and farm the land, the influx reaching an all-time high between 1901 and 1914. In just a few decades it had grown from a small settlement of 241 people in 1871 to Canada's third-largest city in 1911, with a population of 136,000. The Winnipeg Grain Exchange was exporting grain all around the world and the city was the transportation, distribution and financial centre of western Canada.

Winnipeg today

By 1915 the boom was over and Winnipeg entered a period of recession. Poor working conditions and a burgeoning trade union movement resulted in the abortive Winnipeg General Strike in 1919, Canada's most famous strike to date. The situation didn't improve as Canada entered the 1920s in the grip of the worldwide Great Depression.

The economy picked up after the Second World War and Winnipeg once more established itself as the transportation hub of the west. Its prosperity has been undermined, however, by the westward shift of economic development into cities such as Saskatoon and Regina. Today Winnipeg has a population of 666,500 and is the eighth-biggest city in Canada.

GETTING AROUND

The local **bus** service is operated by Winnipeg Transit (☎ 204-986-5700, 🖳 www .winnipegtransit.com). The *Downtown Spirit*, which does a loop taking in Main, Portage, Vaughan and Broadway (calling at The Forks market), is free; otherwise, regular bus routes cost $2.30 per ticket. Taxi companies include Unicity Taxi (☎ 204-925-3131) and Duffy's Taxis (☎ 204-775-0101).

If you'd rather get around by **bike**, you can rent mountain bikes for around $40 per day at Gord's Bike Centre, 2 Donald St (☎ 204-284-2952). Stop off at the Tourist Information Centre and pick up the complimentary *Cyclist's Map of Winnipeg*, which has lots of great routes and tracks, regardless of the season or how good your cycling skills are.

ORIENTATION

The train station is very central, on Main St, and is no more than 15 minutes' walk from most hotels.

The lay-out of the city has developed around the Red and Assiniboine rivers – the downtown area slots into the corner where the two rivers meet. The two busiest thoroughfares are Main St (north–south, parallel to the Red River) and Portage Ave (east–west, parallel to the Assiniboine).

SERVICES

Tourist information
The staff at the **Tourism Winnipeg** office (☎ 204-943-1970, or ☎ 1-800-665-0204 toll-free from anywhere in North America), 259 Portage Ave, are very helpful; the office is open Monday to Friday 8.30am–4.30pm.

There's also a **Travel Manitoba Information Centre** (☎ 204-945-3777 or ☎ 1-800-665-0040) at The Forks, opposite the Johnston Terminal; it incorporates a very interesting if small museum known as the Theme Pavilion which depicts the history of Manitoba and includes a life-size polar bear and other amusing displays. It also has a free internet terminal. Between May and September, the centre is open daily 9am–6pm, and Monday to Friday 9am-5pm in the winter.

Money
There are plenty of banks and exchange facilities about, including the Custom House Currency Exchange at 231 Portage Ave. The Toronto Dominion Bank is at Portage and Main and the Assiniboine Credit Union can be found at 265 Portage Avenue

Consulates
Belgium (☎ 204-261-1415) 15 Acadia Bay; **Denmark** (☎ 204-233-8541) 239 Aubert St, St-Boniface; **Germany** (☎ 204-475-3088) Suite 101, 1200 Pembina,

---

❏ **Winnipeg online**
💻 **www.destinationwinnipeg.ca** Tourism Winnipeg's official website, with lots of practical information on the city; 💻 **www.travelmanitoba.com** Well put-together site with lots of travel information on the whole province and a section with suggestions on what to do in Winnipeg.

Fort Garry; **Italy** (☎ 204-488-8745) 1055 Wilkes; **Netherlands** (☎ 204-487-1211) 69 Shorecrest Dr; **Norway** (☎ 204-489-1626) 603 Pasadena Ave; **Sweden** (☎ 204-233-3373) 1035 Mission St

Post, internet and laundry

Winnipeg's main **post office** is at 266 Graham Ave, at the corner with Smith. **Internet access** is available at the post office, as well as at the public library at 251 Donald (on the corner with Graham) and at Tourism Manitoba at The Forks. There's also Osborne Cyber Café at 118A Osborne St (Monday to Friday 10am–midnight), and Cyber Game Internet Café at 5-709 Corydon Ave. If you need a **laundry**, try the Midland Maytag Laundry Centre at 208 Marion St, in the St Boniface district (☎ 204-237-7223).

WHERE TO STAY

Winnipeg has a good spread of accommodation, particularly in the mid-range bracket. If you've just arrived from Montreal or Toronto you'll notice that you get a lot more for your money here, even at the upper end of the scale.

Budget accommodation

The recently renovated *HI Winnipeg Downtowner Hostel* at 330 Kennedy St (☎ 204-943-5581, 🖥 www.hihostels.ca) comes with clean and comfortable dorms from $29 per person (many with en-suite bathrooms) and private rooms ($69); there's also a pub and restaurant on-site, among other facilities. The location is fairly central, about a 10- to 15-minute walk from the train station, though the area is a little run-down and lone travellers (especially female) should take care when walking around the area at night; taxis are advisable.

A little further from the centre, at 168 Maryland (near the corner with Sara Ave) is the *Backpackers' Guest House International* (☎ 204-772-1272, 🖥 www.backpackerswinnipeg.com), in a converted Victorian house on a leafy street. It has dorm beds (from $22) and private rooms ($52 per double room), cable TV, a games room in the basement, laundry facilities and bike rental. It sometimes closes from November to March so it's best to phone in advance if you're travelling during those months. To get there from the train station, take bus No 29 to Broadway and Sherbrooke, one block east of the hostel.

Mid-range hotels

The *St Regis Hotel* (☎ 204-942-0171, 🖥 www.stregishotel.net) at 285 Smith, just south of Portage Ave, was built in 1911 at the height of the immigration boom. The rooms aren't exactly flash but they're spacious, clean, come with a TV and private bathroom and are very cheap for what you get, starting at $78 for a double. Nudging up the scale in comfort, the *Carlton Inn* (☎ 204-942-0881, 🖥 www.carltoninn.mb.ca), 220 Carlton St, offers neat, well-maintained rooms plus a small pool, with

---

❏ Accommodation prices quoted in this book are for **high season** (normally May or June to September). In low season many hotels offer substantial discounts.

CITY GUIDES

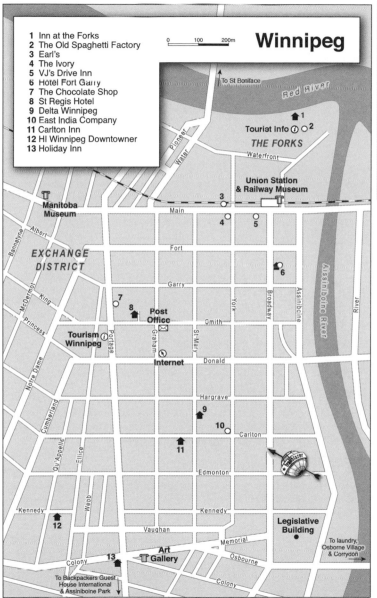

Winnipeg

1 Inn at the Forks
2 The Old Spaghetti Factory
3 Earl's
4 The Ivory
5 VJ's Drive Inn
6 Hotel Fort Garry
7 The Chocolate Shop
8 St Regis Hotel
9 Delta Winnipeg
10 East India Company
11 Carlton Inn
12 HI Winnipeg Downtowner
13 Holiday Inn

0   100   200m

To St Boniface

Red River

Tourist Info ⓘ ○ 2

THE FORKS

Waterfront

Union Station
& Railway Museum

Manitoba
Museum

Main

EXCHANGE
DISTRICT

Fort

Garry

Post
Office

Tourism ⓘ
Winnipeg

Internet

Donald

Hargrave

Carlton

Edmonton

Trailways

Legislative
Building

To laundry,
Osborne Village
& Corrydon

Kennedy

Vaughan

Art
Gallery

Memorial

Osborne

Colony

To Backpackers Guest
House International
& Assiniboine Park

Pioneer

Water

Albert

Bannatyne

McDermot

King

Princess

Notre Dame

Cumberland

Qu'Appelle

Ellice

Webb

Kennedy

Colony

Graham

Portage

Smith

St Mary

York

Broadway

Assiniboine

Assiniboine River

River

CITY GUIDES

rates going from $81 a double. Adjoined to the hotel is the smart Paragon restaurant which serves up great Greek food and has live jazz sets every Friday at 5pm.

The smartest mid-range choice is the *Holiday Inn* (☎ 204-786-7011, 💻 www .holiday-inn.com/winnipegdtwn) at 360 Colony St, which comes with a pool and a small gym; doubles here cost $139 during the week and $109 at weekends. Finally, if you don't mind staying out of the city centre you could always try one of the B&Bs in the leafy residential neighbourhoods: **Heritage Bed and Breakfast Homes of Winnipeg** (💻 www.bbcanada.com/associations/winni peg) offers four large and characterful B&Bs with rates from $65.

Upmarket hotels

Close to the railway station at 222 Broadway, the *Hotel Fort Garry* (☎ 204-942-8251, 💻 www.fortgarryhotel.com) is without doubt Winnipeg's most distinctive and atmospheric hotel. Built in 1913 by the Grand Trunk Pacific Railway, it's wonderfully grand inside, featuring a beautiful domed lounge and a gorgeous lobby. Residents have free use of the adjacent pool and fitness centre. Doubles (including a fine breakfast) start at around $159, going up to $249 for an executive suite. Keep your wits about you if you happen to be on the eighth floor – it is said to be haunted.

The newly renovated *Delta Winnipeg* (☎ 204-942-0551, 💻 www.deltawin nipeg.com) at 350 St Mary Ave is smart and modern with excellent facilities, including an indoor and outdoor pool and large gym. Another nice touch is the heated bathroom floors and hi-speed internet access in all the rooms; standard doubles start from $139. Another stylish hotel is the *Inn at the Forks* (☎ 204-942-6555, 💻 www.innforks.com) which boasts a great location right next to the The Forks market, a short distance from the VIA station. Rooms here are spacious and immaculate, as you might expect from a hotel of this standard, and if you feel in need of some serious pampering the Riverstone Spa, located within the hotel, will do the trick. Rates start at $159.

WHERE TO EAT

The first thing you'll notice about Winnipeg's restaurants is that so many of them are Italian, reflecting the city's immigration history in the early 20th century. Most of them are also very good and reasonably priced to boot.

Budget food

For a really cheap meal you could do worse than try *VJ's Drive Inn*, a shack opposite the train station serving homemade burgers, hot dogs and fries which is apparently famous throughout the prairies. There are also plenty of bargain food stalls at **The Forks market**, ranging from bagels to stir-fries, accompanied by a lively atmosphere.

One of the most popular eating places in town is *Earl's* at 191 Main St (☎ 204-989-0103), where you can eat burgers, pastas, pizzas, fried chicken and the like in a large, bright and invariably packed-out dining room. If the weather is cooperative you can make the most of the spacious outdoor patio overlooking Main St. For something a bit different, try the *East India Company*'s

$14.95 lunch buffet or $19.95 dinner buffet (Monday to Friday; ☎ 204 947-3097) at 349 York Ave, surrounded by sumptuous Indian decorative art. Alternatively, *The Old Spaghetti Factory* (☎ 204-957-1391) is housed in the Old Johnson Railway Storage Building at The Forks. Part of a chain, it offers cheap but dependable food (typically $10 to $15) and friendly, efficient service.

Mid-range and upmarket restaurants

Some of the best places to eat are out of downtown in the surrounding neighbourhoods, where Winnipeg's ethnic communities are concentrated. One of these is **Corrydon Ave**, which is lined with Italian cafés and restaurants (to get there take the No 18 bus from Main St). *Civita* (☎ 204-453-4616), at No 691, has an Italian-meets-Californian feel to it – the food is very satisfying and moderately priced at $10 to $20 for mains, and the atmosphere and service are very friendly.

Another good bet on Corrydon Ave is *Confusion Corner Bar and Grill* (☎ 204-284-6666) at No 500, which brings together Mexican, Asian and European cuisine in an intriguing menu, taking in items as diverse as Szechuan beef wrap to Mexican shrimp salad and New York steak (mains around $14–24). It also has a pleasant second-floor patio.

Closer to the city centre, on the south side of the Assiniboine River, is **Osborne Village**, which has a lot of good-value, interesting eating places. The Village is about a 10-minute walk from the Legislative Building or you can take the No 16 bus from Graham at Vaughan. Places to try here include the *Tomato Pie Co* (☎ 204-477-6609) at 167 Osborne St, which serves delicious thin-crust pizzas with a huge variety of toppings and traditional southern Italian fare from around $15, or friendly *Bangkok Thai* at 100 Osborne St (☎ 204-474-0908), where you'll find popular Thai dishes in an elegant dining room within a historic building on the corner of Osborne and River.

A solid choice in downtown Winnipeg is *The Chocolate Shop* at 268 Portage Ave (☎ 204-947-9109), which claims to be the oldest restaurant in Winnipeg, having opened in 1918. Before then it was a candy and confectionery store – hence its name – but these days specializes in hearty and reasonably priced meat dishes of all descriptions; try the award-winning bison chilli (though fish gets a look in, too, for example with the excellent Manitoba pickerel). For top-notch Indian food, head for *The Ivory* (☎ 204-944-1600) at 200 Main St, not far from the train station, where you can feast from a huge diner buffet ($20 per person) in a funky, imaginative interior. One of Winnipeg's most upscale restaurants is *The Current* at the Inn at the Forks (see p 132; ☎ 204-942-6555), whose smart dining room offers wonderful views of The Forks market, where many of the restaurant's ingredients are sourced. Main courses – mostly traditional meat- and fish-based – are well prepared and fairly good value, mostly within the $15–30 range.

Finally, mention must be made of the fabulous Sunday brunch served at the *Hotel Fort Garry* (see p132), where a breathtaking range of fruits, salads, hams, cold fish, pastries and cakes (as well as traditional hot breakfasts) are spread out in the grand lobby and eaten in the domed lounge (if they try to seat you in the other dining room, insist on waiting for a free lounge table); the buffet costs around $40 per person and reservations are essential, even for hotel guests.

NIGHTLIFE

Thanks to its large student population, Winnipeg has a lively nightlife scene. Curiously, the city has a number of very popular pseudo-British pubs, including *Elephant & Castle*, next door to the Delta Winnipeg at 350 St Mary, and *Toad in the Hole* in Osborne Village at 112 Osborne.

For more authentic stuff you should try out one of the local country and western bars frequented by burly men wearing stetsons and cowboy boots; one of the best, especially for live music and country dancing, is *Palomino Club* at 1133 Portage Ave (a short cab ride from the centre), which is open until 2am.

There's a concentration of nightclubs around the Exchange District, including *Whiskey Dix* on the corner of McDermot and Main, and *Vibe* at 330 York Ave.

One of the best places to listen to jazz in Winnipeg is *The Blue Note Café*, an intimate, relaxed place at 875 Portage. More sedate, and very refined, is the bar at the *Hotel Fort Garry*, which has live piano music most evenings.

A good place for live blues is the *Times Change High and Lonesome Club*,

Charlie Chaplin was here: mural at the Windsor Hotel
PHOTO © JIM MANTHORPE

234 Main St, at St Mary (Thursday to Sunday until 2am). Another, even better one is the *Windsor Hotel Bar* at 187 Garry St. Known to locals as the House of Blues, it's famous for attracting internationally renowned blues artists. It's also famous for putting up Charlie Chaplin who is said to have penned a letter to a friend on the hotel's headed paper declaring his intention to move to Hollywood to pursue a career in acting. A huge Chaplin mural decorates the outside back wall of the hotel.

WHAT TO SEE

The Forks
Right behind Union Station is The Forks, where the Red and Assiniboine rivers meet. It used to be a railway service and repair site but has been converted to a market. The buildings are full of food, crafts, jewellery, clothes, restaurants, cafés and the like, bearing more than a passing resemblance to London (England)'s Covent Garden, and there are plenty of street entertainers outside. It's very lively and has a buzzing atmosphere, especially in the summer, and if the hustle and bustle become too much there are some lovely pathways leading down to the river and beyond.

Union Station and Winnipeg Railway Museum
Close to the Forks, Winnipeg's railway station, which was designed by the same architects as New York's Grand Central Station, is one of the most impressive in Canada, featuring a beautiful domed ceiling above the main hall.

Upstairs on Tracks 1 and 2, the Winnipeg Railway Museum (☎ 204-942-4632) houses several gems including the grand old *Countess of Dufferin*, the first locomotive in the Canadian West, built in 1872. Other exhibits include a Baldwin locomotive that was used to build part of the Canadian Pacific Railway, a CNR Caboose that (if you ask nicely) you can climb aboard, and a 1920s railbus. A recent addition to the museum is an interesting exhibition about the role of women in the success of the railway. There's also a well-stocked gift shop selling everything from fridge magnets to clocks.

The museum, run on a voluntary basis by the Midwestern Rail Association, is open from June to August from Friday to Sunday noon–5pm; and in May and September through November on Saturday and Sunday noon–4pm. They often try to be open when *The Canadian* is passing through, too, when it makes an excellent place to stretch your legs during the four-hour layover. A modest entrance price of $5 is charged.

Manitoba Museum

This is Winnipeg's best museum by a long shot. With an emphasis on the province's natural and human history, highlights include a representation of the Arctic tundra with an impressive polar bear display, a Grasslands gallery with a big tepee and other items typical of life on the plains and, best of all, a full-size working replica of the ketch that brought the founders of the Hudson's Bay Company to Canada (you can climb on board and wander around), as well as a life-size reconstruction of Winnipeg during the 1920s complete with boardwalks, shops, factories and the railway station.

The museum (🖳 www.manitobamuseum.ca) is at the Centennial Centre on Main St, opposite the City Hall. From May 16 to September 7 it's open daily 10am–5pm and during the rest of the year Tuesday to Friday 10am–4pm, weekends 11am–4pm. Admission is $8, or $18.50 for a Value Pass which also gets you into the attached **Planetarium** (excellent multimedia shows which recreate the sky at night, suitable for all ages) and **The Science Centre** (a hands-on science gallery, geared towards kids).

Exchange District

In the boom years of 1880–1915 large numbers of banks, warehouses and other commercial buildings sprang up in Winnipeg. The centre of this expansion was the Exchange District, close to the Manitoba Museum, where the old buildings with their elaborate advertisements painted on the walls have been renovated and gentrified. They now house offices, shops, restaurants and pubs. It's an interesting place to wander around and certainly contains the best examples of Winnipeg's otherwise uninspiring architecture. Guided historic walking tours ($7) are available during summer months; see 🖳 www.exchangedistrict.org.

Winnipeg Art Gallery

At the northern end of downtown, the Winnipeg Art Gallery (🖳 www.wag.mb .ca) houses mainly temporary exhibitions of modern Canadian art which change regularly. One room is used exclusively for Inuit collections and the museum has a reputation for showing the most comprehensive range of Inuit art in Canada.

The museum is located at 300 Memorial Blvd and is open Tuesday to Sunday 11am–5pm (and until 9pm on Thursdays); entrance is $8.

Legislative Building

Dating from 1919, Manitoba's seat of government – a few blocks east of the Art Gallery at 450 Broadway – is an imposing building. Its large dome is topped by Winnipeg's most famous symbol: the Golden Boy, a four-metre-tall gilded statue of a messenger carrying a sheaf of grain in one arm and a torch in the other (and supposedly embodying the spirit of youth and enterprise). During the summer months there are free guided tours around the building.

Winnie-the-Bear
PHOTO © JIM MANTHORPE

Assiniboine Park

About 8km west of downtown is this 376-acre park, containing a zoo (admission $4.55) with over a thousand animals.

Look out for the statue of Winnie-the-Bear near the main entrance, one-time resident of the zoo, named after the city and donated to London Zoo as a cub. It happened that young Christopher Robin named his own teddy bear after the animal, giving rise to the Winnie-the-Pooh stories that his father A A Milne wrote.

The park is also home to a conservatory (with some lovely tropical plants) and the Leo Mol Sculpture Garden, with its religious and wildlife sculptures. To get to the park take the No 18 bus from Main at Pioneer; the park entrance is at 2355 Corydon Ave.

Winnipeg's Book Walk

Any bookworms visiting the city might be interested to know that Winnipeg offers a self-guided tour of its 'Book and Collectible District', centred on the streets off Notre Dame Ave, just west of the Exchange District. The walk takes you on a leisurely stroll through a variety of thrift stores, second-hand bookstores and quirky antique shops – you can pick up a map at either of the town's tourist offices or at the Aqua Books second-hand bookstore at 274 Garry St. If you've a long train ride ahead, this is a good opportunity to stock up on books – and if not, it's still a chance to get to know a different side of Winnipeg. For more information, contact Kelly Hughes on ☎ 204-943-7555 or 🖳 Kelly@ aquabooks.ca, or visit the store.

Old Saint-Boniface

Cross over the river from the VIA station and the Forks and you'll find yourself in Old Saint-Boniface, the heart of Winnipeg's Franco-Manitoban community, which prides itself on its history and ambience. Home to the largest francophone community west of the Great Lakes, the area is steeped in French and Métis culture – eloquently celebrated at the impressive Saint-Boniface Museum (housed in the oldest building in Winnipeg and the oldest log structure in North

America). Saint-Boniface is also the site of the impressive façade of the **cathedral** which burned down in 1968, some modern galleries and shops featuring the works of local artists and craftsmen, and plenty of inviting cafés and restaurants. Guided walking tours of Saint-Boniface, led by knowledgeable staff in period costume, are offered by Tourisme Riel: for more details contact ☎ 204-233-8343 or visit 🖳 www.tourismeriel.com.

Prairie Dog Central Railway

This beautiful early 20th-century train makes the 36-mile round trip (two and a half hours) every Saturday and Sunday between June and September. The *Prairie Dog Central*'s steam engine was built in Scotland in 1882, and for 36 years pulled CPR passenger trains between Fort William and Kenora. These days it runs north from Inkster Junction Station (a 20-minute drive from central Winnipeg) to Grosse Isle, and while it can hardly claim to be the most scenic rail ride in the country it's certainly one of the most stylish; the polished oak and mahogany inside the old coaches are magnificent. The train stops off at Warren before reaching Grosse Isle and local residents set up stalls on the platform selling cakes, hot drinks and local crafts. The staff are all in costume and it really is a great family day out.

Trains depart at 11am; the regular fare is around $20, though check in advance as some special events can mean that the fare is either increased or discounted. It's possible to make advance reservations online or by phone and for those without their own transport, the *Prairie Dog Central* provides its own courtesy shuttle bus to Inkster station, with pick-up points at the Inn at the Forks and the Clarion Hotel, 1445 Portage Ave (☎ 204-774-5110). For more information on the *Prairie Dog Central*, call ☎ 204-832-5259 or visit 🖳 www.pdcrailway.com.

FESTIVALS

● **Winnipeg Jazz Festival**, mid to end of June. Week-long programme of indoor and outdoor jazz concerts.
● **Red River Exhibition**, last week in June. Manitoba's largest fair: music, parades, shows and games.
● **Folk Festival**, mid-July. Huge gathering of Canadian and international folk musicians.
● **Folklorama**, early to mid August. A multicultural celebration of the peoples of the world, housed in over 40 pavilions spread throughout the city, with singing, dancing, arts and crafts, ethnic foods and more on offer.

MOVING ON

The *Canadian* leaves for Vancouver (about 40 hours from Winnipeg) on Wednesdays, Fridays and Sundays, and for Toronto (about 30 hours) on Tuesdays, Thursdays and Sundays.

The *Hudson Bay* leaves Winnipeg for Churchill on Tuesdays and Sundays – the journey takes around 35 hours. The VIA information line is ☎ 1-888-842-7245.

Edmonton

Edmonton, the headquarters of the Hudson Bay Company's Saskatchewan trade... is a large, five-sided fort with the usual flanking bastions and high stockades. It has within these stockades many commodious and well-built wooden houses, and differs in the cleanliness and order of its arrangements from the general run of trading forts in the Indian country.
Butler, *The Great Lone Land*, 1872

Situated on the northern edge of the prairies, Alberta's provincial capital is a city grown rich from wheat and oil. Despite its affluence, however, of all the cities along the line it has the least to recommend itself to the rail traveller. It's not that there's nothing to do or see here; on the contrary there are some great attractions but, unfortunately, most of them are far from the city centre and reaching them by public transport can be tedious.

The downtown area is a little lifeless owing to the collapse of a large number of shopping outlets since the opening of the giant West Edmonton Mall. This shopping and entertainment complex, the largest in the world, ranks as Edmonton's number one tourist attraction – a fact that may well start the warning bells ringing... That said, the rejuvenated district of Old Strathcona, on the south side of the river running through town, makes up for the city centre's lack of vim with its lively atmosphere, attractive old buildings and good supply of shops, restaurants and cafés.

Nonetheless, you may feel that even the charms of Old Strathcona aren't reason enough to delay the spectacular journey into the Rockies, less than four hours away by train.

HISTORY

Fur-trading outpost
Edmonton began life in 1795 when the Hudson's Bay Company (HBC) erected Edmonton House as a fur-trading base. This was established to compete with the nearby Fort Augustus, founded a few months earlier by the HBC's great rival, the North West Company. The two companies traded with the local Cree and Blackfoot Indians for beaver pelts, otter and muskrat furs and Edmonton quickly became the headquarters of the fur trade in the western prairies. It was also a major stopping-off point for travellers to the North or to the Pacific.

Sold to the Dominion
It wasn't until the Hudson's Bay Company sold the best part of its land to the Dominion of Canada in 1870 that settlers began to set up home outside the HBC stockade. Businesses sprang up and by the 1890s the new town was operating coal mines, saw mills and a boatbuilding factory. In 1897 the Yukon gold rush brought thousands of fortune-seekers en route for the goldfields. Many stayed and by the turn of the 20th century Edmonton's population had grown to 4000.

Booming provincial capital

Following its incorporation as a city in 1904, Edmonton became Alberta's capital when the province was created in 1905. By then the population was 9000, a number that grew rapidly in the next few decades. Although it had been ignored in favour of Calgary by the Canadian Pacific Railway, it was a major stop on two new lines by 1915. It also became an important transportation and supply centre with the construction of the Alaska Highway in 1942.

Shortly after this, Edmonton's success was assured when oil was discovered at Leduc Number One Well in 1947. Over the following years, oil was struck in thousands of wells within a 160km radius of the city and Edmonton became known as the 'Oil Capital of Canada'.

Edmonton today

Today over one million people live in Greater Edmonton, making it Canada's sixth-largest city. The wealth bestowed on it by the oil industry has transformed the downtown district into a jumble of glass-plated skyscrapers.

As the impact of oil on Edmonton's economy begins to scale down, businesses such as forestry, pharmaceuticals and electronics are starting to play a more important role.

GETTING AROUND

If you stick to the downtown core you'll be able to get around on foot but for visits to attractions such as the famous Mall you'll need to use Edmonton Transit (☎ 780-496-1611, 🖳 www.edmonton.ca/transportation), a mixture of **bus** and **light-rail** transit (LRT) networks. Fares are $2.50. Ask for a transfer when you board the bus as this allows you to change buses during the following 90 minutes. **Taxi companies** include Alberta Co-Op (☎ 780-425-2525) and Yellow Cab (☎ 780-462-3456).

ORIENTATION

The railway station is at 12360–121 St, 6km north-west of downtown; the only way into the centre is to take a cab, which usually works out at about $15.

Downtown Edmonton, which is surprisingly compact, sits on the northern bank of the North Saskatchewan River, while the popular district of Old Strathcona is on the south bank. The city's biggest and busiest thoroughfare is Jasper Ave. Most of the other avenues and streets are numbered, not named:

❑ **Edmonton online**
🖳 **www.edmonton.com** Provides general information on the Greater Edmonton area. This is the official tourism website for Edmonton; 🖳 **www.discoveredmon ton.com** General round-up of the city's attractions, accommodation and restaurants plus ideas for touring the Rockies from Edmonton; 🖳 **www.travelalberta.com** Heaps of information on the whole province including a good section on Edmonton.

avenues run from east to west, their numbers increasing as you go north; streets run from north to south with their numbers increasing as you move west.

SERVICES

Tourist information
The main **tourist office** (☎ 780-496-8400 or ☎ 1-800-463-4667) is in the World Trade Centre at 9990 Jasper Ave. It's open 7am–7pm from Monday to Friday, and 9am–5pm at weekends during the summer; it stocks a comprehensive range of maps, brochures and other material.

Money
All the major banks can be found along Jasper Ave. There's also an American Express office at 10180–101 St and a Thomas Cook Foreign Exchange in the City Centre Mall.

Consulates
Denmark (☎ 780-426-1457) Suite 1112, 10235–101st St; **Finland** (☎ 780-429-6253) 10135-100th St; **France** (☎ 780-420-6050) 467 Rooney Crescent; **Germany** (☎ 780-434-0430) 8005-102nd St; **Italy** (☎ 780-423-5153) Suite 1900, Merrill Lynch Tower; **Netherlands** (☎ 780-428-7513) 82nd and 83rd St; **Norway** (☎ 780-440-2292) 2310–80th Ave; **Sweden** (☎ 780-886-2501) Now located in Calgary; **USA** (☎ 403-266-8962) Now located in Calgary

Post, internet and laundry
The main downtown **post office** is at 9808–103A Ave. A handy downtown address for **internet access** is Bohemia Cyber Café, 11012 Jasper Ave NW (at 110th St NW). In old Strathcona there's an internet café (called 3rd on Whyte) at 10351 Whyte Ave, near the corner with 104 St.

The most conveniently located **laundries** are Easy Coin Laundry at 10992–124th St (west of downtown) and Soap Time Laundry, 7626–104th St, near Old Strathcona.

WHERE TO STAY

Budget accommodation
Go Backpackers Edmonton at 10209-100th Ave (☎ 780-423-4146 ⌨ www .edmonton@gohostels.ca) is a newly renovated hostel in the heart of downtown with dorms for $25 per person and private doubles at $70. The friendly staff are happy to suggest activities and places to eat and the hostel is connected to *Jekyll and Hyde,* a popular bar which hosts live bands on Friday nights.

The *HI Hostel* (☎ 780-988-6836, ⌨ www.hihostels.ca) is at 10647–81st Ave in Old Strathcona, the lively shopping and restaurant district across the river

---

❏ Accommodation prices quoted in this book are for **high season** (normally May or June to September). In low season many hotels offer substantial discounts.

Edmonton

Where to stay
1 Sutton Place
2 Grand Hotel
5 Westin Hotel
6 Courtyard by Marriott
7 Fairmont Hotel
   Macdonald
9 Go Backpackers
13 Days Inn

Where to eat
3 Hawoli, Old Spaghetti
   Factory & La Crêperie
4 Sorrentino's
7 Harvest Room
8 La Ronde
10 The Hat
11 Russian Tea Room
12 Blue Plate Diner

To railway station &
Chateau Nova Hotels

106th Ave

105th Ave

To Telus World
of Science

104th Ave

103A Ave

Post
Office

103rd Ave

Art
Gallery

98th St

99th St

9 th St

98th St

100th St

Bus
station

103rd Ave

2

102A Ave

3

To Royal
Alberta Museum

102nd Ave

108th St

107th St

106th St

105th St

104th St

103rd St

102nd St

101st St

100A St

4

101A Ave

12

5

Tourist
Information

11

Jasper Ave

7

6

13

10

100th Ave

8

9

99th Ave

To West
Edmonton Mall

0   100   200   300m

North
Saskatchewan River

Alberta
Legislature

To Fort
Edmonton Park

To Old Strathcona, HI Hostel,
Da-De-O New Orleans Diner-Bar,
Tasty Toms, New York Bagel,
Unheardof, internet & laundry

Muttart
Conservatory

from downtown. Beds start from $28 for members and $32 for non-members; there are also a few private doubles with ensuite bathrooms at $87 and $89 respectively. The hostel is directly behind Whyte Ave, otherwise known as 'Party Street', so if it's nightlife you're after this is the place to head.

Mid-range hotels

The cheapest downtown hotel is the *Grand Hotel* (☎ 780-422-6365, 🖳 www .edmontongrandhotel.com) at 10266–103rd St, which has adequate en-suite doubles (with rather lurid 1970s carpets and small beds) for $58 and rooms with a shared bathroom for $38; both types come with full breakfast included. *Days Inn* (☎ 780-423-1925), at 10041–106th St, looks a bit spartan from the outside but its rooms (starting at $105 for a standard bedroom) are neat, modern and good value; breakfast (which costs extra) is served at the friendly Albert's restaurant. Moving up a notch, a short cab-ride from the train station at 159 Airport Rd, *Chateau Nova Hotel and Suites* (☎ 780-424-6682, 🖳 www .chateaunovahoteledmonton.ca) has beautiful, spacious rooms and a business centre with free internet access for all guests. The location is perfect if you just want an overnight stop before getting back on the train but isn't convenient for the downtown area (about a $7 cab ride away).

Upmarket hotels

The *Fairmont Hotel Macdonald* (☎ 780-424-5181, 🖳 www.fairmont.com) at 10065–100th St was built in 1915 by the Grand Trunk Railway and is exquisitely decorated — all ivories, whites and Edwardian elegance. The location is unbeatable as the hotel sits in the heart of downtown Edmonton yet offers spectacular views over the river valley. Guests can admire the views as they sip cocktails in the beautiful Confederation Lounge or perhaps take a stroll in the immaculate hotel gardens, complete with ornate fountain. Standard doubles go from $259 to $489.

Next door, the *Courtyard by Marriott* (☎ 780-423-9999, 🖳 www.marriott .com) offers the same great riverside views from many of its rooms as well as from its outdoor deck area. This recently renovated hotel has a variety of very spacious, pristine suites, some with Jacuzzi baths, and offers free laundry facilities to all guests. Weekend rates start at $139, with standard room prices ranging from $159 to $189 during weekdays.

Across the road, well-appointed *Westin Edmonton* (☎ 780-426-3636, 🖳 www .westin.com/Edmonton) is another good choice with its spacious rooms, contemporary décor and trademark 'Heavenly Beds'. Rates are around $85 to $180 according to demand. The recently refurbished *Sutton Place Hotel* (☎ 780-428-7111, 🖳 www.edmonton.suttonplace.com) at 10235–101st St boasts a fantastic rooftop indoor pool and hot tub and an impressive, elegant lobby. Standard rooms range between $284 and $304 during high season.

WHERE TO EAT

Downtown Edmonton has a reasonable selection of restaurants and cafés but if you want a more vibrant atmosphere at night head over to the livelier district of

Old Strathcona, just across the river (take bus No 6 on 100th St at Jasper Ave, opposite the Fairmont Hotel Macdonald).

Budget food

An excellent downtown choice is *The Blue Plate Diner* at 10145-104th St (☎ 780-429-0740), a quirky restaurant with charming décor and original art on the walls. It serves delicious brunches at weekends as well as a huge array of snacks and meals throughout the week, many of which are vegetarian.

The Hat, at 10251 Jasper Ave (☎ 780-429-4471), has been in existence since 1912 but many of the original features have disappeared and these days the place sports a trendy décor and modern feel. It's still very popular with locals for a quiet coffee or a quick lunch and offers appetizers such as 'Brie with strawberry coulis' and a large selection of good-value main meals such as burgers and salads.

Another inexpensive choice is the *Russian Tea Room* at 10312 Jasper Ave (☎ 780-426-0000). Although the surroundings aren't grand, it offers tasty lunchtime specials as well as plenty of snacks, chicken and beef dishes and large cakes. It also offers psychic readings (from around $22) at the back of the restaurant!

In Old Strathcona, most places to eat are on Whyte Ave, including *Da-De-O New Orleans Diner and Bar* (☎ 780-433-0930) at No 10548A (known for its Cajun chicken) and *Tasty Toms*, on the corner of Whyte and 100th St (☎ 780-437-5761), plus lots of fast-food outlets. Just off Whyte Ave at 8430 Gateway Blvd, *New York Bagel* is a small but appealing café/restaurant serving a wide choice of bagel platters with potato salad and pickle. Although most items are very affordable, the menu also features the 'James Bond's Favourite' – a bagel served with Malosol Beluga caviar at $95!

Mid-range and upmarket restaurants

Downtown, there's a cluster of affordable mid-priced restaurants at the old Boardwalk Market on 103rd St at 102nd Ave, including the always-reliable *Old Spaghetti Factory* (☎ 780-422-6088), *Haweli Indian Restaurant* (☎ 780-421-8100) and *La Crêperie* (☎ 780-420-6656), an intimate, attractive restaurant offering a huge choice of crêpes and some imaginative, well-prepared meat dishes.

You could also try the lovely *Sorrentino's* at 10162-100th St (☎ 780-424-7500), a popular Italian restaurant with smart linen tablecloths and excellent service. They celebrate local produce and food festivals including the August mushroom festival, during which they have an extra 'mushroom-themed' menu. Main courses are $20 and up and they have an extensive wine list.

One of the nicest places to eat in town is The Fairmont Hotel Macdonald's *Harvest Room* (see p 142; ☎ 780-424-5181), which has beautiful views over the river and an outdoor terrace. Most main dishes are around $30 but sandwiches and light snacks are also available.

Another good place for a splurge is *La Ronde*, Edmonton's only revolving restaurant on top of the Crowne Plaza-Chateau Lacombe at 10111 Bellamy Hill (☎ 780-428-6611), where you can admire the views of downtown Edmonton and the river valley and eat from around $40.

Back over on Whyte Ave in Old Strathcona, at No 9602, *Unheardof Restaurant* is popular for both its signature seafood dishes and selection of creative specialities which change on a twice-weekly basis, such as pistachio halibut fillet and caribou schnitzel. Reservations are advised as it can get pretty busy (☎ 780-432-0480 from 5.30pm onwards; closed on Mondays).

NIGHTLIFE

Edmonton's nightlife scene is concentrated in Old Strathcona, which boasts numerous bars and pubs, most of them affecting a British or Irish style. Most are on Whyte Ave, including *Mickey Finn's Tap House* at No 10511, *O'Byrnes* at No 10620 and *The Empress Alehouse* at No 9912; one of the most popular is the *Elephant and Castle* at No 10314, serving generous portions of typical bar food (such as nachos and wings), but it can get packed out during ice hockey season when fans flock there to watch the Oilers play, so get there early to grab a good seat. *Funky Buddha* at No 10341 is an extremely popular bar with a heaving dancefloor – expect to line up outside at weekends. For something a bit calmer, try *The Attic* at No 10407, a very cool place with friendly staff and good music. Drinks offers and a pool table make this a popular hang-out Wednesday through Saturday 8pm-2am.

The best blues can be found at *Blues on Whyte* in the spacious bar of the Commercial Hotel, 10329 Whyte Ave. This Edmonton institution opens every evening and has excellent live blues most nights (expect a small cover charge).

Popular with tourists are the weekend night cruises on the *Edmonton Queen Riverboat*, moored at Rafter's Landing on the south bank of the river, close to the Muttart Conservatory. Drinks are served on the upper deck and you get excellent views onto Edmonton's illuminated skyline as you drift past, sipping cocktails. Another fine venue for a drink is the elegant bar at *Hotel Macdonald* (see p142), where the 1915 décor and soft jazz music lend an air of style and romance.

WHAT TO SEE

In town
● **Art Gallery of Alberta** Fresh from its $88-million renovation, the Art Gallery of Alberta (🖳 www.artgalleryalberta.com) is housed in a dramatic new zinc, glass and steel building at 2 Sir Winston Churchill Square, in the heart of downtown. The museum hosts high-quality temporary exhibitions (recent examples have included sculptures and paintings by Degas and Goya's *Los Caprichos* etchings), and a permanent collection ('From Sea to Sea') taking in Canadian painting from the late 19th century to today, including works by the Group of Seven (see box p121) and Emily Carr. Admission is $12 for adults and opening hours are 10am–7pm Tuesday to Friday and 10am–5pm at the weekend. The gallery also houses a very good restaurant as well as a terrace café.

● **Alberta Legislature** This beautiful neo-classical building (🖳 www .assembly.ab.ca) is worth a visit if only for the tranquillity of its gardens and fountains. It was built in 1912 on the site of Fort Edmonton (the stockade belonging to the Hudson's Bay Company) at 97th Ave and 107th St. The entrance is minutes from the streetcar platform and there are free guided tours inside, lasting roughly 30–45 minutes, throughout the day – for details call ☎ 780-427-2826. Summer hours are daily 9am to 4pm with tours running on the hour from 9am and then on the half hour from midday onwards. In winter, hours are 9am-3pm Monday-Friday and noon-4pm at the weekends, with tours running every hour.

● **Royal Alberta Museum** Upgraded from 'Provincial' to 'Royal' by Queen Elizabeth II during her 2005 trip, the museum (🖳 www.royalalbertamuseum .ca) has some interesting displays falling into three broad categories: natural history, habitat groups and human history. Highlights include some fossils of extinct animals from Alberta and hundreds of examples of Canadian taxidermy at its best. The Syncrude Gallery of Aboriginal Culture looks back at over 11,000 years of aboriginal history and the grounds feature an impressive sculpture park. The museum is open daily 9am–5pm; entrance is $10 or half-price at weekends between 9am and 11am. It's at 12845–102nd Ave; to get there take the No 1 or 20 bus west along Jasper Ave.

● **West Edmonton Mall** This mother of all malls is listed in the *Guinness Book of Records* as being the 'largest shopping and entertainment centre in the world' and having the 'world's largest car park.' It's certainly big, covering an area of 48 city blocks. Inside, not only can you shop 'til you drop, you can also do a spot of bungee-jumping, splash around in the water park and wave pool, take a submarine ride, watch three performing sea lions, take a whirl on the enormous ice rink, lose your money at the casino and wrap it all up with a penitential visit to the chapel. It's quite a fun place to visit and is very well designed with lots of natural light to stop you from feeling claustrophobic. Of course, a shopping mall's really just a shopping mall no matter how much you jazz it up but that doesn't stop over 28 million visitors heading here each year. To join the crowds take bus No 100 west along Jasper Ave; while to find out more about what's waiting for you, check 🖳 www.wem.ca.

● **Muttart Conservatory** Highly recommended as a post-mall relaxation exercise, the conservatory, which consists of four pyramid-shaped greenhouses, lies on the southern bank of the river, not too far from downtown. The plants inside represent three climatic zones: arid, temperate and tropical, while the fourth pyramid houses a changing display. It's a lovely, peaceful place to stroll around and the plants are glorious, especially in the tropical pyramid; one local told me she goes there to cheer herself up in the middle of Edmonton's cold winters. Admission to the conservatory is a steep $9.75. It's at 9626–96A St and is open year round: Monday to Friday 9.30am–5.30pm, weekends and holidays 11am–5.30pm. To get there take the No 85 or 86 bus on 100 St opposite the Fairmont Hotel Macdonald or, if you fancy the short walk, head down the steps behind the Shaw Conference Centre and cross the footbridge. Check the website for more details: 🖳 www.muttartconservatory.ca.

● **Old Strathcona** Also on the south bank of the river, centred on Whyte Ave, Old Strathcona is in many respects the most enjoyable part of Edmonton to stroll around, boasting many well-preserved old buildings and lots of pavement cafés, restaurants and small boutiques. While you're here, you could pay a visit to the **C&E Railway Museum** at 10447–86th Ave which displays a modest collection of railway memorabilia and old photographs. The museum (admission by donation) is open Tuesday to Saturday 10am–4pm during the summer months; if you're not here in the summer, phone ☎ 780-433-9739 to arrange a visit. Another attraction is the lively **farmers' market** at 10310-83rd Ave, where you'll find numerous colourful fresh produce stalls and craft shops. The market's open year-round on Saturdays 8am–3pm.

To get to Old Strathcona from downtown, take bus No 6 from 100th St at Jasper Ave, opposite The Fairmont Hotel Macdonald. Alternatively, if you'd prefer to get there in style you could hop aboard the High Level Bridge Streetcar, 'the world's highest streetcar river crossing', from Jasper Ave over the North Saskatchewan River to 103rd St, behind the farmers' market (🖳 www .edmonton-radial-railway.ab.ca). The views over the river are quite amazing and the three-kilometre trip is a very pleasant way to see the city from above. The streetcar operates at 40-minute intervals between 11am and 4pm daily from mid-May to early September, and Friday to Sunday during the rest of the year. Tickets cost $4.

Out of town
● **Fort Edmonton Park** This 'living museum' (🖳 www.fortedmontonpark .ca) represents four periods of Edmonton's past with reconstructions of the old Hudson's Bay Company fur-trading fort and three streets (1885 St, 1905 St and 1920 St). It makes an excellent day out and is well worth the visit, providing a clear picture of how life and trade were organized in these early outposts. Staff dress in period costume and take on various roles relating to the different areas of the park – you may find yourself drinking tea with a group of friendly cowboys on 1885 St or being waited on at lunch by attentive staff kitted out in immaculate twenties attire in the fantastic Hotel Selkirk on 1920 St. The site is extensive but if you tire of walking around on foot, transport is provided by way of an old steam locomotive, a tram and even a horse and carriage.

It's quite a distance from downtown but you can get there by public transport. First take a southbound train to the University LRT station and from there pick up the No 4 bus from stop 2001, right next to the station. The Park's opening hours are: spring (mid-May to late June) Monday to Friday 10am–4pm, weekends 10am–6pm; summer (late June to early September) daily 10am–6pm; autumn (September) guided wagon tours Monday to Saturday between 11am and 3pm. Entrance costs $13.50 for adults, with family passes for $40.50.

● **Telus World of Science** This excellent complex includes Canada's biggest planetarium and a huge IMAX theatre. Shows are screened on various scientific topics with the help of state-of-the-art audiovisual effects. Visitors can walk through five interactive galleries and there's also an observatory, a centre for live demonstrations and facilities for going on simulated trips in space. Brilliant stuff. For information on schedules call ☎ 780-451-3344 or check 🖥 www.telusworldofscience.com/edmonton. From late June to early September the centre is open daily 10am–9pm and for the rest of the year 10am–5pm. Admission is $13.95, or $22.50 including an IMAX ticket. To get there take the No 5 to Westmount Transit Centre from Jasper Avenue and then switch to the 126.

FESTIVALS

● **Edmonton International Jazz Festival**, late June to early July. Good selection of jazz artists, Canadian and international.
● **Capital EX**, for one week, mid to late July. Big and brash celebration with live music events, including some major bands.
● **Folk Music Festival**, early August. Internationally renowned event attracting huge crowds. A wide range of styles represented.
● **Edmonton International Fringe Theatre Festival**, mid-August. More than 800 performances are spread over nine days. The quality is highly variable, as with any fringe festival, but on the whole it's worth visiting.

MOVING ON

The *Canadian* leaves for Vancouver on Mondays, Thursdays and Saturdays, and for Toronto on Mondays, Wednesdays and Saturdays. For more details call VIA on ☎ 1-888-842-7245.

Jasper

A ride of two miles took us to Jasper's, where we arrived exactly fifteen days after leaving Edmonton... This station is now all but abandoned by the Hudson's Bay Cy. It was formerly of considerable importance, not only from the number of fur-bearing animals around, but because it was the centre of a regular line of communication between Norway House and Edmonton on the one side, and the Columbia District and Fort Vancouver on the other. An agent and three or four men were then stationed at it all the year round...Now, the houses are untenanted, locked and shuttered. Twice a year an agent comes up from Edmonton to trade with the Indians of the surrounding country and carry back the furs.
Rev Grant, *Ocean to Ocean* (1873)

Jasper is a quieter, calmer alternative to busy Banff. Nestled deep in the Canadian Rockies, the town sits in the largest national park in the Rocky Mountains, Jasper National Park. Founded in 1907, the park covers an incredible 10,878 square kilometres and is home not only to stunning scenery but to a variety of wildlife, with 277 species of birds and just under 70 species of mammals, including mountain goats, moose, bison and elk to name but a few.

Unlike the more popular tourist resorts of Banff and Whistler, Jasper is surprisingly uncommercial and retains a definite charm, even though thousands of visitors flock here each year to admire and explore the surrounding wilderness. The backdrop of the Rocky Mountains, the sparkling turquoise waters of the winding Athabasca River, the animals grazing nonchalantly by the side of the road – Jasper is a nature-lover's heaven and a photographer's dream. If you're passing through on *The Canadian*, don't miss the opportunity to spend a few days here, whatever you do.

ARRIVING IN JASPER

By train

The train station is right in the centre of the downtown core on Connaught Drive; you should be able to pick up a taxi right outside to take you the short distance to your lodgings. If none are there, call Mountain Express (☎ 780-852-4555) or Jasper Taxi (☎ 780-852-3600).

By bus

Greyhound (🖳 www.greyhound.ca) provides a daily service to Jasper from Edmonton which takes roughly five hours and costs around $65 for a single ticket (with discounts for HI members); the Greyhound terminal is centrally located at 606 Connaught Drive. The Sundog shuttle (🖳 www.sundog tours.com) is the best option when travelling up from Banff, Lake Louise or Calgary. Sundog buses will drop you at 414 Connaught Drive.

ORIENTATION AND GETTING AROUND

Jasper town is so compact that you'll be able to take it all in on foot. The two main streets where the majority of shops, restaurants and bars are situated are Connaught Drive, on which the rail station is located and, running parallel behind it, Patricia St. If you need a taxi, Mountain Express (☎ 780-852-4555) are reliable or try Jasper Taxi (☎ 780-852-3600). Alternatively, if you're staying in the HI hostel (see p149) or venturing up to the Jasper Tramway, the town offers a great **shuttle service** which runs frequently throughout the day from 9am to 8pm (summer months); a single ticket costs $3. The shuttle stops next to the VIA Rail station on Connaught Drive and heads up to the Tramway, with plenty of rooftop space for luggage.

SERVICES

Tourist information

The friendly **Parks Canada Visitor Centre** (☎ 780-852-6176, 🖳 www.jasper canadianrockies.com) is housed in a beautiful historic building at 500

❏ **Jasper online**

🖳 **www.jaspercanadianrockies.com** Official website of Jasper Tourism and Commerce; 🖳 **www.visit-jasper.com** Independent but useful site on Jasper; 🖳 **www.canadianrockies.net/jasper** Site on Jasper National Park

Connaught Drive. The centre is open year round, from 8.30am to 7pm in high season, 9am until 4pm in winter.

Money

There are several banks in the centre of the town including a TD Waterhouse bank at 606 Patricia St and a CIBC bank at 416 Connaught Drive.

Post, internet and laundry

The **post office** lies on Patricia St, or you can head to More Than Mail on Connaught Drive which offers facilities such as **faxing**.

The fantastic Coin Clean **laundry** at 607 Patricia St (at Miette Av) has huge washing machines and dryers and a little counter selling coffee and muffins to help pass the time away. Directly above is one of the town's many **internet cafés**, offering competitive prices.

WHERE TO STAY

There is no shortage of accommodation in Jasper, ranging from campsites and rustic cabins to luxurious hotels and resorts. It can, however, easily become booked up in high season so reserve ahead of time; that said, some hotels do offer last-minute deals so if you're willing to take a risk outside the high season you can sometimes get a great deal.

Budget accommodation

Jasper National Park has five HI hostels within its boundaries. The nearest one to the town site (and the least primitive!) is the *HI Jasper Hostel* (☎ 780-852-3205; 🖳 www.hihostels.ca), which lies a short distance out of the town centre on Whistler's Mountain. The building is rather like a slightly run-down wooden cabin but has a spacious, fully fitted kitchen, hot showers and a cosy lounge area. Private rooms are available (from $63) as well as two very large dormitories ($22 per person), one specifically for females, the other mixed. The Jasper Shuttle runs between the town centre and the hostel (en route to the Jasper tramway) several times a day ($3) or you can walk (45 minutes-plus), though watch out for the wildlife!

Mid- and upper-range hotels

One of the best-value deals in town, a few minutes' walk from the centre, is the very welcoming *105 Patricia Street* (☎ 780-852-4346; 🖳 www3.telus.net/105 patriciastreet), where the friendly owners offer two spotless self-contained suites ($100) adjoined to their own home, each with fridge, microwave and kettle.

More centrally located at 200 Connaught Drive, *Amethyst Lodge* (☎ 780-852-3394, 🖳 www.mpljasper.com) is a much larger affair, with 97 rooms, most with balconies or patios boasting splendid mountain views. It also has good

❏ Accommodation prices quoted in this book are for **high season** (normally May or June to September). In low season many hotels offer substantial discounts.

CITY GUIDES

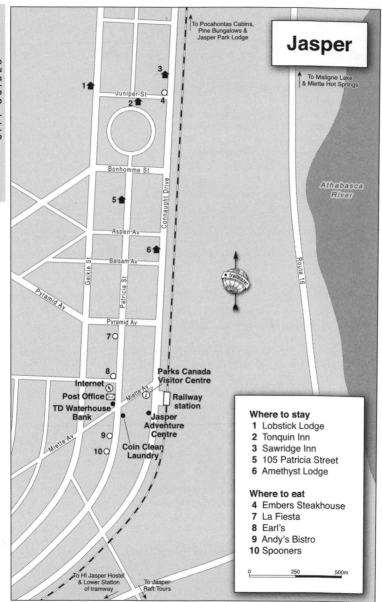

To Pocahontas Cabins,
Pine Bungalows &
Jasper Park Lodge

Jasper

To Maligne Lake
& Miette Hot Springs

Juniper-St

Bonhomme St

Connaught Drive

Athabasca River

Aspen-Av

Balsam-Av

Pyramid Av

Geikie St

Patricia St

Route 16

Pyramid Av

Parks Canada
Visitor Centre

Internet
Post Office
TD Waterhouse
Bank

Miette Av

Railway
station

Jasper
Adventure
Centre

Coin Clean
Laundry

Miette Av

Where to stay
1 Lobstick Lodge
2 Tonquin Inn
3 Sawridge Inn
5 105 Patricia Street
6 Amethyst Lodge

Where to eat
4 Embers Steakhouse
7 La Fiesta
8 Earl's
9 Andy's Bistro
10 Spooners

To HI Jasper Hostel
& Lower Station
of tramway

To Jasper
Raft Tours

0   250   500m

facilities, including two outdoor hot tubs and a decent restaurant. High-season rates here start at $219.

There's a cluster of places to stay about five blocks north of the train station. Among them is the recently renovated **Tonquin Inn** at 100 Juniper Street, (☎ 780-852-4987, 🖳 www.tonquininn.com), which offers a mix of standard double rooms and self-catering suites of various sizes with full kitchen facilities. Rates vary accordingly, from $199 to $400.

Close by, at 94 Geikie St, the **Lobstick Lodge** (☎ 780-852-4431, 🖳 www .mpljasper.com) is part of the same local chain (Mountain Park Lodges) as the Amethyst Lodge. Its 139 rooms (around $199) are spacious and comfortable and some have kitchen facilities. The lodge also has a range of amenities including a pool, sauna, indoor and outdoor Jacuzzis, laundry facilities and restaurant.

Also near here, the warm and hospitable **Sawridge Inn**, at 82 Connaught Drive (☎ 780-852-5111; 🖳 www.sawridgejasper.com), is naturally lit with an abundance of skylights and comes with 153 bedrooms and suites, its own spa – complete with two hot tubs, a sauna and pool – as well as cosy Champs bar, with its leather couches, a pool table and flatscreen TV. Doubles start at around $175.

There are also a number of options to choose from out of town, where you can generally be guaranteed a peaceful and scenic setting. An excellent out-of-town choice is award-winning **Pine Bungalows** (☎ 780-852-3491; 🖳 www .pinebungalows.com), a 30-minute walk (or $10 taxi ride) north-east from the centre at 2 Cottonwood Creek Rd, on a wooded 11-acre site on the bank of the Athabasca. This family-owned business puts an emphasis on enjoying the natural surroundings, which is why you won't find televisions or phones in your room. Most accommodation is in wooden cabins, some with kitchen facilities (from $155), though 'motel' rooms are also available (from $140).

A similar but larger scale set-up (cabins from $129) can be found at **Pocahontas Cabins** (☎ 780-866-3732; 🖳 www.mpljasper.com) on Highway 16 East – but the downside is that it's a 25-minute drive from town, so is really only an option with your own hire car.

Finally, mention must be made of the most spectacular accommodation in Jasper: the **Fairmont Jasper Park Lodge** on Old Lodge Road, just outside Jasper town itself. Originally established by the Grand Trunk Pacific Railway in 1915, the complex now comprises 446 luxurious cabins surrounding one of the Rockies' many lakes, nestled in a valley, with incredible views of Mount Edith Cavell. Facilities include a heated outdoor swimming pool, hot tub, tennis courts and a golf course, and kayaks and pedalos can be hired for use on the lake. High-season rates weigh in at around $500 for a standard suite, going up to around $700 for the luxury lakefront 'signature cabins'.

WHERE TO EAT

There is no shortage of places to eat out in Jasper, from friendly breakfast cafés like **Spooners** at 610 Patricia St, where you can tuck into their tasty bagels and burritos on the balcony surrounded by flower baskets and fantastic views of the Rockies, to cosy Mexican restaurants like **La Fiesta**, 504 Patricia St (☎ 780-

852-0404), which offers very affordable Spanish-Mexican fusion cuisine such as tapas dishes, fajitas and enchiladas. A staple favourite is the chain restaurant *Earl's*, on the 2nd floor at 600 Patricia St, (☎ 780-852-2393) which has great steaks and salads and appealing drinks offers practically every night of the week (the martinis are great). Also popular with locals but a notch up in price and quality, is intimate and cosy *Andy's Bistro* at 606 Patricia St, owned and run by chef Andy Allenbach. The menu changes seasonally but you can expect to find Canadian cuisine with hints of exotic flavours such as 'orange marinated lamb sirloin with citrus infused polenta'. Main courses are around $25.

Many of the hotels also feature appealing restaurants such as *Embers Steakhouse* (☎ 780-852-4471), part of the Mountain Park Lodges chain, which serves hearty breakfasts and dinners and has events throughout the year, such as Scotch tasting in January.

NIGHTLIFE

The Whistlestop, located between Patricia and Connaught opposite the Tourist Information office, is a snug pub with worn-in couches and a friendly atmosphere that draws in plenty of locals and visitors. For those who prefer to dance the night away, the two main hotspots are *Pete's Club*, upstairs at 614 Patricia St, which fills up every weekend with a young and lively bunch, and the *Atha-B* nightclub, 510 Patricia St, which rivals Pete's with its packed-out dancefloors and fun clientele.

THINGS TO DO

You can take in Jasper National Park's breathtaking scenery in a multitude of ways, from quiet walks or bike rides along the Athabasca River to guided excursions, cable-car rides, raft trips and even helicopter rides. Aside from the immediate environs of Jasper itself, there are numerous possibilities for day-trips to outlying beauty spots and attractions. A good one-stop place to help work out what to do and where to go is the **Jasper Adventure Centre**, opposite the train station at 604 Connaught Drive (☎ 780-852-5595; 🖥 www.jasperadventure centre.com), where you can book everything from rafting, canoeing and horse-riding excursions to coach trips to the Columbia Icefields (see p154), as well as buy tickets for the Jasper Tramway (see below).

Jasper Tramway

For those with a head for heights, a cable-car ride known as the Jasper Tramway provides breathtaking views of the national park. Climbing to 2277 metres at the top of Whistler's Mountain, the Tramway begins its journey ten minutes out of town at the lower station (1304m), situated at the top of Whistler's Mountain Road. The Tramway journey takes roughly ten minutes. At the end you can admire the views over a drink from the Treeline Restaurant or, if you're feeling adventurous, venture out on the summit hiking trail which leads to even more spectacular views (appropriate footwear essential).

The Tramway runs 9am–8pm from late June to late August ($29 per adult, discounts for children and seniors). To reach the lower station from downtown

❏ **Renting a car in Jasper**
If you're not keen on organized tours, you might prefer to rent your own vehicle. The following car rental companies all have offices in Jasper: **Avis**, 414 Connaught Drive ☎ 780-852-3970; **Budget**, 638 Connaught Drive ☎ 780-852-3222; **Hertz**, at the train station ☎ 780-852-3888; **National**, 607 Connaught Drive ☎ 780-852-1117.

you can take the shuttle bus from the car park next to the train station on Connaught Drive; a return journey, including Tramway tickets, costs $33 and can be bought from the driver. The Tramway gets very busy in summer so it's worth booking your ride in advance. This can be done online or by phone (☎ 780-852-3093, 🖳 www.jaspertramway.com), or through the Jasper Adventure Centre (see p152) opposite the train station.

Maligne Lake

If you have time to make only one day-trip during your stay, then spend it exploring the largest and most photogenic lake in the Canadian Rockies. Maligne Lake (🖳 www.malignelake.com) is an hour's drive from Jasper; you can get there in comfort by booking a seat on the **Maligne Lake Shuttle** which runs from outside its office at 616 Patricia St three to four times a day. On the way, keep your eyes peeled for wildlife – the last time we did this trip we were lucky enough to see a mother black bear and her cubs idling up the side of the road! At the lake you can sit back and enjoy the views or take the 90-minute Spirit Island Scenic Cruise (☎ 780-852-3370) out onto the beautiful turquoise glacial waters, which calls in at a wonderfully picturesque stretch of shore on the way. A return ticket on the shuttle costs $40; the boat cruise is $55 and the two can be purchased as a package for $85. The guided boat cruise departs on the hour between 10am and 5pm in high season.

Miette Hot Springs

Perfect after a strenuous day of sightseeing, enjoying a wonderful setting, the Miette Hot Springs are about an hour's drive from the town centre. The mineral-rich waters come straight from within the Rockies at 54°C before being cooled to a bearable 40°C in two pools, with a third 'cool pool' nearby. They can get very crowded, though: thousands of people flock here in the height of summer to soak in the waters and enjoy the wildlife, with bighorn sheep and deer grazing in the nearby parking area. The springs are open from May to mid-October, with opening hours of 10.30am–9pm in May and September, 8.30am–10.30pm in summer. Admission costs $6.05. Unless you have access to a vehicle, you'll need to take a shuttle to the springs. Jasper Adventure Centre (see p152) offers regular tours to the springs for around $70.

Rafting

Whitewater rafting is a very popular activity in Jasper National Park with the Athabasca and Sunwapta rivers providing opportunities for people of all ability levels. **Jasper Raft Tours** (☎ 780-852-2665; 🖳 www.jasperrafttours.com)

provide a great way to enjoy the river in a relaxing way, with round trips down the Athabasca on a raft that can seat between 12 to 20 people, led by an experienced guide who steers you through gentle rapids graded at a pleasant 1–2. The tours run between mid-May to late September and cost $55 for adults and $15 for children under 15.

For a more challenging experience, try **Jasper's Whitewater Rafting** (☎ 780-852-7238, 🖳 www.whitewaterraftingjasper.com), which offers two- to three-hour trips down the Athabasca or Sunwapta rivers. The Sunwapta is the more challenging of the two, with exciting class 3 rapids, suitable for fit, strong swimmers. Prices are from $59 per person.

Guided walks
Former Parks Canada interpreter and long-time Jasper resident Paula Beauchamp offers a choice of small-group guided walks enhanced by illuminating commentary through her company **Walks & Talks Jasper** (☎ 780-852-4994, 🖳 www.walksntalks.com), which also employs other local guides. Walks are carried out a leisurely pace, suitable for all fitness levels, on trails through outlying areas such as Mount Edith Cavell Meadows or the Maligne Canyon.

Prices range from $55 for a morning nature hike (2 hours) to $125 for a 6- to 7-hour trail around the Columbia Icefields; transport to the trailheads and back is included but you'll need to bring your own picnic lunch. The company's downtown booking office is in the Edge Control Ski & Outdoor Store at 626 Connaught Drive.

Columbia Icefields
At the very southern end of Jasper National Park, about 1½ hours from Jasper itself, the Columbia Icefield is a large icefield covering some 325 square kilometres and feeding eight major glaciers. During the summer, visitors can travel onto the icefield on special vehicles known as 'snow coaches'. Brewster Tours offer a very popular **Columbia Icefield Glacier Experience**, which takes you from Jasper to the Columbia Icefields Visitor Centre by ordinary coach, where you transfer to a massive *Ice Explorer* snow coach which travels over the ice to the middle of the Athabasca Glacier. Here passengers can get off, walk around and drink the melted glacier water, accompanied by a guide, before travelling

---

❏ Helicopter Rides
Although very expensive, if your budget will stretch to it a helicopter ride over the Columbia Icefields is a truly memorable experience. The views are absolutely spectacular and the sheer thrill of soaring over the Rockies is unforgettable. The tours range in price from expensive to astronomical, with the most affordable being the 'Cline Glacier Tour' at $165 per person for a 20-minute ride over over gigantic rock faces, mountains and turquoise-blue glacial lakes. Additional extras can also be purchased, such a stop in the forest for champagne and chocolates – incidentally this is a prime spot for proposals! A full 55 minutes over the Columbia Icefields costs $499. For more information, contact **Icefield Helicopter Tours** on ☎ 1-888-844-3514 or 403-721-2100, 🖳 www.icefieldheli.com.

back to the Visitor Centre. The day-trip ($5^{1}/_{2}$ hours) from Jasper, which includes a stop at the beautiful Athabasca Falls, costs $124 per person, including the 90-minute tour on the *Ice Explorer* (buses depart from Jasper's bus terminal daily from May to October at 8.30am). If you have your own transport to the Columbia Icefields, the glacier tour itself costs $49.

For more information see ⌨ www.explorerockies.com/columbia-icefield or call ☎ 1-800-760-6934 or 403-760-6934. Alternatively, tickets can be booked at the Jasper Adventure Centre (see p152).

MOVING ON

By rail

The *Canadian* leaves for Vancouver on Tuesdays, Fridays and Sundays and for Toronto on Mondays, Wednesdays and Saturdays. For more information visit ⌨ www.viarail.ca.

The *Rocky Mountaineer* leaves for Vancouver via Kamloops on Tuesdays, Thursdays and Sundays, and for Whistler via Quesnel on Tuesdays, Thursdays and Saturdays. Both Rocky Mountaineer routes are seasonal (April/May to late October) so check in advance for alternative transportation if you are visiting during the winter months. For more information visit ⌨ www.rockymoun taineer.com.

By bus

There are frequent daily departures from Jasper to Edmonton and limited (and long) indirect services to Banff and Calgary on the **Greyhound** bus service (⌨ www.greyhound.ca). The quickest way to travel from Jasper to Lake Louise ($3^{1}/_{2}$hrs; $57), Banff ($4^{1}/_{2}$hrs; $68) or Calgary ($7^{1}/_{2}$hrs; $115) is on the **Sundog** shuttle service, with departures year-round. Their office in Jasper is at 414 Connaught Drive or contact them on ☎ 780-852-4056, ⌨ www.sundogtours.com.

Calgary

Affluent, self-confident, youthful and lively, Calgary is an attractive, compact city that is one of the fastest growing in Canada. Seen from a distance, its down-town core is a glittering island of glass and steel sitting in rolling grassland near the foot of the mighty Rocky Mountains. It is the accessibility of these moun-tains – less than an hour's drive away – that makes Calgary such an appealing place to visit, combining all the advantages of a modern city with on-your-doorstep wilderness. Also, one of the most famous events in Canada takes place here each July: the annual Calgary Stampede, featuring ten days of rodeos, country dancing and wild celebrations.

Although no longer served by national trains – the historic CPR passenger service stopped operating in 1989 and *The Canadian* goes via Edmonton, 294km north – the success of the privately run *Rocky Mountaineer* has revived

Calgary's role as a railway city and today thousands of rail travellers pass through to travel on the old CPR route through the Rockies.

HISTORY

Fort Calgary

Calgary has one of the shortest histories of all Canada's cities, dating back to 1875 when a detachment of the North West Mounted Police (NWMP) built Fort Calgary at the confluence of the Bow and Elbow rivers. They'd been sent to establish order in a region disrupted by whisky traders and general lawlessness as the fur trade pushed west into the prairies. This area was home to thousands of Cree, Blackfoot and Stoney natives who lived off the vast numbers of buffalo that inhabited the region at that time; the Canadian government, however, had plans to settle the region with immigrants who would be transported west on the new transcontinental railroad under construction. Sending the NWMP was the first step in its plan to 'civilize' the region and create conditions that would encourage white settlement.

The CPR

Following the completion of the CPR railroad in 1885 hundreds of settlers arrived, principally from Britain, the Ukraine and Scandinavia, to claim land and farm it. Quickly, Calgary was transformed from the collection of rough wooden shacks it had been under the NWMP to a fledgling town with streets, stores and proper houses.

On 7 November 1884, Calgary was officially declared a town and, a decade later in January 1894, it was made a city. Throughout the town's early days the role of the CPR was very prominent: not only did it bring settlers here by rail and export their produce to other markets, it also owned much of the land Calgary was built on and even named many of the new town's streets after CPR officials.

From ranching to oil

By the early 20th century, Calgary was a booming little city with an economy based firmly on ranching. This was supplemented by a second major industry in 1914 when the Turner Valley oil fields were discovered 35km south-west of the city. There was no looking back and in 1947 Calgary's importance as an oil and gas supplier was confirmed with the discovery of the spectacular Leduc oil field, followed by further discoveries throughout the province.

Today, Calgary houses the headquarters of many energy companies and is the nerve centre of Canada's oil and gas industries.

ARRIVING IN CALGARY

By air

Many international airlines have direct flights to Calgary, which is a popular arrival point in Canada. There are no direct public transit buses from the airport to downtown. However, regular private shuttle buses (☎ 403-299-9555, 🖳 www .airportshuttlecalgary.ca) run every half-hour during the day between the airport and various downtown hotels, including the Sandman, Westin, Palliser and Marriott. Tickets cost $15 per person. A taxi to downtown will cost around $30-45.

❏ In-line skating
Certain areas of Calgary provide the perfect terrain for rollerblading, or **in-line skating** as it's known in North America. You can pick up a free leaflet from the Visitor Information Centre at the Calgary Tower Centre detailing the different pathways around town (basic to advanced). Alternatively, if you'd like to take a lesson, contact the City of Calgary Recreation on ☎ 403-268-3800. For more information see 💻 www .calgary.ca/parks and go to the section named 'Pathways'.

By bus
If you've come to Calgary to combine your trip on *The Canadian* with *The Rocky Mountaineer* train, the chances are you've arrived by bus from Edmonton. The **Greyhound** terminal is south-west of downtown at 877 Greyhound Way. A taxi from the Greyhound station to downtown should cost around $10. The **Red Arrow** terminal is more central at 205–9th Ave SE.

By train
The train station is right underneath the Calgary Tower at 131–9th Ave, in the heart of downtown. The Visitor Information Centre (see p158) is just one level above, so you can pick up maps and other tourist information while you're here.

GETTING AROUND

The downtown core is very compact and easily covered on **foot**. Several attractions, however, are out of the centre but can be reached by public transport, operated by Calgary Transit (☎ 403-262-1000, 💻 www.calgarytransit.com). This consists of a network of **buses** plus the **C-Train**, an overground light-rail service running through the city centre along 7th Ave and out into the suburbs.

The downtown portion of the C-Train trip service between 10th St and the City Hall is free. Otherwise, C-Train and bus fares are $2.50 for a single ticket (exact change required), $23 for a book of 10 tickets, or $7.50 for a day pass, available at some convenience stores or the Calgary Transit Customer Service Centre at 224–7th Ave SW. If you need to change buses, ask for a transfer when you buy your ticket. A reliable **taxi** company is Checker Cabs (☎ 403-299-9999).

ORIENTATION

Calgary is divided into four quadrants: NW, NE, SW and SE. The dividing lines are the Bow River, running east to west, and Central St to Macleod Trail, running north to south. The quadrant is always included on addresses and should

❏ Calgary online
💻 **www.tourismcalgary.com** Good, city-focused site produced by Calgary Convention and Visitors' Bureau. Questions can be emailed to 💻 destination@visitor .calgary.ab.ca;
💻 **www.traveldiscoveralberta.com** Information on the province by Tourism Alberta.

be noted carefully to avoid going to the same address in the opposite quadrant. Most of downtown Calgary falls into the SW quadrant.

The focus of downtown is the pedestrianized stretch of 8th Avenue, known as **Stephen Avenue Walk** – an attractive street lined with boutiques, bars and restaurants. Note that avenues run east–west and streets north–south.

SERVICES

Tourist information

The downtown **Visitor Information Centre**, run by the Calgary Convention and Visitors' Bureau, is on the ground level of the Calgary Tower Centre at Centre St and 9th Ave SE. In summer (mid-May to October) it's open Monday to Friday 9am–8pm and Saturday and Sunday 9am–5pm; during the rest of year it's open daily 9am–5pm. Phone enquiries should be made to the Bureau's central office on ☎ 403-263-8510 or 1-800-661-1678.

Money

Downtown, you'll find plenty of banks with ATMs on Stephen Avenue Walk and the surrounding streets. Foreign exchange outlets include: Calgary Foreign Exchange, 307–4th Ave SW; Alberta Treasury Branch, 239–8th Ave SW; and Royal Bank, 339–8th Ave SW.

Consulates

Austria (☎ 403-283-6526) 1131 Kensington Rd NW; **Denmark** (☎ 403-251-5052) 132 Parkwood Place; **Germany** (☎ 403-247-3357) 550–11th Ave SW, Suite 600; **Hungary** (☎ 403-229-4800) Suite 5Fl-1111 11 Ave SW; **Italy** (☎ 403-276-9389) Bay 9, 3927 Edmonton Trail NE; **Netherlands** (☎ 403-266-2710) Suite 708, 304–8th Ave SW; **Norway** (☎ 403-208-2264) Suite 1753, 708–8th Ave SW; **Sweden** (☎ 403-532-8020) 111-5th Ave SW; **Switzerland** (☎ 403-208-3296) 700 Sunlife Plaza, N Tower; **USA** (☎ 403-266-8962) Suite 1000, 615 Macleod Trail SE.

Post, internet and laundry

The main **post office** is at 207–9th Ave. The best place to go for **internet access** is the public library at 616 Macleod Trail SE (you get 15 minutes free per day if you are a visitor), or you could try Wired at 1032–17th Ave SW, or at the Greyhound bus terminal (see p157).

WHERE TO STAY

Downtown accommodation is fairly thin on the ground in the mid-range bracket but many of the upmarket hotels offer discounts at weekends so it's worth checking in advance to see what deals are available. During Stampede (ten days in early July; exact dates at 🖳 www.calgarystampede.com) all accommodation is more expensive and needs to be reserved well in advance.

Budget accommodation

The *HI Hostel* (☎ 403-269-8239, 🖳 www.hihostels.ca) is at 520–7th Ave SE, three blocks east of the City Hall; take the free C-Train to the corner of 7th Ave

CITY GUIDES

To Canada Olympic Park
University of Calgary residence
& Greyhound terminal

Calgary

Louise Bridge

9th St SW

C TRAIN

8th St SW

7th St SW

3rd Ave

Calgary
Transit

1st Ave

6th St SW

4th Ave

2nd Ave

5th St SW

Eau Claire Ave

5th Ave

4th St SW

Prince's
Island
Park

3rd St SW

1st Ave SW

Eau
Claire
Market

Toronto
Dominion
Square

Devonian
Gardens

2nd St SW

To Chianti

Post
Office

1st St SW

Railway
station
& Calgary
Tower

Stephen Ave Walk

C TRAIN

Centre St

Glenbow
Museum

1st St SE

Red Arrow
bus terminal

2nd St SE / Macleod Trail SE

To Stampede Park
& Heritage Park

City
Hall

Library &
internet

3rd St SE

To
Fort Calgary
(200m)

4th St SE

To Zoo

Bow River

Bow River

Where to stay

1 Sandman Hotel
4 Westin
6 The Fairmont Palliser
10 Calgary Marriott
13 HI Hostel

Where to eat

2 Chicago Chop House
3 Earl's
5 Bistro Piq Niq
7 Divino's
8 Blink Restaurant and Bar
9 Avenue Diner
11 World Delicatessen
12 Teatro

0   100   200m

❏ Accommodation prices quoted in this book are for **high season** (normally May or June to September). In low season many hotels offer substantial discounts.

and 3rd St then walk a couple of blocks east. The area is rather downtrodden and it might be best not to wander around alone at night but the hostel itself offers clean, comfortable dorm rooms, a bright and airy reading/internet room and a large kitchen. Beds cost $30, although prices do increase slightly during the Calgary Stampede.

In addition, the *University of Calgary Residences* offers visitor accommodation on the 200-acre university campus in north-west Calgary, at 2500 University Drive NW. For more information, contact ☎ 403-220-3203, or see 🖳 www.ucalgary.ca/residence.

Mid-range hotels

Due to the recent closure of a few hotels in Calgary, the downtown mid-range market is rather bare. The best option is the highly recommended *Sandman Hotel* (☎ 403-237-8626, 🖳 www.sandmanhotels.ca) at 888–7th Ave SW, literally straight off the free downtown C-train at 7th St. It has a smart, welcoming lobby, spruce rooms, a great indoor pool and fitness room and a fresh, modern feel to it. The hotel also boasts a business centre and a trendy bar as well as Moxie's, a rather stylish grill and steakhouse. Doubles start at $139.

Otherwise, the **Bed and Breakfast Association of Calgary** offers a wide range of comfortable B&B accommodation, although many are out of the downtown area. For a complete list, see 🖳 www.bbcanada.com/associations/bbac.

Upmarket hotels

By far the most beautiful and romantic hotel in town is *The Fairmont Palliser* (☎ 403-262-1234, 🖳 www.fairmont.com), at 133–9th Ave, built by the CPR in 1914. The opulent lobby is a sea of marble, bronze and crystal and the rooms have a classic old-world charm. The hotel also boasts a superb restaurant and a lovely pool and spa – this is the place to stay if you're in search of some serious pampering. Doubles range between $129 and $500 depending on availability and day of the week (weekend rates are lower); be sure to check online for special offers.

Alternatively, you could try the *Westin* (☎ 403-266-1611, 🖳 www.westin .com), at 320–4th Ave SW, with a 24-hour fitness centre, a Starbucks coffee house on the premises and rooms from $285, or the *Calgary Marriott* (☎ 403-266-7331, 🖳 www.calgarymarriott.com), in a wonderfully leafy and peaceful yet central location at 110–9th Ave SE – it's a smart, crisp, modern hotel where weekday rates are a steep $309 but weekend prices (Fri/Sat nights) drop to around $159.

WHERE TO EAT

Calgary has a good spread of downtown restaurants including plenty of budget choices. Alberta beef ranks among the best in the world and a highlight of eating out in Calgary is sampling the locally produced prime ribs and steaks.

Budget food

The best place for a cheap, filling lunch is the **Eau Claire Market** by Prince's Island (see p162-3), which has a food court with several outlets. For something more substantial, try the always-packed *Chianti*, a few blocks out of the centre at 1438–17th Ave SW (☎ 403-229-1600). It serves excellent pasta dishes for around $10 and the atmosphere is good.

If you're looking for a filling breakfast before a big day of sightseeing, head to the *Avenue Diner* on Stephen Avenue Walk (105A–8th Ave) where you can tuck into delicious omelettes and other great breakfast fare in a typical American-style diner. The lunches are good here, too – try the very tasty and filling homemade macaroni cheese.

One block south on the main level of the Calgary Tower, *World Delicatessen* is popular with locals for its cheap and filling homemade sandwiches and snacks for under $10.

Mid-range and upmarket restaurants

The best place to head for lunch or dinner is downtown's bustling Stephen Avenue Walk (8th Ave), home to numerous restaurants, many of them lively and attractive. A good number of them are decidedly meat-focused, such as the trendy *Chicago Chop House* at No 604 (☎ 403-265-3000), impeccably chic with its stripped beech floor, stainless-steel open kitchen and bar in the middle of the dining room. A prime Alberta beef steak here will cost around $43.

A few blocks east down the Avenue, between 2nd and 3rd streets, always-popular *Earl's* (☎ 403-228-4141) offers well-priced steaks, pasta, fish and more; the décor's pretty standard but the atmosphere's good and the cheesecake delicious.

Continuing east, on the corner of Stephen Avenue Mall and 1st St SW you'll find *Bistro Piq Niq* (☎ 403-263-1650) which offers comforting French bistro cuisine accompanied by a live jazz band on Wednesday and Thursday evenings (7–9pm); light meals like *confit de canard* and salade niçoise are around $16–18, while more substantial *grands plats* are in the $22–28 mark.

One block east at No 113, the bistro theme continues with similarly priced *Divino's* (☎ 403-234-0403), a small restaurant with exposed brickwork and modern décor serving delicious Canadian and European cheese platters as well as a full menu of more substantial bistro fare. Just opposite, smart *Blink Restaurant and Bar* at No 111 (☎ 403-263-5330) offers upmarket comfort food like burgers, sausages and mash, and fish and chips (lunches around $16–18), as well as a more sophisticated dinner menu (around $30).

A few blocks east along the Avenue at No 200, opposite Glenbow Museum, *Teatro* (☎ 403-290-1012) serves 'Italian market cuisine' in a splendid old building that was originally the Toronto Dominion Bank, boasting incredibly high ceilings and gleaming white pillars. It serves spectacular meat, fish and pasta dishes, like 'lasagne with lobster and scallops in a pomodoro sauce'. Main-course prices range from $18 to $45 and there's also a tasting menu at $95 per person.

WHAT TO SEE

Downtown

● **Calgary Tower** A good starting point for taking in the lie of the land and getting great views onto the mountains is this 190m-high tower (🖥 www.calgarytower.com) on the corner of Centre St and 9th Ave SW (it's also conveniently located next to the Visitor Information Centre). The observation tower has a large, vertigo-inducing glass floor which, we are reliably informed, 'can hold the weight of several elephants'. There's also a revolving restaurant, Sky 360, if you want to combine your visit with a meal. From June to November the tower is open 7am–11pm (last ride leaves at 10.30pm), and for the rest of the year 9am–11pm (last ride at 9pm). Tickets cost $12.95. Entry is free or half price if you have a booking at the revolving restaurant.

● **Glenbow Museum** A few steps from the tower is the excellent Glenbow Museum (🖥 www.glenbow.org), a must-see while you're in town. The museum explores the Canadian West's history with a fascinating range of exhibits – displays include an enormous stuffed buffalo; fabulous native beadwork; old 'Mountie' uniforms; personal belongings of the first immigrants; indigenous art and crafts; a Blackfoot tepee, and a pioneer's log cabin. There's also a display on the CPR and its crucial role in shaping the West's development. Look out for the scale model of the Stoney Creek Bridge, built in 1886, the highest on the line and still crossed today by *The Rocky Mountaineer* (see p230). Another interesting display is the 'Warriors' section, where visitors can walk through five centuries of war stories, weapons and armoury. The museum is open daily 9am–5pm with the exception of Sunday (open from noon–5pm). Entrance costs $14.

● **Fort Calgary Historic Park** On the eastern edge of downtown, bordering 6th St SE, Fort Calgary Historic Park (🖥 www.fortcalgary.com) covers the land occupied by the original log stockade built in 1875 by the North West Mounted Police when they arrived to impose law and order on the region. They stayed there until 1914, when the buildings were demolished. You can now walk around an exact replica of the 1888 barracks complete with the canteen, recreation room and library. In addition there's a museum with reconstructions detailing life at the fort, along with stacks of memorabilia from Calgary's early days. Exhibits include NWMP uniforms, which you can try on and have your photo taken in; a reconstructed jail cell where you can try the handcuffs; a hospital room; a drugstore, and an old streetcar. The museum and site are open daily 9am–5pm; entrance is $11.

● **Devonian Gardens** One of Calgary's biggest surprises is this luxuriant indoor garden on the top floor of the Toronto Dominion Square building, at 317–7th Ave. Opened in 1977 and covering two and a half acres, the garden boasts a glorious array of flowers and trees arranged around streams and waterfalls, making a relaxing place to stroll on a sunny afternoon or if you want to escape the crowds in the Toronto Dominion Mall.

● **Eau Claire Market and Prince's Island** Six blocks north of the Devonian Gardens, on the corner of 3rd St SW and 1st Ave SW, the Eau Claire

Market features craft shops and interesting boutiques as well as a small food court where you can grab a bite to eat. It's a popular place with a pretty location on the banks of the Bow River. The market features a Latin-American dance studio where you can take lessons in cha cha or tango or, if you've two left feet, just sit back and enjoy the entertainment and the atmosphere. Opposite the market a bridge leads across to Prince's Island, an attractive park and the site of evening outdoor performances of 'Shakespeare in the Park' during the summer months

Out of Downtown

● **Canada Olympic Park** East of downtown at 88 Olympic Park Rd, the complex created to host the 1988 Winter Olympics is open to the public as an attraction. You can follow a self-guided tour for $16.80 and take a look at the bobsleigh tracks and the ski-jump tower or even take a luge ride for $25. There's also an extensive mountain-bike trail on the slopes of the park; you can hire bikes at the bottom, take them up on the chairlift and cycle down. For details about the many activities, packages, passes and lessons available, check 🖳 www.winsportcanada.ca or call ☎ 403-247-5452.

● **Heritage Park Historical Village**
Sixteen kilometres south of the city centre, Heritage Park (☎ 403-268-8500, 🖳 www.heritagepark.ca) is a recreation of a 1910 prairie town, an 1880s pre-railway settlement and an 1860s fur-trading outpost, with over 150 meticulously restored buildings salvaged from other locations and brought here to be preserved.

The three sites are fairly spread out and connected by a circular railroad served by steam trains. The three stops house original CPR log stations, including the first station erected at Laggan, now known as

Visitors to the **Calgary Heritage Park** are transported around the site in carriages dating from 1885, 1907 and 1912, with a former CPR conductor as a guide.
PHOTO © MELISSA GRAHAM

Lake Louise. Just behind Shepherd station you'll find a collection of beautiful old locomotives and trains, including the splendid train constructed by the CPR to transport the then Duke and Duchess of Cornwall (the future King George V and Queen Mary) on their tour of Canada in 1901; you can wander through their sleeping quarters and admire the luxury. You can also take a short cruise on *SS Moyie*, a beautiful steamboat which makes regular circular trips and has the added bonus of the Rocky Mountains as a backdrop.

Heritage Park is open from mid-May to early September daily between 9.30am–5pm, and then to mid-October weekends only. Entrance is $20, except mid-week during winter when it's $9.50 (and when some attractions are closed). The park offers special deals such as a free pancake breakfast before 10am; check the website for more details. To get here, take the C-Train towards Somerset/Bridlewood and get off at Heritage Station, then transfer to bus No 502.

● **Calgary Zoo** Calgary's zoo (🖳 www.calgaryzoo.com) is one of the best in Canada and quite progressive, with its animals in large areas that mimic their natural habitat as closely as possible. Of the 1200 animals, highlights include a family of gorillas in the Primates section; tigers and snow leopards in the Eurasia section; kangaroos and wallabies in the Australia section and lions, giraffes and hippos in the Destination Africa area. If you're not going to get the chance to see the real thing in the Rocky Mountains, you can see moose, bighorn sheep, Rocky Mountain goats and grizzly bears among other local wildlife in the Canadian Wilds area. The zoo also has beautiful botanical gardens and waterfalls and is currently creating a new habitat for the zoo's Asian elephants. The Calgary Zoo is a great family day out and is open daily 9am–5pm, with an admission fee of $18 for adults and $10 for children between 3 and 12. The zoo is very accessible from downtown Calgary: to get there take the C-Train towards Whitehorn and get off at the stop named Zoo.

FESTIVALS

● **Calgary International Children's Festival**, May. Games and events for kids.
● **Calgary Stampede**, around the first two weeks of July (check on ☎ 1-800-661-1767, or 🖳 www.calgarystampede.com). One of Canada's most famous events, with ten days of rodeos, chuck-wagon racing, pancake breakfasts, country dancing and much more.
● **Calgary International Blues Festival**, August. A four-day long annual event with bands and artists playing throughout the day and night. Day passes are available as well as passes for the entire festival.

MOVING ON

By rail
The *Rocky Mountaineer* departs from the CPR station directly underneath the Calgary Tower at 131–9th Ave (☎ 403-294-9298 or 1-800-665-7245).

By bus
There are frequent departures from Calgary to Banff, Lake Louise, Edmonton, Vancouver and other destinations in western Canada. Most services are provided by **Greyhound** (☎ 403-265-9111, 🖳 www.greyhound.ca), operating from 877 Greyhound Way, but if you're going to Edmonton note that **Red Arrow** (☎ 403-531-0350, 🖳 www.redarrow.ca) buses are more comfortable with just three seats to an aisle: they leave from 205–9th Ave SE. If you're heading up to Lake Louise or Jasper, your best bet is with **Sun Dog** (☎ 1-888-786-361, 🖳 www.sundogtours.com), whose shuttles depart from downtown Calgary or the airport (they also serve Banff).

By air
Minibus shuttles to the airport are provided by Allied Airport Shuttle for about $15 (☎ 403-299-9555, 🖳 www.airportshuttlecalgary.ca), who pick up from a number of major hotels; you need to book a place in advance of collection.

Vancouver

A great sleepiness lies on Vancouver as compared with an American town; men don't fly up and down the streets telling lies, and the spittoons in the delightfully comfortable hotels are unused; the baths are free and their rooms are unlocked.
Rudyard Kipling, *From Sea to Sea*, 1900

Vancouver just doesn't have to try. In front is the ocean, behind are the snow-capped mountains and in between is this bustling city full of cafés, restaurants, boutiques and healthy, long-limbed people. It is utterly seductive.

The city is situated on a peninsula in the south-west corner of British Columbia. It has a mild, temperate climate and its inhabitants have a reputation for taking a laidback attitude to life (it is said that Vancouver is more Californian than Canadian). Its easygoing ambience, however, conceals a vigorous commercial, financial and industrial sector that has made it the economic hub of western Canada. Its port handles 65 million tonnes a year, real estate in the city continues to boom and its population is the fastest-growing in North America.

Meanwhile, the city's tourist infrastructure has recently benefitted from a major injection of cash, thanks to the Winter Olympics which were hosted in Vancouver and nearby Whistler in 2010 – an event which also saw many of the city's hotels thoroughly revamped and spruced up.

HISTORY

Early visitors
It is thought that Coast Indian tribes inhabited the area as early as 5000BC and developed a number of fishing communities. The first European to visit the site where Vancouver now stands was the Spanish sailor, José Navéz, in 1791. The following year the English explorer, Captain George Vancouver, made a fleeting one-day visit on his way to search for the North West Passage. The site was then largely ignored by Europeans until the 1858 Fraser River gold rush brought fortune-seekers to the area.

Gastown
Of these fortune-seekers, three intrepid Englishmen decided to stay and set up (rather curiously) a brickyard on the shore of the Burrard Inlet. The venture failed, but a more astute entrepreneur moved in to establish the highly success-ful Hastings Saw Mill. A small settlement soon sprang up and became known as Gastown after a garrulous local bar-owner named 'Gassy' Jack Deighton. In 1869 it was incorporated as a town under its official name of Granville, only to go up in flames later that year.

CPR terminus
The rapidly rebuilt Granville would probably have remained a small coastal town if it hadn't been for Van Horne's decision, on a visit to the area in 1884,

CITY GUIDES

Vancouver's Chinese immigrants

When Andrew Onderdonk began work on his section of the transcontinental rail line through the Fraser Valley, he knew he had a serious labour shortage on his hands. British Columbia's population was very small and Onderdonk needed at least 10,000 men. The solution was found in the large numbers of Chinese labourers in California who had worked on the Union Pacific Railway and were more than willing to come and work for Onderdonk at a cheaper rate than the locals. When still more workers were needed they were shipped over from Canton – between 1881 and 1885 more than 15,000 Chinese came to work on the railway.

Once the line was completed many of these stayed on, to the disgust of British Columbians who regarded the Chinese with contempt. In an attempt to curb immigration the Chinese 'head tax' imposed on new arrivals was increased to a drastic $100 in 1900. Two years later, as anti-Chinese feelings reached hysterical proportions, a Royal Commission on Chinese and Japanese Immigration produced a report which concluded that Asians were 'obnoxious to a free community and dangerous to the state' and, accordingly, 'unfit for full citizenship'.

In 1903 the head tax was raised to $500 and the Immigration Act of 1923 effectively banned Chinese immigration (the day the act was passed is known as 'Humiliation Day' by Canadian Chinese). Amazingly, it was not until 1947 that this appalling legislation was repealed, and it was not until 1967 that the final restrictions on Chinese immigration were removed.

to make it the terminus of the new transcontinental railway instead of Port Moody (about 20km away). He also decided that Vancouver would be a more fitting name than Granville. Thus, Vancouver officially came into existence on 16 April 1886 and the first through train from Montreal arrived on 23 May the following year. The railway brought a massive boom to the town, which by the end of the century outstripped Victoria in size and commercial importance. Before long it had also replaced Winnipeg as the most important city in western Canada.

Vancouver today

Vancouver's commercial success has been built on its fishing, lumber and minerals industries and on its huge port which today is the largest on the west coast of North America. Most exports are bound for Asia and include wheat, timber, ore and cellulose. In little more than a hundred years Vancouver has grown from a tiny outpost to Canada's third-largest and fastest-growing city. Some 600,000 people live in the city proper and over 2.1 million live in Greater Vancouver.

❏ Vancouver online

💻 **www.tourismvancouver.com** Tourism Vancouver's attractive site, with information on the city and day trips to the surrounding area; 💻 **www.travel.bc.ca** A look at the whole province with Tourism British Columbia; 💻 **www.martiniboys.ca** Up-to-the minute reviews of Vancouver's restaurants, bars, nightlife, shops and more, pitched to a young and trendy clientele.

ARRIVING IN VANCOUVER

By air

Vancouver International Airport is 12km south of the city centre – about a 20-minute drive. The SkyTrain Canada line can take you directly from the airport to the city centre in 24 minutes. It costs $5 for a single ticket. The same ride by taxi will cost around $23–26.

By rail

Trains arrive at the stately Pacific Central Station in a slightly insalubrious corner of town. It's a bit of a walk from downtown but is directly linked to the centre by the SkyTrain (Vancouver's fully automated light-rail transit – fares are $2.50 or $9 for a day-pass). Otherwise there are plenty of taxis at the station (about $10 to downtown).

GETTING AROUND

Local transport is operated by BC Transit (☎ 604-953-3333, 💻 www.translink.bc.ca). In addition to their vast network of buses they run a **ferry service** (known as the SeaBus) across the Burrard Inlet between downtown and North Vancouver, and the state-of-the-art driverless **SkyTrain** connecting downtown Vancouver with the airport and the suburbs of Richmond and Surrey. Single zone fares are $2.50 for all three modes of transport. You can buy day passes for $9, available at many convenience stores, the Vancouver Tourist InfoCentre and the SeaBus terminal and SkyTrain station. BC Transit produces an excellent free pocket guide which tells you how to get to all Vancouver's attractions by public transport; pick it up in the Vancouver Touristinfo Centre.

You can hire **bikes** and **rollerblades** from a number of rental outlets around the corner of Denman and Georgia, including Spokes Bicycle Rental & Espresso Bar (☎ 604-688-5141) and Bikes 'n' Blades at 718 Denman St (☎ 604-602-9899). For **taxis** try Black Top Cabs (☎ 604-731-1111) or Yellow Cabs (☎ 604-681-1111)

ORIENTATION

Downtown Vancouver sits on a small peninsula framed by Burrard Inlet to the north and False Creek to the south. Stanley Park covers the western tip and the city centre pretty much fills the rest of the peninsula, spilling south onto the other side of False Creek. The main downtown artery is Robson St; the focal point of the waterfront is Canada Place. Be sure to avoid Hastings St East, Vancouver's skid row and certainly not a safe place to be after dark.

SERVICES

Tourist information

The excellent **Vancouver Touristinfo Centre** (☎ 604-683-2000) is on the Plaza Level at 200 Burrard St, close to the waterfront. As well as providing the usual information the office has an accommodation booking service and a Tickets

Tonight kiosk which sells tickets for upcoming events and attractions. The office is open daily 8.30am–6pm.

Money

There's no shortage of downtown banks, with a cluster around Georgia at Burrard and Howe. Foreign exchange offices include American Express at 1040 West Georgia St, International Foreign Exchange at 1169 Robson St, Custom House Currency Exchange at 375 Water St and Thomas Cook Foreign Exchange at Suite 130, 999 Canada Place.

Consulates

Austria (☎ 604-980-0035) 2255 Ennerdale Road; **Britain** (☎ 604-683-4421) Suite 800, 1111 Melville St; **Denmark** (☎ 604-982-8892) Suite 101, 245 Fell Ave; **Finland** (☎ 604-688-4483) 1480–1188 West Georgia St; **France** (☎ 604-681-4345) Suite 1100, 1130 West Pender St; **Germany** (☎ 604-684-8377) Suite 704, 999 Canada Place; **Ireland** (☎ 604-683-9233) 10th Floor, 100 West Pender St; **Italy** (☎ 604-430-3337) 3075 Slocan St; **Japan** (☎ 604-684-5868) Suite 800, 1177 West Hastings St; **Netherlands** (☎ 604-684-6448) Suite 821, 475 Howe St; **New Zealand** (☎ 604-684-7388) Suite 1200, 888 Dunsmuir St; **Norway** (☎ 604-682-7977) Suite 1200, 200 Burrard St; **Sweden** (☎ 604-683-5838) Suite 1480, 1188 West Georgia St; **Switzerland** (☎ 604-684-2231) Suite 790, 999 Canada Place; **USA** (☎ 604-685-4311) 21st Floor, 1095 West Pender St.

Post, internet and laundry

Vancouver's main **post office** is 349 West Georgia. The cheapest **internet access**, at just $1.50 per hour, is at 119 Computer World, just around the corner from the HI Hostel at 1221 Thurlow St. You'll also find internet access at Kinko's Copies & Internet (open 24 hours a day) at 789 West Pender; Lingo Cyberbistro at 547 Seymour St; and Websters Internet Café at 340 Robson St.

The most central downtown **laundries** are Davie Laundromat at 1061 Davie St (near the corner with Thurlow) and The Clothesline Laundry at 1070 Davie St.

WHERE TO STAY

Budget accommodation

Vancouver boasts three HI hostels (🖳 www.hihostels.ca). The excellent *HI Vancouver Downtown Hostel* (☎ 604-684-4565) is at 1114 Burnaby St in a quiet, leafy corner of town. Beds are in small shared rooms for up to four people, with single-sex bathrooms on each floor. One of the highlights of staying here is the free continental breakfast served each morning between 8am and 9.15am, consisting of bagels, cereals, fresh fruit and juices. A dorm bed costs from $27 for members, and there are a few private en-suite doubles from $75 for members and $83 for non-members; free linen and towels are included in the price. The new *HI Vancouver Central Hostel* (☎ 604-685-5335) at 1025 Granville St has an even more central location, though it's consequently less leafy and peaceful. The hostel organizes a weekly pub crawl every Monday, Wednesday and Friday night in association with the HI Downtown hostel. Rates are the same as in HI Downtown, with continental breakfast again included in the price (served 8am–10am).

The original *HI Vancouver Jericho Beach Hostel* (☎ 604-224-3208), at 1515 Discovery St, is a little more basic but the location, right by Jericho Beach, is fantastic. Beds here are from $26; to get there take the No 4 bus from Granville St.

Centrally located at 300–310 Cambie St, in the historic Gastown area, *Cambie International Hostel* (☎ 604-684-6466, 🖳 www.thecambie.com) is one of three Cambie hostels in Vancouver and Vancouver Island. With dorm beds from $25 and a few private rooms available for $60 (or $70 with a private bathroom), the hostel offers clean rooms, laundry facilities and a free coffee and muffin each morning from the bakery next door.

A little scruffy but very cheap is the *American Backpackers Hostel* (☎ 604-688-0112, 🖳 www.ameribackpackers.com) at 347 Pender St, where dorm beds cost a mere $10, single rooms $25 and double rooms $35. Though not in as inviting an area as the other hostels, the rates are certainly appealing if you're travelling on a tight budget; note that there is an upper age limit of 35!

Mid-range hotels

Definitely more hotel than hostel, the immaculate *YWCA Hotel* (☎ 604-895-5830, 🖳 www.ywcahotel.com), at 733 Beatty St, has a range of rooms from singles with shared bathrooms for $68 right up to five-bed rooms with private bathroom for $160 (a double with private bath costs $125). The YWCA has its own cosy coffee shop, internet and laundry facilities and there's air conditioning and mini fridges in all the rooms. More old-fashioned but great value is the *Kingston Hotel Bed and Breakfast* (☎ 604-684-9024, 🖳 www.kingstonhotelvancouver com), at 757 Richards St, which styles itself as a European-type B&B. Its rooms are cheerful and well maintained, with singles from $75 (shared bath) and doubles from $85 (shared bath). Continental breakfast is included and other facilities include sauna, coin-operated laundry and a secure underground car park.

For a step up in comfort, try the *Barclay Hotel* (☎ 604-688-8850, 🖳 www.barclayhotel.com), excellently located at 1348 Robson St, seconds from the shops and cafés and a short walk to Stanley Park. It has pleasant rooms at fair rates, with singles/doubles from $79/99. Across the road at No 1393 is the newly revamped *Greenbrier Suites* (☎ 604-683-4558, 🖳 www.greenbrier hotel.com), whose spacious self-catering apartments (from $129) all have kitchenettes and full bathrooms; some also have lovely views across the harbour.

With similar rates, the *Sunset Inn and Suites* (☎ 604-688-2474, 🖳 www. sunsetinn.com) is another apartment-hotel, this time in peaceful, leafy Burnaby St at number 1111. Rooms range from standard studio suites with full kitchen, dining area, wireless internet access and private bathroom (from $149) to large

---

❏ Accommodation prices quoted in this book are for **high season** (normally May or June to September). In low season many hotels offer substantial discounts.

CITY GUIDES

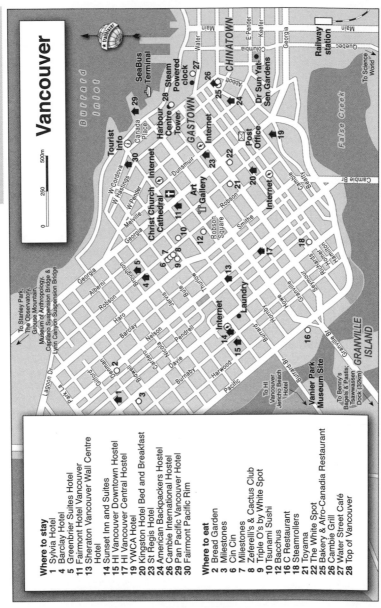

Vancouver

Where to stay
1 Sylvia Hotel
4 Barclay Hotel
5 Greenbrier Suites Hotel
11 Fairmont Hotel Vancouver
13 Sheraton Vancouver Wall Centre Hotel
14 Sunset Inn and Suites
15 HI Vancouver Downtown Hostel
17 HI Vancouver Central Hostel
19 YWCA Hotel
20 Kingston Hotel Bed and Breakfast
23 St Regis Hotel
24 American Backpackers Hostel
26 Cambie International Hostel
29 Pan Pacific Vancouver Hotel
30 Fairmont Pacific Rim

Where to eat
2 Bread Garden
3 Milestones
6 Cin Cin
7 Milestones
8 Zeferelli's & Cactus Club
9 Triple O's by White Spot
10 Tsunami Sushi
12 Bacchus
16 C Restaurant
18 Steamrollers
21 Toyama
22 The White Spot
25 Bakery & Afro-Canadia Restaurant
26 Cambie Grill
27 Water Street Café
28 Top of Vancouver

one-bedroom suites with balconies (starting at $199). Down at English Bay, a stone's throw from the beach, *Sylvia Hotel* at 1154 Gilford St (☎ 604-681-9321, 🖥 www.sylviahotel.com) is a charming, ivy-covered hotel offering pleasant rooms from $109 to $189 depending on size.

Over in Gastown, at 602 Dunsmuir St, the newly renovated *St Regis Hotel* (☎ 604-681-1135, 🖥 www.stregishotel.com) is a very comfortable option with smart, attractively decorated rooms from $189 including breakfast.

Upmarket hotels
The four-diamond *Sheraton Vancouver Wall Centre Hotel* (☎ 604-331-1000, 🖥 www.sheratonvancouver.com) is one of the most luxurious hotels in Vancouver. This 35-storey building is sheathed in glass from top to bottom; each of the 744 rooms has floor-to-ceiling windows that can be opened and $300,000 worth of BC art is scattered around the building. It's at 1088 Burrard St and standard rates range between $259 to $299, though 'Super Saver' rates are sometimes available and there are often discounts if you book online.

Another glitzy four-diamond job is the *Pan Pacific Vancouver Hotel* (☎ 604-662-8111, 🖥 www.vancouver.panpacific.com) down in Canada Place, with spectacular waterfront views and an elevated reception area on the 3rd floor (which you reach by escalator). There's a wonderful, airy atmosphere to the building; rates start at $300 for a city view and $360 for a harbour view.

On a more traditional note, the beautifully refined *Fairmont Hotel Vancouver* (☎ 604-684-3131, 🖥 www.fairmont.com) can be found at 900 West Georgia St, at the corner with Burrard. Opened in 1939 for the arrival of King George V and Queen Elizabeth I, who stayed here while in Vancouver, this old CPR railway hotel is now a heritage building and one of the most elegant establishments in the city. As well as a large indoor pool, a charming lounge (where high tea is served between 2pm and 4pm in summer) and stylish bedrooms, the Fairmont Hotel Vancouver even has its own mascot in the friendly form of Mavis the dog, who can often be seen wandering around the reception area. Rates can be anywhere between $270 and $450.

The Hotel Vancouver's new sister hotel, the *Fairmont Pacific Rim*, was built for the 2010 winter Olympics and boasts an excellent position on the waterfront and spectacular state-of-the-art facilities – even a standard room (from around $300) comes with flat-screen TV and surround sound in the bathroom, as well as high-tech computer systems which can do anything from changing the temperature to closing the curtains.

WHERE TO EAT

Vancouver offers a huge choice of places to eat, from dirt cheap to super-extravagant and with so many people eating out, most have a lively atmosphere.

Most popular and common is Asian food (particularly Chinese, Japanese, Vietnamese and Korean) and 'West Coast' cuisine, which is a sort of fusion of Asian and Mediterranean food, with an emphasis on fresh, locally available produce and beautiful presentation.

Budget food

A good spot for a quick lunch is *Steamrollers* at 437 Davie, a tiny place with a take-away counter and a sit-down bar serving steamed burritos and a selection of tasty wraps for under $10.

Also good for lunch are the many sushi bars around town: a couple to try are *Tsunami Sushi* at 1025 Robson, where diners choose their food from a conveyor belt in front of their seats (a plate of mixed sushi here costs around $10), and *Toyama*, at No 757 Seymour, which does an 'all you can eat buffet' and meal combos which are delicious and really good value.

A little bit too close to the seedy part of town but worth hunting out is the *Cambie Grill*, below the hostel of the same name at 300 Cambie St. Claiming to be Vancouver's oldest pub, it's a real spit-and-sawdust place with cheap, filling bar food. Next door there's a good bakery selling sandwiches and salads and, further along at No 324, you'll find the *Afro-Canadian Restaurant* (☎ 604-682-2646) with healthy meals, including some great Ethiopian and other African dishes, for around $10.

Healthy, attractive food is on offer at the *Bread Garden* chain of local sit-down delis; branches include 1040 Denman St and 812 Bute St, both of which stay open until midnight through the week and until 2am at the weekend. Rather more predictable but very filling food is available at *The White Spot*, a popular local chain with a large branch at Georgia 580 (☎ 604-662-3066), serving burgers, milkshakes, sandwiches and grills. Part of the same chain is *Triple O's by White Spot* at 805 Thurlow St (☎ 604-609-7000), a friendly diner complete with 'Guys' and 'Gals' toilets and a juke box playing classic Fifties and Sixties tunes. Breakfast dishes and burgers are around $3–6.

Enjoying a choice location at 2503 West Broadway, with a patio looking onto English Bay Beach, is *Benny's Bagels*, a pleasant place for sandwiches, 'melts' and bagels by the ocean – but be warned that it gets busy and you may have to wait a while to be served.

Mid-range and upmarket restaurants

Vancouver has plenty of appealing places to eat in the mid-range bracket – typical prices might be around $16–18 for lunches or light evening meals, going up to around $28–38 for more substantial dinner mains.

Milestones is a very popular mid-priced local chain serving fairly standard meat, fish and pasta dishes in colourful surroundings; there are downtown branches at 1145 Robson (☎ 604-682-4477) and 1210 Denman (☎ 604-662-3431), which both get packed out on Friday and Saturday nights. There's a proliferation of restaurants along Robson St, one of the best being *Cin Cin* at No 1154 (☎ 604-688-7338), serving Italian/West Coast (and rather pricey) food in a rustic-style dining room with a lovely outside terrace. *Zeferelli's*, nearby at No 1136 (☎ 604-687-0655), is also 'West Coast' and very good. A cheaper option is the *Cactus Club Café* (☎ 604-687-3278) below Zeferelli's (with other branches around town); it's very lively and the Tex/Mex menu isn't bad at all. Gastown's another place with plenty of eating spots, including the *Water Street*

Café at 300 Water St (☎ 604-689-2832), with its very pleasant outdoor terrace looking onto the steam clock.

Vancouver's high-end restaurants are well worth a splurge. One of the best in the city is *C Restaurant* (☎ 604-681-1164) at 1600 Howe St, looking across the water to Granville Island. As well as lovely views it boasts a stylish, minimalist interior, a buzzing crowd and superb seafood – try the lobster bisque with cured spring salmon and basil mayo, or Alaskan sable fish. Lunch mains are around $19, with dinner mains double that – or come for an early *prix fixe* 3-course dinner for $45 between 5pm and 6pm.

Another first-rate restaurant is award-winning *Pastis*, a short cab ride from downtown at 2153 West 4th Ave (☎ 604-731-5020), an upmarket bistro specializing in classic French dishes such as duck à l'orange ($29) and sole meunière ($42). Diners are greeted with a pastis cocktail when they arrive and the atmosphere manages to be both informal and classy. Centrally located *Bacchus* (☎ 604-608-5319) at 845 Hornby St is definitely a place for dinner rather than lunch, with its dark corners and low lighting. The choice of food is agonizing, ranging from 'risotto of golden chanterelles' to 'pine-nut and parsley crusted rack of lamb'; dinner mains start at $37. For a post-dinner digestif, the adjoining bar is one of the most appealing in town.

Finally, mention must be made of those restaurants that boast outstanding views. *Top of Vancouver* (☎ 604-669-2220), the 167-metre-high revolving restaurant at the Harbour Centre, is undeniably touristy but you're unlikely to care when you can look across your dinner plate to a range of snow-capped mountains rising from the ocean. Most mains here are in the $35–40 range; diners don't have to pay for the ride up in the elevator.

The Observatory (☎ 604-980-9311), at the top of Grouse Mountain (see p180), boasts superb views and is the sort of place where marriage proposals are regularly made. The most romantic place to sit is the smaller, corner room attached to the main dining room; you can request (but aren't guaranteed) a window seat when you reserve. There's a six-course *prix fixe* menu for $125, or you can go à la carte for less; note that those with a dinner reservation get a free ride up the mountain in the cable car.

NIGHTLIFE

Vancouver's nightlife scene is extremely lively, offering a huge choice of bars, pubs, live music, jazz venues, nightclubs and much more. Among the current favourites, *La Bodega* at 1277 Howe (near Davie) is a colourful tapas bar with great sangria and Spanish and Latin music.

On Granville Island at 1585 Johnston, *The Arts Club Theatre Backstage Lounge* makes a more mellow alternative, with live blues and jazz at the weekend and views across the water. A couple of upmarket, stylish places for a drink are *Gerard's* at 845 Burrard, featuring lots of dark wood and leather armchairs, and *Bacchus* at 845 Hornby, which has a roaring fire when the weather turns chilly. Both places have live piano music at the weekend and are popular with a slightly older, professional crowd. A little younger and rowdier is the *Yaletown Brewing Company* at 1111 Mainland St, a large pub-restaurant which brews its own beer on the premises.

The self-proclaimed oldest pub in Vancouver, *The Cambie*, at 300 Cambie St, is very rustic and always busy night and day. For live music, one of the most enduringly popular venues is *The Railway Club* at 579 Dunsmuir (at Seymour), which puts on a different act (from folk to rock to jazz) every night except Sunday, when there's a movie showing instead. Among the city's nightclubs, you could try the eternally popular *The Cellar* at 1006 Granville or the hyper-trendy *Mars* at 1320 Richards.

WHAT TO SEE

Vancouver is a relaxing place in which to spend time. It's not packed full of museums and obligatory sights. The best thing to do here is just wander round and take in the atmosphere in the city's many 'people's places' (to use Vancouver-speak).

A fun way to get a quick overview of the city is to take a tour aboard one of the Vancouver Trolley Company's replica turn-of-the-century trolley buses. The tours take in 24 stops, including Gastown, Chinatown and Stanley Park, and as tickets are 'hop-on/hop-off', you can jump off at any point along the way and then join the tour again later on in the day, with trolleys running every 20 minutes. Tickets ($35.25) can be purchased from drivers or at the ticket booth in Gastown (157 Water St), and are valid for two consecutive days; for more information contact ☎ 604-801-5515 or 🖳 www.vancouvertrolley.com.

Robson St to English Bay

Another good way to get a feel for the city is to take a walk down Robson, starting at Robson Square. Nicknamed 'Rodeo Drive of the North', it's Vancouver's liveliest street and is lined with clothes boutiques, bookstores, record shops, cafés and restaurants. By night it's packed with young people out on the town.

If you turn south off Robson down Denman (more cafés and restaurants) you'll end up at English Bay Beach. The views from here are lovely and it's a very relaxing place to go and lie with a book in summer. The walk to English Bay from Robson Square takes about half an hour; the No 5 bus follows the same route.

Vancouver Art Gallery

Close to Robson Square, the Vancouver Art Gallery (🖳 www.vanartgallery.bc.ca) is well laid-out and worth a visit. The highlight of the permanent display is the excellent collection of works by Emily Carr, whose swirling greens and blues depict the landscape and Indian communities of the West Coast. There's also an extensive collection of contemporary visual art, with contributions from Stan Douglas and Ian Wallace to name just two. Otherwise, the museum is given over mainly to temporary exhibitions, either visiting or from the gallery's own collection.

Located at 750 Hornby St, the Vancouver Art Gallery is open daily 10am–5pm and 10am–9pm on Tuesday. Entrance is $19.50 (with 'pay by donation' on Tuesday 5–9pm).

Christ Church Cathedral

Should Vancouver's busy streets become too much, there are a number of downtown churches where you can gather your thoughts and enjoy some peace and quiet. Close to the Vancouver Art Gallery at 690 Burrard St, Christ Church Cathedral was built as an Anglican church in 1888 and features 32 beautiful stained-glass windows, a magnificent cedar ceiling and a most impressive organ. It sits just across from the Fairmont Hotel Vancouver and was attended by King George and Queen Elizabeth during their visit to Vancouver in 1933. As well as holding services throughout the week, it opens to visitors from 10am to 4pm from Monday to Friday, with extended hours at weekends during the summer (Saturdays 9.30am–12.30pm, Sundays 12.30–5pm).

Canada Place and Harbour Centre Tower

Canada Place, down by the waterfront, was built as the pavilion for Expo '86. The complex, with its roof of billowing sails, was designed to resemble a large ship and is worth visiting if just for its excellent vantage point over the harbour.

You can get an even better view, though you have to pay $13 for it, from the 177-metre-high observation platform at the nearby **Harbour Centre Tower** (🖥 www.vancouverlookout.com) at 555 West Hastings St. On clear evenings the views over the surrounding mountains, streaked with pink, are absolutely stunning. The tower is open daily 8.30am–10.30pm from May to mid-October and 9am–9pm for the rest of the year (last ride up 30 minutes before closing time).

Gastown

Named after 19th-century entrepreneur 'Gassy Jack', whose nickname derives from his talkative nature rather than his digestive system, Vancouver's oldest quarter was given a huge facelift in the 1970s and today is one of the most popular spots in town. With its cobbled streets lined with gift shops and cafés, Gastown is shamelessly tourist-orientated but it's a lively, fun place to take a stroll, especially Water St, the core of the area. Not to be missed is the hilarious spectacle of tourist crowds silently waiting – breath held, cameras poised – for the **steam-powered clock** on Water St to start chiming and hissing vapour, which it obligingly does every 15 minutes.

Chinatown

Chinatown is a frenetic tangle of streets packed with restaurants, markets, bakeries, herb shops and thousands of Chinese people. The main thoroughfares are Pender and Keefer streets (a 20-minute walk from Robson Square, or a short bus ride on the No 22 eastbound on Pender; if you're walking to Chinatown from Gastown, try to avoid crossing the rundown area of East Hastings St).

If the relentless bustle gets too much for you, the **Dr Sun Yat-Sen Classical Chinese Garden** (🖥 www.vancouverchinesegarden.com) will sort you out. Modelled on the Ming Dynasty gardens in the city of Suzhou and incorporating the Taoist philosophy of yin and yang, the garden is an oasis of harmony and tranquillity. In summer, live Chinese music is often performed in the gardens; for information call ☎ 604-662-3207. It's located at 578 Carrall St, next to the Chinese Cultural Centre. Entrance is $10 and opening hours are daily

10am–6pm May to mid-June, 9.30am–7pm mid-June to late September and 10am–4.30pm October to April (closed on Mondays between November and April). Tea and a 45-minute tour are included in the price of the ticket.

Science World

A few blocks south of the Chinese Gardens, near the train station at 1455 Quebec St, this fascinating centre (🖳 www.scienceworld.ca) is full of hands-on exhibits and allows you to crawl through a beaver lodge among other things. It's also home to Canada's largest Omnimax Dome cinema. Entrance to the centre is $18.75, or $23.75 with an Omnimax film thrown in. The building is open daily from 10am to 5pm and until 6pm at weekends; Omnimax hours change depending on what film is currently being shown.

Granville Island

Southwest of the downtown core, across False Creek, Granville Island was developed as an industrial site in 1915 largely to provide space for the railway yards of the Canadian Northern Railway and the Great Northern Railway. After years of disuse it received a handsome redevelopment package from the federal government in 1972 and was soon transformed into a colourful and lively centre of cafés, artists' workshops and boatyards. The area works much better than Gastown, partly due to the fact that it's as popular with locals as with tourists. While you're here, don't miss the lively Granville Market, packed with fresh vegetables, fruit and pasta and some delicious baked goods.

To get here by public transport, take either the No 50 bus south down Granville St or a ferry from False Creek Ferries' dock on Sunset Beach Park, at the southern end of Thurlow St (🖳 www.granvilleislandferries.bc.ca). Ferries run from 7am to 10.30pm in high season and single tickets are $4. Alternatively, the Vancouver Trolley stops off here (see p174).

Vanier Park Museum Site

Close to Granville Island, the Vanier Park Museum Site is home to three of the city's main museums: the Vancouver Museum, the HR Macmillan Space Centre and the Maritime Museum. The grounds are very pretty and there's an attractive coast path leading from the park to **Kitsilano Beach**. To get there by bus, take the No 2 or 22 from Burrard St and get off at the first stop after the bridge, or you can take a False Creek Ferry (see above). If you're travelling on the Vancouver Trolley, there's a designated stop at the museum site.

● **HR Macmillan Space Centre** The centre (🖳 www.hrspacecentre.com) combines flight-simulators and displays on space exploration with a planetarium specializing in astronomy and rock laser shows (for showing times call ☎ 604-738-7827; tickets cost $15 for adults and $10.75 for children). It also has an observatory next door where you can look at the stars under the guidance of astronomers (Friday and Saturday nights, weather permitting).

● **Vancouver Maritime Museum** In addition to the usual wooden models and old photos, the Vancouver Maritime Museum (🖳 www.vancouvermaritime museum.com) is home to the *St Roch* – a gem of an exhibit. This two-masted

Arctic patrol ship, built in 1928, was only the second vessel to navigate the treacherous North West Passage and the first to do it in both directions; there are guided tours around the ship every half hour. In recent years the museum has acquired more fascinating artefacts such as the clock from *HM Bark Resolute*, one of six ships that went in search of Sir John Franklin when he went missing in the mid-19th century (see p223). From May to September the museum is open daily 10am–5pm and for the rest of the year the hours are: Tuesday to Saturday 10am–5pm and Sunday noon to 5pm; entrance is $10.

● **The Museum of Vancouver** Concentrating on local history, this museum (🖳 www.museumofvancouver.ca) takes you through the city's initial settlement and later development with exhibits ranging from clothes and canoes to photographs and replicas of turn-of-the-20th-century shops. The displays are well presented and the accompanying text is thoughtfully written but the museum has a very parochial air to it and is, on the whole, a bit disappointing.

The museum is open daily 10am–5pm (Thursdays till 9pm); closed Mondays from September to June. Entrance is $11.

Stanley Park
Visit Stanley Park and you begin to see why Vancouverites look so happy: they have a thousand acres of green space on their doorstep in which to unwind. Situated on the tip of a peninsula, most of the park is surrounded by ocean.

You can walk all the way round its edge on the 10km seawall promenade or take a free bus on the road running parallel. From the eastern side are excellent views over Vancouver's downtown skyline and from the west are equally fine views of the mountains looming over West Vancouver across the Burrard Inlet. To get to Stanley Park, take the No 19 bus from West Pender St (at Burrard).

CITY GUIDES

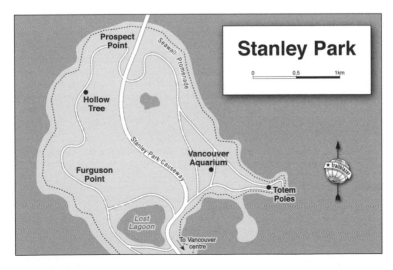

❏ Visiting Victoria, Vancouver Island

It would be a great shame to visit Vancouver and not take the opportunity to travel across to beautiful Vancouver Island, only a $1\frac{1}{2}$-hour ferry ride away. **Victoria**, its biggest city and the capital of British Columbia, sits on the south coast of the island. An important British centre during colonial times, it still sports the air of an old-fashioned English seaside town with its quaint streets, genteel tearooms and fine Victorian architecture – a fact the tourist industry exploits to the full. Commercialism aside, Victoria's laidback ambience and picturesque setting make it a very enjoyable place to visit.

Getting there

BC Ferries (☎ 250-381-1401, 💻 www.bcferries.com) operate frequent crossings from Tsawwassen Dock (32km southwest of downtown Vancouver) to Swartz Bay near Victoria; tickets cost $13.50 each way for foot passengers. To get to the ferry terminal from downtown Vancouver take the SkyTrain on the Canada line to Bridgepoint and then the No 620 bus to Tsawwassen Dock (the bus fare is $5 weekdays or $2.50 at weekends; make sure you ask for a three-zone transfer). The bus ride to the terminal will take about 1 hour 30 minutes and then the ferry crossing is a further 1 hour 35 minutes. When you get to Vancouver Island, pick up the No 70 bus from the ferry terminal to downtown Victoria, which takes about an hour to reach (the bus fare is $2.25 for an adult).

A simpler option is to take a coach tour: Pacific Coach Lines (☎ 604-662-7575, 💻 www.pacificcoach.com) do great deals, with hourly departures from Pacific Central Station (where Vancouver's main bus terminal adjoins the train station) during summer, and regular departures during the rest of the year. Tickets cost $41.60 single, $81.29 return, including the ferry crossing – buy tickets in advance at the station or from the bus driver when you board. The journey from Vancouver to downtown Victoria takes about four hours and fifteen minutes.

Tourist information

Tourism Victoria's **Visitor Centre** (☎ 250-953-2033, 💻 www.tourismvictoria.com) is centrally located on the harbourfront at 812 Wharf St. It's open daily, from May to September 8.30am–8.30pm and for the rest of the year 9am–5pm.

Where to stay

At a stretch you could visit Victoria as a day-trip from Vancouver but it's far more agreeable to spend at least one night here. The best budget option is the *HI Victoria Hostel* at 516 Yates St (☎ 250-385-4511, 💻 www.hihostels.ca), five minutes from the waterfront in a great downtown location. Dorm beds start at $24 for members and $28 for non-members, with a few private en-suite rooms available as well ($62–70).

A very good mid-priced choice is the *James Bay Inn* at 270 Government St (☎ 250-384-7151, 💻 www.jamesbayinn.bc.ca), whose neat, simple rooms (from $125) occupy a handsome Edwardian building that was once the home of painter Emily Carr.

If you'd prefer to pull out all the stops and spend an evening in total luxury then there's only one place to do it: *The Fairmont Empress*, overlooking the harbour at 721 Government St (☎ 250-384-8111, 💻 www.fairmont.com). With its beautiful gardens and ivy-covered exterior, it certainly is an impressive building; high-season rooms go for around $450. If you can't afford to stay here, then drop by for **afternoon tea** instead (noon onwards; from $55) and you'll be treated to an exquisite selection of sandwiches, scones and clotted cream. Reservations are required so be sure to book ahead on ☎ 250-389-2727.

Where to eat

Victoria has some great restaurants, bars and cafés, many of them very reasonably priced. All you really need to do is wander along by the harbour and see what takes your fancy. A firm local favourite, sitting right on the harbour at 500 Fort St, is *The Keg*, with a lively atmosphere and delicious steaks. Alternatively, at 515 Yates St, *Fiamo Italian Kitchen* offers affordable Italian cuisine with a fantastic outdoor patio and a lovely atmosphere.

What to see

One of the most popular activities on Vancouver Island is **whale-watching**, with a number of companies offering excursions, such as The Prince of Whales (☎ 250-383-4884, or toll-free 1-888-383-4884, 💻 www.princeofwhales.com) on the harbourfront, directly below the Visitor Centre. Three-hour trips cost from $95 but it's worth every penny – there's nothing quite like being a few metres away from a pod of orcas (though sightings are not guaranteed), and you should also get to see sea lions and seals.

Back on dry land, the most appealing thing to do is just wander around the **harbourfront** and **Old Town** area and soak up the atmosphere. Of the individual attractions, the three stand-outs are the Royal British Columbia Museum, the Parliament building and the out-of-town Butchart Gardens.

● Royal BC Museum

At 675 Belleville St, the Royal BC Museum (💻 www.royalbcmuseum.bc.ca) takes you through British Columbia's history with a range of outstanding galleries and exhibits. Check out a replica of a section of Captain Vancouver's 18th-century ship, *HMS Discovery*; walk through a turn-of-the-20th-century town complete with silent movie-theatre, Chinatown alley and railway station; admire a series of native totem poles and ceremonial masks; and visit a First Nations longhouse and learn about shaman practices. The museum is open daily 9am–5pm (and until 10pm on Fridays and Saturdays from June to September); admission is $15 (however, when a special exhibit is in town prices can jump to $27.50).

● Parliament Buildings

An imposing edifice overlooking the harbour, Victoria's Parliament Buildings were designed by a 25-year old architect in 1893 in honour of Queen Victoria's sixtieth year on the throne. Completed in 1915, the stately domed building was the subject of much controversy owing to its hefty construction costs. Today, the Parliament Buildings are open to the public for regular tours led by staff in period costume, with a visit from a youthful 'Queen Victoria' herself. Tours are free and take place every 30 minutes in the summer between 9am and 5pm, with the last tour leaving at 4.30pm. The building is particularly striking at night when it's illuminated by hundreds of tiny lights.

● The Butchart Gardens

Established in the early 20th century, what was originally a hobby for Jennie Butchart has today become a gardener's paradise attracting over a million visitors each year (💻 www.butchartgardens.com). Located on an old limestone quarry, Jennie's 'Sunken Garden' is breathtaking with its stunning flowerbeds and different types of shrubs spreading out as far as the eye can see. In summer the gardens stay open late on Saturday nights and feature a fireworks display. The gardens are a forty-minute bus ride from town; take the No 75 bus from downtown (Blanchard St at Fairfield). Opening hours are 9am–10.30pm from mid-June to early September and 9am–5pm for the rest of the year; entrance is $23.

Points of interest to look out for include: the **Lost Lagoon**, home to Canada geese, ducks and swans; a collection of magnificent **totem poles**; **Prospect Point** (excellent views) and the **Hollow Tree**, an incredible red cedar thought to be up to 1000 years old, with a circumference that would take three or four adults holding hands to encircle. Another highlight is the beautiful **Rose Gardens**, featuring an array of immaculate flowerbeds filled with different types of roses.

Also inside the park is the excellent **Vancouver Aquarium** (🖳 www .vanaqua.org). Entrance is a steep $22 (seniors and students $17) but with 8000 marine species represented, including sea otters, beluga whales, sea lions and sharks, it's a fascinating place. There's also the opportunity to book either a Trainer Tour or a Beluga Tour which allows you to get up close and personal with whales and sea otters (call ahead on ☎ 604-659-3546). The aquarium is open daily 9.30am–7pm during July and August and 9.30am–5pm for the rest of the year.

UBC Museum of Anthropology

Located out of town on the university campus, this outstanding museum (☎ 604-822-3825, 🖳 www.moa.ubc.ca) is well worth the trip. Its modern, award-winning buildings house a vast collection of artefacts with an emphasis on cultures of BC's Pacific Coast Natives. Exhibits include masks, jewellery, textiles, ivory carvings and a fine collection of totem poles. Particularly arresting is *The Raven and the First Men*, an enormous cedar sculpture designed by Haida artist Bill Reid.

In summer (mid-May to early October) the museum is open daily 10am–5pm and on Tuesdays until 9pm; outside these months it's open Wednesdays to Sundays 10am–5pm, Tuesdays 10am–9pm. Entrance is $11 ($6 on Tuesday evenings between 5pm and 9pm).

To get to the museum take the southbound No 4 or 10 bus from Granville to its final stop near the campus.

Grouse Mountain and Capilano Suspension Bridge

Rising up from North Vancouver, just across Burrard Inlet, the 1250-metre summit of **Grouse Mountain** (🖳 www.grousemountain.com) can be easily reached by the Skyride cable car, giving sweeping views for miles around. The ride up is exhilarating but very expensive at $37.95, although your ticket does include a number of different activities from ice skating and sleigh rides in the winter to visits to a Refuge for Endangered Wildlife in the summer. Admission to Grouse Mountain is free for those with advance dinner reservations at the restaurant at the top (well worth considering; see p173). Alternatively, you can hike up the thigh-killing Grouse Grind trail in about one and a half to two hours, and in winter (November to April) you can ski down. To get to Grouse Mountain, take the SeaBus across to Lonsdale Quay and then bus No 236. Opening hours are 9am–10pm 365 days a year.

The same bus also passes the entrance to the 137-metre-long **Capilano Suspension Bridge** (☎ 604-985-7474, 🖳 www.capbridge.com) which wobbles precariously over a narrow gorge and river some 70m below. Crossing the bridge certainly gets your heart pounding but you have to pay a staggering $29.95 (students $23.75) for the thrill; note that a ticket up Grouse Mountain gets you $1.50 off the entrance to the bridge. Entrance to the Capilano

Suspension Bridge also includes some interesting pathways through surrounding woodland and you have the opportunity to head up into the trees and amble along a series of raised walkways, known as the **Treetop Adventure**. The bridge is open daily 8.30am-8pm from late May to early September and 9am–5pm for the rest of the year.

Lynn Canyon Suspension Bridge and Park
A more economical alternative to the Capilano Suspension Bridge is the very similar Lynn Canyon Suspension Bridge (💻 www.lynncanyon.ca), which is free; it is a 20-minute bus ride (No 229) from Lonsdale Quay. An added bonus of visiting this bridge is the adjoining 617 acres of walking trails in lush forest. The park is open 7am–9pm in summer, 7am–7pm in spring/autumn, and 7am–dusk in winter.

FESTIVALS

● **International Dragon Boat Festival**, late June. Lively three-day event featuring boat races, music and theatre shows.
● **International Jazz Festival**, late June to early July. Balmy summer evenings of jazz and blues – a highly pleasurable festival (💻 www.jazzvancouver.com).
● **Firework competition**, early August. Music and firework extravaganza.
● **International Comedy Festival**, early August. Usually has an excellent line-up; great location, too, on Granville Island.
● **Vancouver Fringe Festival**, usually first two weeks in September. Excellent range of material encompassing drama, comedy, dance and musicals. Very popular.

MOVING ON

By rail
The Canadian leaves Vancouver's Pacific Central Station for Toronto on Tuesdays, Fridays and Sundays; the journey takes four days (three nights). You can get to the station from downtown on the SkyTrain; alternatively, a taxi should cost no more than about $10.

There's also an Amtrak connection from Vancouver to Seattle (☎ 1-888-842-7245) leaving from the same station.

The Rocky Mountaineer trains, on the other hand, leave from *The Rocky Mountaineer* station, a short distance away from the VIA station at 1755 Cottrell St, just off Terminal Avenue.

The Whistler Mountaineer leaves from North Vancouver station; passengers are taken there by shuttle bus from a number of downtown hotels.

By air
The SkyTrain Canada Line can take you from the heart of Vancouver's downtown straight to the airport with trains around every 8 minutes. Note that you must pay an airport improvement fee when flying out of Vancouver: this is $5 for destinations within BC, $10 for other destinations within North America and $15 if you're travelling outside North America. Taxis from downtown to the airport are around $23-26.

Air Canada: ☎ 604-689-0300; American Airlines: ☎ 1-800-368-1955.

Churchill

Churchill gives a whole new meaning to the phrase 'the end of the line'. As remote a place as you're ever likely to visit, this is a bleak, inhospitable little town, made up of straggling, utilitarian-looking houses shivering by the edge of the great Hudson Bay – over a thousand kilometres from the nearest major city. Its residents are friendly and welcoming but there's no masking the feeling of neglect about the place. Unemployment is fairly high among its 1000-strong population, especially among the natives.

The town's main attraction, of course, is the local wildlife and nature, especially the polar bears that gather close to town in October while waiting for Hudson Bay to freeze over. Besides the bears, you can see beluga whales on the Churchill River, sight wildlife such as arctic foxes and arctic ptarmigans, admire tundra lichens, mosses and flowers during spring, and – if you're lucky – observe the northern lights.

On top of this, there's something deeply alluring about visiting a place with no roads to it, a town that can't be reached by car. This is a frontier, edge-of-the-world kind of place, and getting here on *The Hudson Bay* is a railway journey you'll never forget.

HISTORY

Inuits and settlers

There have been Inuit settlements in this area for thousands of years, though sadly there's little trace left of them today. The first Europeans arrived when the Danish navigator Jens Munk led an expedition in search of the North-West Passage (1619–20). Forced to winter his ship near the mouth of the Churchill River, out of a crew of 48 only he and two others survived.

Fur-trading post

Later, in 1717, the Hudson's Bay Company established a fur-trading post here which remained active for the next 150 years. To judge by the entry for 16 July in the journal of Captain James Knight, it was not a popular posting: 'I never did See such a Miserable Place in my Life'. When the post was no longer used, Churchill was left virtually abandoned for several decades.

Grain port

Following the grain boom on the prairies at the beginning of the 20th century, politicians and farmers campaigned for a port on Hudson Bay from where grain could be exported to European markets. Eventually one was established at Churchill, connected to Winnipeg by the new railway line, whose last spike was driven in 1929. The first two shiploads of grain left Churchill – Canada's only Arctic port – in 1931.

The port is still in use today, though its success has always been limited by the fact that the Hudson Bay is frozen over for nine months of the year. Sold off by the Canadian government in the late 1990s, the port is now in the hands of an American company.

SERVICES

Tourist information

The railway station houses a small **tourist information office** that is generally open 1–4.30pm, although staff are also there when *The Hudson Bay* arrives on Tuesday and Friday mornings. The best online travel resource is 🖳 **http:// everythingchurchill.com**. Put together by Travel Manitoba, the site has lots of suggestions on what to do in Churchill, as well as plenty of accommodation and tour operator listings.

Money

Churchill has one bank, the Royal Bank of Canada, centrally located in Bayport Plaza. It's open Monday to Friday 10.30am–3pm, and has a 24-hour ATM. There's also an ATM at the Seaport Hotel, 299 Kelsey Boulevard.

WHERE TO STAY

Accommodation gets booked up very quickly during the wildlife seasons so you're advised to book ahead. The prices we quote below are for the summer months of July and August; note that rates can rise sharply during the polar bear season (see box p185). Most hotels in Churchill are warm enough and do the job but – in keeping with their rather bleak surroundings – have a functional, rather than a homely, atmosphere.

The most appealing place to stay in town is the *Lazy Bear Lodge* on Kelsey Boulevard (☎ 204-663-9377, 🖳 www.lazybearlodge.com), a timber lodge with spacious, well appointed rooms with good facilities (including cable TV and wifi), as well as a nice café. It's also, however, the most expensive: doubles here cost $385, and during the polar bear season are available only as part of an all-inclusive package (3 nights' accommodation, four days on a tundra vehicle and meals for $2600 per person).

A less pricey alternative is the *Seaport Hotel* (☎ 204-675-8807; 🖳 www .seaporthotel.ca) at 299 Kelsey Boulevard, about 100m from the train station, which offers clean, comfortable rooms in a very central location. The hotel has its own restaurant serving food throughout the day and there's also a complimentary airport shuttle service. Rooms start at $115.

Another popular hotel in town is the *Polar Inn* (☎ 204-675-8878; 🖳 www. polarinn.com), further along the road at number 153, which offers not only clean, comfortable guest rooms but also has kitchenette suites and one-bedroom apartments. Rates start from $133 for standard rooms, and $150 for kitchenette suites.

Just off Kelsey Boulevard, at 34 Franklin St, *Tundra Inn* (☎ 204-675-8831, 🖳 www.tundrainn.com) is another friendly hotel with 31 spacious rooms and a dining room serving decent meals. Standard doubles are $121, including breakfast.

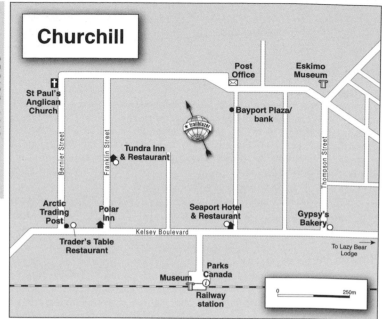

WHERE TO EAT

Many hotels provide meals as well as accommodation; besides this, Churchill has only a small selection of restaurants and cafés. The *Trader's Table Restaurant* (☎ 204-675-2141), at 124 Kelsey Blvd, has warm, filling fare, while *Gypsy's Bakery* is a popular café/restaurant that lies further along Kelsey Boulevard past the Seaport Hotel. If the cold weather gets too much, it's the perfect place to warm up over a cup of hot coffee and enjoy a home-baked pastry.

WHAT TO SEE

The main activities for visitors to Churchill are wildlife viewing and dogsled rides (see box opposite for when to see what).

For a complete list of Churchill's **tour operators**, see 🖳 http://everything churchill.com. The following is a selection of established operators, many of whom offer a spread of activities.

● **Blue Sky Expeditions** (☎ 204-675-2001, 🖳 www.blueskymush.com) Dogsled tours from $90 per person.

● **Churchill Nature Tours** (☎ 204-636-2968, 🖳 www.churchillnature tours.com) Wildlife safaris and birdwatching tours led by experienced naturalists and ornithologists.

- **Great White Bear Tours** (☎ 204-675-2781, 🖳 www.greatwhitebear tours.com) Tundra buggy tours for $350 per day.
- **Kayak Churchill** (☎ 204 -663-9377, 🖳 www.kayakchurchill.com) Attached to the Crazy Bear Lodge and offering kayaking tours on the Churchill River (around $120).
- **Nature 1st** (☎ 204- 675-2147, 🖳 www.nature1sttours.ca) Adventure walking tours around the Hudson Bay; half days cost $85, full days $150.
- **Sea North Tours** (☎ 204-675-2195, 🖳 www.seanorthtours.com) Boat tours on the Churchill River and Hudson Bay; from $90 per half day. Also offers kayaking ($120) and snorkelling ($170).
- **Tundra Buggy Tours** (☎ 204-675-2121 between 1 July and 30 November; ☎ 1-204-949-2050; 🖳 www.tundrabuggytours.com) Hotel-based packages including tundra buggy tours to view polar bears, accommodation in Winnipeg and Churchill and transport to Churchill from Winnipeg. See website for package details and rates (typically 5 or 6 nights at around $5000).
- **Wapusk Adventures** (☎ 204-675-2887, 🖳 www.wapuskadventures.com) Award-winning operator offering dog-sled tours from $90.

❑ When to see what in Churchill
- **Polar bears**: October and November, when the bears move back from the tundra onto the frozen Hudson Bay.
- **Beluga whales**: late June to mid-August, when thousands of belugas feed in the Seal and Churchill rivers that empty into the Hudson Bay. Tours are expensive at around $80 but from the boats you'll also get to see **Fort Prince of Wales**, built in the 18th century and now a National Historic Site. If you're feeling very adventurous, you can kayak or snorkel with the whales.
- **Birds**: April–June and October–November, when migratory birds such as snow and Canada geese head north or south. Native birds include peregrine falcons, snowy owls, tundra, terns and gulls.
- **Iceberg tours**: June.
- **Dogsled rides**: November to May.

Other wildlife you might spot here includes Arctic fox, ptarmigan, and caribou. If you visit between January and April you may also see the **northern lights**, while you can enjoy the Arctic wildflowers from late June to early August.

Other places of interest in this small town include **St Paul's Anglican Church**, which overlooks Hudson's Bay; look out for the stained-glass window, which was originally presented to **York Factory** in 1887 by Lady Franklin in memory of her husband (see p223). The factory was the HBC's headquarters in the region and their main supply base and port. Founded in the late seventeenth century, it lay approximately 250km southeast of Churchill and remained in operation right up to 1957. The site is now maintained by Parks Canada as a National Historic Site. The glass window remains in one piece despite being air-lifted from York Factory to Churchill in the 1960s.

If you'd like to learn more about the Inuit in Canada then head to the **Eskimo Museum**, just off Kelsey Blvd at the end of Selkirk St. The museum has been around since 1944 and is filled with fascinating artefacts and a lifesize replica of a polar bear. The opening hours vary depending upon the time of year though it's always open 1–4.30pm from Monday to Saturday, year-round. You can buy good value souvenirs here.

The railway station also has its own fun **museum**, too, which is free and displays the history of Churchill and York Factory. The staff are most helpful and can provide lots of information regarding the local wildlife.

Finally, if you'd like to take home something to remind yourself of northern Manitoba, head to the **Arctic Trading Post** on Kelsey Boulevard, a charming store with equally charming staff, selling everything from Inuit jewellery to furs to local crafts and produce.

MOVING ON

By rail
The Hudson Bay leaves Churchill on Tuesdays, Thursdays and Saturdays at 8.30pm, arriving at Winnipeg $35^1/_2$ hours later (Thursdays, Saturdays and Mondays) at 8.05am.

By air
If you can't face the journey back by train, **Calm Air** offers regular $2^1/_2$-hour flights from Churchill to Winnipeg – currently three daily on weekdays and one daily on weekends, costing from around $550 per person (one-way). For up-to-date schedules and prices check out 💻 www.calmair.com or call them on ☎ 204-675-8858, or toll-free on 1-888-225-6247. There's no bus service to Churchill's airport but some hotels and tour companies offer a shuttle service; alternatively book a taxi with Churchill Taxi on ☎ 204-675-2345 (approximately $20).

Alternatively, if you'd like to take an adventurous detour from Churchill into Canada's far, far north, **Kivalliq Air** (www.kivalliqair.com) flies to nine communities in Nunavut – primarily as a medical service but also with scheduled passenger flights.

Using this guide

You can follow your route on the strip maps in this guide and read about the points of interest along the way in the accompanying text.

Where something of interest is on only one side of the track, it is identified by the letters N (north), S (south), W (west) and E (east). Note that in some cases these compass directions are only approximate. Since the direction of travel from Toronto to Vancouver is due west, when you're on this journey north is on the right-hand side of the train.

Railway subdivisions
Each line is divided into subdivisions. These are usually about 125 miles long, which was the average distance a steam train could travel in 12 hours when the railways were built. If you take the train all the way from Halifax to Vancouver, you'll pass through 20 subdivisions. These are shown as —— **RAILWAY SUBDIVISION** —— in the text.

Mile markers
The mileage within each subdivision is indicated by mile markers at the side of the track. Subdivisions run from east to west or south to north, so Mile 0 will always be at the eastern or southern terminal of a subdivision. When you reach the end of a subdivision the next one begins. This is known as a railway divisional point and the miles go back to '0'. The mile markers are usually white rectangular boards on metal posts or telegraph poles. They can be on either side of the track.

Signal masts
You'll also notice numbers marked on signal masts along the way. You can work out which mile you're at by inserting a decimal point before the last digit. For instance, if the number on the signal mast is 562 that means you're at Mile 56.2.

Station names
Of course the foolproof way to find out where you are is to look out for the names of the stations you're passing. These are conveniently announced on signposts a mile before each station. The names of sidings or junctions are often displayed by the track as well.

> **Miles or kilometres?**
> While travelling through Canada you may well be struck by the odd mixture of kilometres and miles, feet and metres in use throughout the country. Conversion to the metric system from the British Imperial system began here in 1971 and while the process is more or less complete, many traces of the old method of measurement remain. The result can be a little confusing; for instance, VIA's timetables give all distances in kilometres, but the CN subdivisions are still broken down by miles and marked by mileposts at the side of the track.

Stops

Most of the stops are for only a few minutes, giving the crew just enough time to whisk passengers on and off. Longer stops are always indicated in the timetable and are shown in this guide in brackets after the station name. You'll notice that some of the stops in the timetable have asterisks after them; these are 'flag stops' which means the train will stop here only when someone wants to get on or off. Flag stops are also marked by an asterisk in this guide, eg **Clearwater***.

Time zones

Most of the routes described take you through at least two time zones; *The Canadian* takes you through four. When you enter a new time zone this will be indicated in the text using the following abbreviations: AT (Atlantic Time); ET (Eastern Time); CT (Central Time); MT (Mountain Time); PT (Pacific Time). See pp47-8 for more on time zones.

❏ **Speed calculations**
You can work out how fast you're travelling by measuring the time it takes the train to get from one mile marker to the next one, then consulting this table.

Seconds	kph	mph	Seconds	kph	mph
36	170	100	80	72	45
38	153	95	85	68	42
40	145	90	90	64	40
42	138	86	95	61	38
44	132	82	100	58	36
46	126	78	105	55	34
48	121	75	110	53	33
50	116	72	115	50	31
52	111	69	120	48	30
54	108	67	130	45	28
56	103	64	150	39	24
58	100	62	160	37	23
60	96	60	170	34	21
65	88	55	210	27	17
70	82	51	240	24	15

The Ocean:
Halifax to Montreal

The Ocean follows the meandering lines of the old Intercolonial Railway; indeed the line loops around so much, swinging off to tiny villages, that it was said the contractors were paid by the mile.

It's a line with a history – the first passenger train ran from Halifax to Lévis, opposite Quebec City, back in 1876. The train following this route has been known as *The Ocean* since 1904, making it the longest-running service in Canada.

The line takes you through three provinces and two time zones and, as you might expect, past a good deal of water: you'll see plenty of lakes, harbours, bays and rivers, including the great St Lawrence, which the train follows for a large portion of the journey. The trip from Halifax to Montreal takes 21 hours.

[MAP 1]

Mile 0: Halifax [AT] For a detailed guide to Halifax, see pp69–81.

Mile 4 (S): The train passes **Fairview Cemetery** where 125 victims of the *Titanic* tragedy are buried. There's also a large common grave here for the unidentified men and women who died in the Halifax Explosion (see p79).

Mile 18–27: As you leave the city you move into a landscape of spruce forest and lakes. Look east at Mile 18 for a view of Kinsac Lake, and west between Mile 24 and 27 for lovely views over Shubenacadie Lake.

Mile 63: Truro There was an Acadian settlement here as early as 1701 but these unfortunate people were forced to make way for New England settlers in 1755. Since then it's become a major railway centre and a thriving farming, lumbering and dairy area. It's a pretty town though the station, set in the middle of an ugly shopping mall, would suggest otherwise.

ROUTE GUIDES AND MAPS

The expulsion of the Acadians
Acadia (or Acadie) was the name given to the original French settlements on the Atlantic Coast that date from around 1610. This land was also claimed by the British who renamed it Nova Scotia. They finally acquired Acadia in the Treaty of Utrecht in 1713, though they more or less left it alone until 1750–60 when thousands of New England settlers were moved in to colonize the area.

Britain demanded of the Acadians an oath of unconditional allegiance to the British Crown but the French refused, vowing neutrality instead. In response, the Acadian population was rounded up, herded onto ships and forcibly deported. Up to 10,000 of these people were expelled between 1755 and 1762 and the event has gone down as one of the greatest tragedies of the French-speaking people of Canada.

———————————— RAILWAY SUBDIVISION ————————————

Mile 11: Just after crossing the Debert River the train swings around a great, sweeping curve of track known as the **Grecian Bend**, apparently laid at the behest of an influential local ironworks owner.

Mile 23(N): Folly Lake Formed by a melting glacier 10,000 years ago, it's supposed to be a watering spot for moose and bear.

Mile 25: For the next five miles the train rides high above the Wallace River, along the Wentworth Valley. As you leave the valley behind, look south for a view of Sugarloaf Mountain in the distance.

Mile 59: Springhill Jct* Springhill used to be an important coal-mining centre but its pits were dogged by tragedy: in 1891 125 miners were killed in an explosion; 39 died in an accident in 1956; just two years later a tunnel collapsed

Nova Scotia
Nova Scotia is Canada's second smallest province, covering just over 55,000 square miles. It sits in the North Atlantic Ocean on a lobster-shaped peninsula, surrounded by 7579km of coastline. One of the three Maritime Provinces, practically everything about Nova Scotia – its history, its climate, its industries, its people – is intricately bound up with the sea. The first Europeans in the area were fishermen, lured over by the legendary supplies of cod here, and the first towns were set up as ports, first by the French and then by the British. The biggest, Halifax, was and remains an important naval base as well as being the province's capital.

It's an area of great natural beauty, particularly around the coast with its incredible variety of fjords, bays, coves, inlets, mudflats, sand dunes, beaches, lagoons and salt marshes. This rugged terrain, added to the province's isolation from central Canada, lends a remote and slightly sleepy feel to the place – qualities that draw significant numbers of tourists here each year. Nova Scotia's population is 873,000; about 75% of these are of British extract, and 11% of French descent (with German and Dutch origin making up the rest). The average income per capita is less than 80% of the national average but Nova Scotians generally claim, with good reason, to enjoy a fine quality of life in an unspoilt environment.

New Brunswick

The official name of this province is New/Nouveau Brunswick. Over a third of its population of 938,000 is French-speaking and New Brunswick is Canada's only officially bilingual province. It was originally administered as part of Nova Scotia but when its population expanded with the arrival of about 14,000 English Loyalists after the American War of Independence, it was made a separate province in 1784. It's bordered by Quebec to the north and Maine (USA) to the west and is connected to Nova Scotia by the Chignecto Isthmus.

In the early decades of Confederation, New Brunswick was the most prosperous region of Canada. Its economy was based on the massive boatbuilding industry centred in Saint John, which exploited the enormous quantity of timber available from the province's interior forest land. However, when the industry began using steel instead, New Brunswick's fortunes declined rapidly and have never properly recovered, due in some part to Canada's national policies which restrict individual provinces from setting their own competitive tariffs. New Brunswick is one of the Maritime Provinces, along with Nova Scotia and Prince Edward Island. Its capital is Fredericton.

killing a further 74 men. Today the pits are all shut down but the bravery of the men who once worked there is still honoured in the **Springhill Miners' Museum**.

Mile 76: Amherst The town was once a booming industrial centre of Nova Scotia but large numbers of the population left for New England after World War I and the local economy has never recovered its former success.

Mile 80: Here you cross the Missaquash River which separates Nova Scotia from New Brunswick.

Mile 81(N): On top of the hill you can see **Fort Beauséjour**, built by the French between 1750 and 1755, then promptly captured by the British the year it was completed. This low-lying building doesn't exactly dominate the skyline, so keep your eyes peeled if you want a glimpse of it.

Mile 86: Sackville This is a small, pretty town with old timbered houses and, surprisingly for its size, a university, Mount Allison, founded over 150 years ago. What's more, this university was the first in Canada to grant degrees to women, when Grace Anne Lockhart was made a Bachelor of Science here in 1875. Sackville is surrounded by the saltwater **Tantramar Marshes**. Keep a look out for Canada geese, marsh hawks, blue-winged teal, black ducks and numerous other waterfowl; the area is a national wildlife reserve and is one of the densest breeding grounds in the world for many species.

Mile 125: Moncton   **[15-minute stop]**
The original name of this town was The Bend; sadly it was renamed Moncton (losing a 'k' along the way) in 1855, in honour of General Robert Monckton, a British commander who became lieutenant-governor of Nova Scotia. Efforts to officially respell the town's name in the 1920s were vigorously opposed by the locals, and Moncton it remained. Today about a third of the population is French-speaking. The 15-minute stop provides a good opportunity to stretch your legs.

> 'From Moncton, westward, there is much along the line worthy of description, but thousands of Railway tourists will see it all with their own eyes in a year or two – the deep forests of New Brunswick, the noble Miramichi River with its Railway bridging on a somewhat gigantic scale, the magnificent highway scenery of the Baie des Chaleurs, the Restigouche and the wild mountain gorges of the Matapédia.'
> **Rev Grant**, *Ocean to Ocean* (1873)

— RAILWAY SUBDIVISION —

Mile 62: Here you cross the **Miramichi River** and then, immediately after, the Little Miramichi. Anglers reportedly flock to these waters from all over the world, lured by their silver Atlantic salmon.

Mile 66: Newcastle The local economy revolves around the town's thriving salmon fisheries. It also boasts a large radio station which met its moment of glory during World War II when it was selected as the British government's receiving station. It's no longer a main stop.

Mile 110: Bathurst This small copper-mining and fishing town marks the beginning of the Caraquet coast. The sandy beaches and old Acadian fishing villages along this coast have made the area a popular tourist resort.

Mile 120: Petit Rocher* This small seaside village is a popular summer resort. Villagers celebrate the Acadian National Holiday every year here on August 15.

Mile 138: Jacquet River* This town was founded by a Mr J Doyle in 1790 who, according to local legend, was its only inhabitant for many years. To the north is the Bay of Chaleur; the train will hug its shores for the next 35 miles. The views over the bay are particularly pretty between miles 165 and 170.

[MAP 2]

Mile 154: Charlo* This little fishing and forestry town has its own local airport with regularly scheduled flights to Montreal.

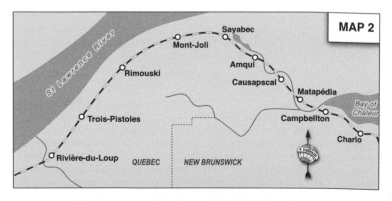

Mile 173: Campbellton The town was originally settled by the dispossessed Acadians back in 1757, but they were once more forced out of their homes by the English a few years later.

The skyline at Campbellton is dominated by the 300-metre high Sugarloaf Mountain – a huge lump of volcanic rock – but it may be too dark to get a good look by the time you arrive.

———————————— **RAILWAY SUBDIVISION** ————————————

Mile 12: Matapédia (ET) Matapédia gets its name from a Micmac word which means 'The river that breaks into branches'. You are now in Quebec Province.

The **Micmac** (sometimes spelt Mi'kmaq) occupy the coastal regions of the Gaspé and Maritime provinces. It is not certain how long they have been there, though it could be anything up to 10,000 years. Their settlements were traditionally located around bays or rivers, and their community and economy revolved around fishing and hunting. As with most native tribes, however, their society was virtually dismantled with the arrival of the Europeans. Attempts by the government to integrate Micmacs with white Canadians resulted in few advantages for the natives and the loss of most of their land, villages and customs. Today there are about 20,000 people of Micmac origin living in this part of Canada.

Mile 47: Causapscal* A lumbering and farming village touched by romance. It was here that Donald A Smith of the CPR (see p64) fell in love with and married his beautiful Indian bride.

Mile 60: Amqui Again, this place name is derived from a Micmac word, this time intriguingly meaning 'Place of amusement'.

Quebec

Quebec is Canada's largest province, covering 1.65 million sq km. The UK would fit into this vast area seven times over but Quebec's population is a fraction of the UK's at 7.7 million. The province stretches right up to the Hudson Strait, not far from the Arctic Circle, but most of the land is covered by the Canadian Shield (see p35) and is virtually uninhabitable. Subsequently, almost all Quebeckers live in the fertile valley of the St Lawrence River, with over a third in Montreal alone.

Quebec is unique in North America in being an almost wholly French-speaking region: over 90% of its people have French as their mother tongue. Its distinctness from the rest of Canada has given rise to a vigorous separatist movement over the last few decades and Quebec has been teetering on the brink of independence in recent years (see p40).

In 1995 a referendum was held in which Quebeckers voted to stay with Canada by just 1%, a figure that indicated how finely the province's future hung in the balance – though the strong feelings concerning the sovereignty issue do seem to have died down somewhat since then. If Quebec were to become a separate nation it would break up the rest of Canada into two blocks, as the province separates Ontario from New Brunswick, Nova Scotia, Newfoundland and Prince Edward Island. Quebec also borders four American states: Maine, New Hampshire, Vermont and New York.

Mile 76: Sayabec* The train passes through this town late at night but, if you haven't gone to bed yet, you may be able make out the striking silhouette of Sayabec's church (E), standing on a hillside.

Mile 105: Mont-Joli The moose- and deer-hunting capital of Quebec, this little town is also known as 'Gateway to the Gaspé'.

Mile 123: Rimouski With a population of around 30,000, this is the first sizeable town since Moncton. The Roman Catholic cathedral is the centre of the diocese. Much of the town was destroyed by a fire in 1950 but there are few signs of this left today.

Mile 161: Trois-Pistoles No one knows for sure how this village got its name but legend has it that a sailor sent to fetch water from a stranded ship lost the silver goblet he was carrying, which was worth three gold *pistoles* (a French coin).

These days Trois-Pistoles is a popular whale-watching spot: beluga, blue and finback whales are all common in this part of the St Lawrence.

Mile 188: Rivière-du-Loup This town used to be called Fraserville but the large packs of wolves that once gathered around the river gave the place its more poetic name.

———————————— RAILWAY SUBDIVISION ————————————

[MAP 3, opposite]

Mile 41: La Pocatière This town of about 5000 people is home to a modern, avant-garde cathedral containing works by an eminent Quebec sculptor.

Mile 78: Montmagny* Probably the most noteworthy feature of this biscuit-manufacturing town is its curious ten-sided church.

———————————— RAILWAY SUBDIVISION ————————————

Mile 8: Charny Now that *The Ocean* no longer stops at Lévis, on the opposite bank of the St Lawrence from Quebec City, this is where passengers wanting to visit Quebec City get off the train. From here, a minibus will take you on the half-hour ride into town (for around $12; tickets bought inside the train station), where it'll drop you at the Gare du Palais in the city's Basse-Ville (see p84).

As you pull out of Charny the train crosses a wide bridge over the Chaudière River. The river takes its name from the 'boiling waters' of its falls, the tallest being forty metres high. Once out of Charny you move into a rural landscape of forests or pastures dotted with tiny villages, pretty church spires and farms.

This fertile land stretches most of the way from here to Montreal. Most of the trees that you pass along this stretch are maple trees, used to produce that great Canadian staple, maple syrup. A hole is bored in each tree so that the sap can be removed, drop by drop; this is then heated under controlled temperatures and the sap turns into syrup. It's then transferred to a cute glass bottle that ends up on your breakfast table next to your pancakes.

Mile 98: Drummondville Note the huge hydroelectric station the train passes just before you get to this busy industrial town.

Mile 40: St-Hyacinthe The mileage suddenly goes down to Mile 40 following a railway junction just before the town. The great gothic building to the south is the St-Hyacinthe Seminary, supposedly modelled on Amiens Cathedral. It is said of St-Hyacinthe that until very recently it had a higher concentration of religious institutions than any other town in the world. It's also the birthplace of Canada's greatest organ builder, Joseph Casavant.

Mile 50: There's a dramatic change of scenery as two of the **Monteregian Hills** suddenly loom up. These huge volcanic mounds were formed 120 million years ago when the area was covered by sea. Particularly impressive is the dark and somewhat menacing Mont Rouge, towering over the track at **Boloeil** (Mile 56). Altogether there are seven of these hills, the westernmost being Mont Royal in Montreal.

Mile 55: As you cross the Richelieu River, spare a thought for the victims of the terrible rail accident at this spot in 1864. A Grand Trunk train carrying mainly German and Polish immigrants was unable to stop for the rising drawbridge and went plunging between the gap into the river; 100 passengers died.

Mile 70: *The Ocean* crosses the St Lawrence Seaway into greater Montreal, stopping briefly at the suburb **St-Lambert**. Look north as you cross the bridge for excellent views of Montreal's skyline. A few miles on from St-Lambert you're in Montreal's Central Station. For more information about **Montreal**, see pp93–109.

The Corridor route: Montreal to Toronto

VIA's modern LRC (Light, Rapid & Comfortable) trains travel along the old Grand Trunk inter-city route, following first the St Lawrence River (which drifts in and out of sight) to its source at Lake Ontario, and then the shores of the lake as far as Toronto. The journey takes from 4½ hours.

ROUTE GUIDES AND MAPS

[MAP 4]

Mile 0: Montreal [ET] See pp93–109.

Mile 11: Dorval The train makes a brief stop just outside Montreal, near the southern international airport. Moving out of Dorval the tracks run parallel to the highway (Route 20) which will remain in view for the next hour or so.

Mile 21 and 23: Here you cross the Ottawa River. Look north for fine views down the river to the Lake of Two Mountains studded with little islands. In the distance you can see the Laurentian Highlands.

Mile 25: Around here the urban landscape peters out and the train moves into a rural setting. The land is as flat as a pancake and the only things to look at are trees and farms.

Mile 41: The train crosses the boundary between Quebec and Ontario.

Mile 58: The peculiar igloo-shaped buildings you can see standing by the track are used by the government to store sand to sprinkle on the roads in the winter.

Mile 65–105: The track running along this stretch was re-laid in the late 1950s when the original track was submerged by the artificial widening of the St Lawrence River. This was part of the construction of the huge **St Lawrence Seaway**, a system of canals and locks connecting the Atlantic Ocean to the St Lawrence River and the Great Lakes. The biggest section is the one you're now running alongside (though it's just out of sight), linking Montreal with Lake Ontario; it can take vessels of up to 222.5m long and 23.2m wide. The railways weren't the only thing submerged by the Seaway: over 500 homes and 6500 people had to be relocated to two newly built towns; you'll pass one of them, **Ingleside**, at Mile 80.

Mile 68: Cornwall Site of one of the province's oldest courthouses (1833) and a restored 'Regency Cottage' museum. If you look south here you can make out the original route of the track before it was re-laid.

Mile 109 (S): Over the trees you can see a huge bridge; this is the International Bridge linking Canada with the US. Right by the bridge are several enormous grain elevators.

Mile 112: A large water-storage tower signals your arrival at **Prescott**. In contrast to this modern edifice is Prescott's beautiful stone station, about 150 years old.

Mile 125: Brockville (or 'Gateway to the Thousand Islands') Between here and Kingston the St Lawrence River is dotted with hundreds of little islands covered with rock and trees. The area, an extension of the Canadian Shield, is very beautiful and has attracted tourists since the early 1800s but unfortunately not much of it can be seen from the train.

Mile 135–145: The rolling pastures suddenly give way to ten miles of beautiful limestone rock and wild-looking trees – a brief glimpse of the scenery covering the Thousand Islands just to the south.

Mile 155: Gananoque The other 'Gateway to the Thousand Islands.' It also has a bridge across the St Lawrence to the US.

Mile 169: The train crosses the **Rideau Canal** that links Kingston with Ottawa. The canal was completed in 1832 and was originally designed (following the War of 1812) to guarantee a supply route north of the US border in the event of another war. In winter this canal turns into a busy skating rink and is used by many locals to skate to work.

Mile 176: Kingston This town's claims to fame include being the former capital of the Province of Canada (1841–67) and the birthplace of Sir John A Macdonald, Canada's first Prime Minister.

Mile 180: As the train passes attractive Collins Bay, with all its pleasure yachts bobbing in the water, you get your first glimpse of Lake Ontario.

Mile 182: A big water tower stands by the track (N) with 'Amherst View' written on it. About a mile further on you can snatch a bit of this view for yourself – the beautiful Amherst Island on Lake Ontario (S).

Ontario

Sandwiched between Quebec and Manitoba, Ontario sprawls over a million square kilometres, from the Great Lakes in the south up to Hudson Bay in the north. A large part of this area is Shield country, with its boreal forest, granite outcrops and countless lakes. 'Ontario' is an Iroquoian word meaning 'Shining waters', a most appropriate name since the province contains a full quarter of the world's fresh water.

It is the most populated province in Canada (with nine million people) and has been so since the first census was taken in 1871. It is also the wealthiest, with the highest degree of urbanization and industrialization, and the most diversified economy. Its manufacturing sector is particularly important, with about half of all goods produced in Canada coming from Ontario. Another major source of revenue is the rich mineral deposits discovered with the construction of the railroad across the Canadian Shield.

Ontario attracts many tourists each year, being home to the nation's capital (Ottawa), its largest city (Toronto) and the Niagara Falls. Less well-known attractions include popular wilderness retreats such as Georgian Bay, the Thousand Islands and Algonquin Park (a mecca for canoeists with its 1600km of water trails).

ROUTE GUIDES AND MAPS

[MAP 5]

Mile 199: Nepanee Just before you get here look south as you cross the river and you'll see a series of pretty waterfalls. The picturesque view continues with Nepanee's beautiful town hall (S) and then its charming old railway station.

Mile 220: Belleville This town has been, in its time, an important fur-trading, saw-milling and cheese-making centre. Like Nepanee it boasts an attractive, well-preserved station dating from the 1850s.

Mile 233: Trenton Jct Chosen as the base for the Royal Canadian Air Force during World War II, this little town was the training centre for Commonwealth pilots.

Back in the 1920s, however, not content with the usual saw-milling and lumbering industries, Trenton tried to establish itself as a film production centre. Unfortunately the glamorous plan didn't really take off and only a handful of films were produced here.

Mile 260 (S): Over the next few miles there are lovely views of Lake Ontario.

Mile 265: Cobourg Among this small town's architectural highlights is a court which is a replica of London's Old Bailey. You may also be interested to know that Cobourg was the site of one of Canada's oldest railways – a 48km track to Peterborough across Rice Lake. The line was not a success; right at the beginning most of the construction team was wiped out by cholera and then when the track was finally laid in the mid-1850s the 5km Rice Lake Bridge proved rather unstable. When the Prince of Wales visited the area in 1860 it was considered best that he shouldn't cross the bridge in case it collapsed – and collapse it did less than one year later, leaving Cobourg with an inoperable and bankrupt railway.

Mile 268: By now the train is running right alongside the lakeshore; the views are stunning so keep your camera at the ready.

Mile 270: Port Hope This town has one of the best preserved turn-of-the-20th-century main streets in Canada. You won't see much of it from the train but its beautiful little railway station is equally well kept.

Mile 271: More superb views of Lake Ontario – sandy beaches, clay bluffs and holiday homes dotted along the shore.

Mile 300: Oshawa This manufacturing city (predominantly of cars) was the birthplace of industrial unions in Canada, following a strike by 4000 men at General Motors in 1937. The controversy surrounding the company's – and the government's – response to the strike resulted in two cabinet ministers resigning. Eventually the company gave in to the strikers' demands – the first union victory in the country. You can see the GM site on the other side of the rail tracks from the station.

Mile 315: Once more the tracks sweep right by the edge of the lake. Take your fill of the beautiful views before the train heads off into Toronto's suburbs where a stop is made at **Guildwood** at Mile 321.

Mile 333: Toronto Your journey ends at Union Station. For more about Toronto, see pp110–26.

The Canadian:
Toronto to Vancouver

This epic journey of 4424km takes four days You'll travel through some of the most diverse landscape contained within a single country. The highlight of the journey is without question the ride through the Rocky Mountains, with the stretch between Jasper and Kamloops taking you through some of the most spectacular scenery in the world.

TORONTO TO WINNIPEG

[MAP 6, p200]

Mile 1–50 [ET]: For the first half hour or so the train chugs through the dismal Toronto suburbs before the landscape gives way to the fertile pastures and picturesque farms that characterize southern Ontario. Travelling this way in 1872, Rev Grant noted: 'The first half of the journey, or as far as Lake Simcoe, is through a fair and fertile land; too flat to be picturesque, but sufficiently rolling for farming purposes. Clumps of stately elms, with noble stems, shooting high before their fan-shape commences, relieve the monotony of the scene.' (*Ocean to Ocean*).

Mile 99: Washago* Sounding alarmingly like a shampoo, this tiny village is situated on the northern shores of Lake Couchiching. The name is actually taken from the native 'Wash-a-go-min' which means 'Sparkling waters.' To the west lies the beautiful **Georgian Bay**, an arm of Lake Huron, one of the Great Lakes. The waters are studded with islands and holiday cottages are dotted around the shore.

Mile 100: *The Canadian* now crosses the Severn River which flows into Hudson Bay. The river was used by fur traders in the 17th and 18th centuries as a route between the bay and Lake Winnipeg. Beyond the river the landscape alters dramatically as you move into the wild, rugged terrain of the **Canadian**

ROUTE GUIDES AND MAPS

MAP 6

TORONTO

Newmarket

Barrie

Lake Simcoe

Orilla

Lake Couchiching

Washago

Severn River

Georgian Bay

Parry Sound

Pickerel River

French River

Sudbury Jct

Shield (see p35). For the next few hours the train winds its way between great outcrops of pink and grey granite, surrounded by a dazzling array of lakes, waterfalls and streams. The scenery is utterly beautiful – though sadly current scheduling has trains travelling through this section of the route at night.

Mile 150: Parry Sound* This town has a peculiar history. The land was bought in the mid-19th century by a Mr W H Beatty who laid out a settlement and encouraged families to move there. As it grew into a successful logging centre, Mr Beatty's son became a sort of self-appointed squire. He was known by everyone as 'The Governor,' enforced prohibition on the villagers and even began to circulate his own money! These days Parry Sound is a bustling tourist resort in the summer. It's known as 'Gateway to the Thirty Thousand Islands' on Lake Huron – the world's largest concentration of islands. You can see some of these (S) over the next few miles if you're on an eastbound train.

Mile 215: After crossing the Pickerel River, the train crosses the **French River**, part of a historic fur-trading route. It's still popular with canoeists who share its shallow waters with large numbers of bass, pike and muskellunge.

Mile 260: Sudbury Jct* As you approach Sudbury look south (if you're awake) for a view of the towering 381-metre INCO smokestack. The region's rich nickel and copper deposits were discovered during the construction of the trans-Canada railway and since then Sudbury has become the largest nickel-mining centre in the world. The mining and smelting were responsible for ravaging the surrounding landscape, earning the area the nickname 'Lunar garden', but extensive reforestation and redevelopment projects have improved the environment.

Mile 276: Capreol [MAP 7] [25-minute stop]
Besides being a railway divisional point, this small town serves as a distribution centre for Sudbury's mining industry. *The Canadian* now enters what is

known as the 'Thousand mile gap' cutting through the Canadian Shield.

Mile 5: Moving out of Capreol the train enters the increasingly remote interior of northern Ontario. It's mind-boggling to think that the exposed bedrock you can see is 500 million years old. You can begin to understand why it took more than 20,000 men to get the track from here to the prairies: the train is forced to weave and loop around numerous lakes, all the while cutting through the rock or bogland of the Shield. The communities that have sprung up along the track remain isolated and sparsely populated (Farlane, for instance, has fewer than 40 inhabitants) and most of the stops between here and Winnipeg are flag stops. Only the occasional trapper, fisherman or lumberjack is likely to get on or off.

Mile 86: Gogama* This is a typical logging village. The area between here and **Folyet** (Mile 150) is renowned for moose and bear so keep your eyes peeled.

Mile 258: Oba* A railway junction amidst the wilderness! The trans-Canada line crosses the tracks of the Algoma Central Railway (from Sault Ste Marie to Hearst), hence the little railway hotel in this village of a hundred people.

[MAP 8, p202]
Mile 295: Hornepayne **[35-minute stop]**
Once a gold-mining town, Hornepayne now relies on its pulp mill to keep its workforce employed. It has about 1500 inhabitants.

Mile 76: Caramat* Like many sites along the line, Caramat sprang up as a logging town and then almost vanished once the area was logged and the workmen moved on.

Mile 100: Longlac* This former gold-mining settlement sits on the northern banks of Long Lake which drains into Lake Superior. The lake is forty-five miles long and just two miles wide. Almost half the village's population (of over 2000) is French-speaking.

ROUTE GUIDES AND MAPS

MAP 8

Hornepayne

Hillsport

Caramat

Longlac

Nakina

Auden

Jackfish Creek

Ferland

Mud River

Lake Nipigon

Armstrong

Mile 131: Nakina* This little fur-trapping town also boasts an airfield and a radio station.

Mile 210: *The Canadian* goes over a viaduct high above Jackfish Creek. Look south for fine views over Lake Nipigon, the fourth largest lake in Ontario.

Mile 219: Mud River* Another viaduct takes you across the murky waters that give the village its name.

Mile 243: Armstrong* The landscape by now is monotonous: trees, trees and more trees. This continues for several hours but you'll think fondly of them as you cross the treeless prairies. To the south are fine views of Lake Nipigon, almost 100km in length.

[MAP 9]

Mile 264: Collins* [CT] You've now crossed over into Central Time.

———————— RAILWAY SUBDIVISION ————————

Mile 67: Flindt Landing* This fishing resort is on a little island. Look north to see the cabins and huts.

Mile 78: Savant Lake* Another long, narrow lake, 25 miles long and just five miles wide. This settlement is visited mainly by people out fishing.

Mile 139: Sioux Lookout **[25-minute stop]** Sioux Lookout sounds as if it's going to be interesting but it's not. The place was far more glamorous in days gone by: it was the home of the Ojibway natives who used the nearby hills as a lookout during an attack by Sioux Indians.

———————— RAILWAY SUBDIVISION ————————

Mile 12: Hudson* This tiny settlement was once the main centre for flights to the far north during the gold-rush years.

Mile 90: Canyon* The train skirts the shores of Canyon Lake for about ten miles.

Mile 113: Farlane* This tiny settlement was once a favourite fishing resort of Winnipeg's affluent middle class.

Mile 137: Minaki* This used to be a fashionable riverside tourist resort in the 1920s and '30s.

Mile 153: Malachi* If you're awake, look south for a beautiful view over Lake Malachi. The attractive hamlet by the lake is still popular with tourists.

[MAP 10, p204]

Mile 160: Rice Lake* Just short of the Ontario/Manitoba border, Rice Lake is a popular fishing destination. You're now in **Whiteshell Provincial Park**, a wilderness area with over 200 lakes. One of these, West Hawk Lake, is 111 metres deep and is supposed to have been created by a giant meteorite. Keep your eyes open for the black bear, deer, moose, coyotes and beavers that live in the park.

Mile 180: Brereton Lake* The last of the lakes. The trees begin to thin out here, giving way to fields and farms.

Mile 197: Elma* Look south as you approach this little hamlet for a view of a Ukrainian church with its striking, onion-shaped dome. This is typical of the ethnically diverse settlements dotted across the prairies; immigrants were encouraged to come here from all over the world to populate the region once the railway was built and a large number came from Eastern Europe.

Mile 244: Transcona* Just before arriving in this Winnipeg suburb you cross the Red River Floodway on a viaduct 275 metres long. The canal was built to divert floodwaters around Winnipeg following the massive flood of 1950 which forced 100,000 Winnipegers to evacuate their homes.

Mile 252: Winnipeg   **[4-hour stop]**
A welcome four-hour-long break to stretch your legs and get some fresh air. You could call in at the Winnipeg Railway Museum, located in the train station, or visit 'The Forks' (the market/café/people-watching centre of Winnipeg), directly behind the station. If you're staying in Winnipeg, see pp127–37 for a guide to the city.

———————— **RAILWAY SUBDIVISION** ————————

WINNIPEG TO EDMONTON

Mile 15: As you pull out of Winnipeg the train rolls into some of the most fertile land in Canada.

MAP 10

ONTARIO

Rice Lake

MANITOBA

Ophir

Brereton Lake

Elma

Red River Floodway

Transcona

WINNIPEG

Portage-la-Prairie

Brandon North

Rivers

Enormous fields stretch all around, the flatness broken only by farms and grain elevators standing by the rail track.

Mile 55: Portage-la-Prairie* A portage is the connecting overland stretch of a water route. For the fur traders, this area was a portage between the Assiniboine River and Lake Manitoba. The activities pursued at Portage-la-Prairie today are not quite so exotic: it's a food-processing centre specializing in mushrooms and frozen foods.

Passing through in 1872, Rev Grant noted: 'Portage la Prairie is the centre of what will soon be a thriving settlement and, when the railway is built, a large town must spring up. On the way to the little village we passed, in less than ten miles, three camps of Sioux – each of them with about twenty wigwams ranged in a circular form. The three camps probably numbered three hundred souls. The men were handsome fellows, and a few of the women were pretty. We did not see many of the women, however, as they kept to the camps doing all the dirty work, while the men marched along the road, every one of them with a gun on his shoulder.'

Mile 128: Brandon North* Brandon is Manitoba's second largest city (about 39,000 people) – you can just about make it out, five miles south of the station.

Mile 143: Rivers* You approach this little town on a 27-metre-long bridge high above the Minnedosa (Cree for 'Swift waters') River. Look out for the colourful grain elevators alongside the track.

[MAP 11]
Mile 180: For the next 25 miles the train follows the **Qu'Appelle Valley**. Look south for lovely views over the lakes and waterways threading through the emerald-green land. The name is derived from the French translation of an Indian legend which told of a young man who, on hearing his name called as he crossed the valley, cried out 'Qui appelle?' ('Who calls?') The only reply was the echo of his voice: 'Qu'appelle....qu'appelle....' He later discovered that the voice he had heard was his lover crying out for him at the moment of her death. A cheery little story to ponder on as the train chugs along the valley.

MAP 11

> 'The broad, open valley of the Qu'Appelle stretched out along to the west, making a grand break in what would otherwise have been an unbroken plateau of Prairie. Three miles to the south of this valley, and therefore opposite us but farther down, two or three small white buildings on the edge of the plateau were pointed out as Fort Ellice. To the north of the Qu'Appelle, the sun was dipping behind woods far away on the edge of the horizon, and throwing a mellow light on the vast expanse which spread around in every direction.'
>
> **Rev Grant**, *Ocean to Ocean* (1873)

Mile 213: Manitoba/Saskatchewan border As the train moves into the Saskatchewan prairies the land gets flatter and flatter. VIA's scheduling thankfully has you travelling through most of Saskatchewan in the dark (in both directions) – presumably to avoid the risk of 'prairie madness' breaking out on the trains.

Mile 280: Melville This town (it's officially a city but the word seems inappropriate for a prairie community of 5000 people) was established by the Grand Trunk Pacific Railway in 1908. It was named after Charles Melville Hays, the GTP president who died in the sinking of the *Titanic*.

———————— RAILWAY SUBDIVISION ————————

Mile 129: Watrous* This town sprang up on the banks of Manitou Lake to house the thousands of visitors who came by rail to bathe in the lake's mineral-rich (and supposedly curative) waters. The buoyancy of these waters is greater than that of the Dead Sea.

Mile 189: Saskatchewan River A 457-metre bridge brings you into the 'City of Bridges', Saskatoon.

Mile 191: Saskatoon [25-minute stop] Saskatchewan's second city (with a population of 185,000) started out as a Temperance Colony in 1882. The Temperance Movement aimed to curb or eliminate the consumption of alcohol in pursuit of a better society. The growth of Saskatoon was slow

ROUTE GUIDES AND MAPS

Manitoba

Manitoba is in the very centre of Canada, and borders Ontario to the east and Saskatchewan to the west. It covers 650,000 sq km but is sparsely populated with about 1.2 million inhabitants – over half of them in its capital city, Winnipeg. Its northern regions are covered by the frozen tundra of the Hudson lowlands but the province's dominant geographic feature is the Canadian Shield, spreading over half the land. To the south is the flat, fertile wheat belt that provides Manitoba with most of its wealth.

This vast territory was originally part of Rupert's Land, owned by the Hudson's Bay Company who used the intricate system of lakes and rivers for their fur-trading activities. After this land was purchased by the first Canadian government, Manitoba became a separate province largely due to the efforts of the rebellious Louis Riel (see p39). When it was incorporated in 1870 it was known as the 'postage stamp province' because its area was so tiny, covering little more than a small rectangle around Winnipeg. It quickly grew, especially following the completion of the transcontinental railroad which allowed wheat to be exported and brought in thousands of settlers from eastern Canada and eastern Europe. Today it's one of the most ethnically diverse provinces of Canada, with thousands of Manitobans of Ukrainian, German, French, Italian, Dutch, Polish, Hungarian and Scandinavian origin.

until the Grand Trunk Pacific brought its northern transcontinental tracks here in 1906. Today it's a small but very prosperous prairie city, its economy revolving around oil and wheat.

For those spending time here, attractions include the **Ukrainian Museum of Canada**, the **Western Development Museum** and **Wanuskewin Heritage Park**. As for accommodation, you could try the *Patricia Hotel* (☎ 306-242-8861) at 345 2nd Ave – the rooms are pleasant and reasonably priced at around $80 a night. A taxi from the station to downtown will cost you around $15.

[MAP 12]

Mile 247: Biggar 'New York is big, but this is Biggar!' is this little town's slogan. It sprang up when the Grand Trunk Pacific decided to locate a railway divisional point here. As well as being a railway centre, Biggar is the tractor-manufacturing capital of Saskatchewan.

───────────────── **RAILWAY SUBDIVISION** ─────────────────

Travelling across this area in 1872, Butler was moved to write: 'No solitude can equal the loneliness of a night-shadowed prairie: one feels the stillness, and hears the silence, the wail of the prowling wolf makes the voice of solitude audible, the stars look down through infinite silence upon a silence almost as intense.' (*The Great Lone Land*).

Mile 57: Unity* The first attempt to mine potash in Canada took place in Unity. It wasn't an overly successful venture but the subsequent mining of salt was a huge success and continues today.

Mile 101: [MT] Saskatchewan/Alberta border As you move into Alberta you also move into the Mountain Time Zone.

Mile 140: Wainwright* This town was created by transplanting another settlement, Denwood, 4km from its original location. Everything was moved – houses, stores, the church – and the settlement was promptly rechristened Wainwright in honour of William Wainwright of the Grand Trunk Pacific.

A huge, brightly coloured grain elevator towers by the railway station (sadly no longer in view, thanks to VIA's new scheduling).

Mile 147: As you move out of Wainwright the relentless flatness of the land starts to give way to gently rolling plains. Look north for an impressive view over the mile-wide Battle River Valley. The river looks like a little stream as it snakes along, far below the train. You soon cross it on an 884-metre-long steel trestle.

Mile 184: Viking* This small town was settled at the beginning of the 20th century by Scandinavians, hence its name. Not far from the town are **The**

Saskatchewan

Saskatchewan is true prairie country – over two thirds of its land is part of the Great Plains, largely composed of fertile, arable soil. It's known as 'The bread basket of Canada' owing to its prodigious wheat production, which meets 60% of the nation's consumption and 12% of total world demand. Saskatchewan has also carved a niche for itself in the manufacturing and distribution of agricultural implements, which it exports around the world. To add to its economic feathers are a range of abundant mineral deposits including uranium, copper, gold and potash.

The region belonged to the Hudson's Bay Company for two centuries and was not settled by Europeans until the 1870s. Until then it had been largely the preserve of the Plains Indians (whose tribes included Cree, Assiniboine, Chipeweyan and Blackfoot) and vast herds of buffalo. After Confederation, the area was first administered by the government as part of the Northwest Territories (most of western Canada) and it wasn't until 1905 that Saskatchewan became a separate province, along with Alberta. Its name was derived from the Cree word for the Saskatchewan River, meaning 'Swiftly-flowing water'. Its capital is Regina and its population is now just over one million.

ROUTE GUIDES AND MAPS

Alberta
Alberta is one of Canada's most prosperous and attractive provinces, stretching across the rolling prairies in the east and centre to some of the most dramatic Rockies scenery at the province's western border. Jasper National Park, the biggest of the four Rocky Mountain parks, lies entirely within Alberta, and the most heavily visited parts of Banff National Park sit inside the province.

Alberta is just over one hundred years old, created in 1905 along with Saskatchewan. (These provinces are, incidentally, the only two in Canada not to have any salt-water coast.) It was named after Queen Victoria's fourth daughter, Princess Caroline Alberta, who was married to a former Governor-General of Canada. The two mainstays of Alberta's economy are wheat and oil, the latter bringing a great boom to the two main cities, Calgary and Edmonton, in the 1970s. These cities have been engaged in fierce rivalry for many years, and while Edmonton scored the coup of being made the province's capital, Calgary has managed to win hands down in most other areas. Alberta's population is 3.6 million and it is the fourth largest province in Canada.

Ribstones, two massive rock carvings created by the Plains Indians about one thousand years ago, depicting a buffalo backbone and ribs.

Mile 205(N): The train passes **Holden**. The town's onion-domed Ukrainian Church looms dramatically on the horizon.

Mile 240(S): Look out for moose and elk in North Cooking Lake.

Mile 260: Edmonton   [45-minute stop]
The train crosses the North Saskatchewan River on a 500-metre-long bridge taking you into Edmonton. Your approach to the city is heralded by the enormous oil refineries that have brought Edmonton its wealth. For Edmonton, see pp138–47.

───────────────── **RAILWAY SUBDIVISION** ─────────────────

EDMONTON TO JASPER   [MAP 13]
Mile 32(N): The train passes another ornate Russian Orthodox church. Strangely, these buildings are as much a part of the prairies as the grain elevators.

Mile 44(S): The train skirts the shores of Wabamun Lake for the next ten miles. Wabamun is the Cree word for 'mirror'.

Mile 45(N): The tranquillity of the scene is interrupted by the huge power stations on the lakeshore. These are coal-fired power generators; the biggest one is called the Sundance Power Plant.

'After breakfast we entered on a vast plain that stretched out on every side to the horizon. This had once been the favourite resort of the buffalo, and we passed in the course of the day more than a score of skulls that were bleaching on the prairie. All the other bones had of course been chopped and boiled by the Indian women for the oil in them.'   **Cumberland**, *The Queen's Highway* (1887)

(side tab) ROUTE GUIDES AND MAPS

Mile 67: The train crosses the Pembina River, once used as a water route to the Cariboo gold fields.

Mile 68: Evansburg* A small coal-mining village named after Harry Evans, a former mayor of Edmonton.

Mile 73–122: The train crosses five bridges over a series of rivers and creeks. The most impressive crossings are at Mile 121 (over Wolf Creek) and Mile 122 (over McLeod River); both bridges are 40m high.

Mile 130: Edson* This little lumbering town was established as a railway divisional point in 1910 by the Grand Trunk Pacific. It was named after Edson J Chamberlain, the company's vice-president.

Mile 136(N): Look down for an attractive view of Sundance Creek.

Mile 150: The terrain becomes increasingly hilly and you can feel the train begin to climb higher. To the south are sweeping views over the McLeod River valley.

Mile 165: At last – the Rocky Mountains! Look towards the front of the train for your first view of the distant snow-capped peaks. The excitement on board is palpable as all the passengers start 'oohing' and 'aahing' and pressing their faces to the windows.

Mile 184: Hinton* As you pull out of this busy town the views of the mountains suddenly become quite breathtaking.

Mile 190: The train passes a little village, charmingly named **Entrance**. It marks, of course, your official entrance into the Rocky Mountains.

Mile 192(N): The **Athabasca River** comes into view. On a sunny day its waters are a beautiful jade-green. The train follows its course from here to Jasper.

Mile 197: For the next eight miles the train skirts **Lac Brulé**, named after Etienne Brulé, the famous 17th-century explorer who was the first Frenchman to live among native Canadians.

Mile 200: By now the train is right in the middle of the mountains; they tower above you on both sides

MAP 13

North Cooking Lake

EDMONTON

Wabamun Lake

Evansburg

Wolf Creek

Edson

McLeod River

Athabasca River

Hinton

Entrance

Lac Brulé

Jasper Lake

JASPER

ROUTE GUIDES AND MAPS

> 'Looking west, I beheld the great range in unclouded glory... An immense plain stretched from my feet to the mountain – a plain so vast that every object of hill and wooded lake lay dwarfed into one continuous level, and at the back of this level, beyond the pines and the lakes and the river courses, rose the giant, solid, impassable, silent – a mighty barrier rising midst an immense land, standing sentinel over the plains and prairies of America, over the measureless solitudes of this great lone land. Here, at last, lay the Rocky Mountains.'
>
> **Butler**, *The Great Lone Land* (1872)

of the track. To the north is the Bosche Range and to the south the Miette Range.

Mile 206: Here you cross the boundary of **Jasper National Park**. It's staggeringly vast, covering over 10,880 sq km, with peaks as high as 3747 metres. It's the biggest of Canada's mountain national parks, and also one of the best for wildlife.

Mile 215: Now known as the **Devona Siding**, this was once the site of Jasper House, a supply post used by travellers crossing the mountains for the fur trade. It was built in 1817 by a merchant called Jasper Hawe whose name has proved a more enduring feature of the region than his store.

Mile 216(S): Jasper Lake This lake is less than one mile wide and is getting narrower and narrower because of the silt deposits carried here from the mountains by the Athabasca River.

Mile 225: Henry House Elk are a common sight along this stretch of the Athabasca Valley.

Mile 235: Jasper [75-minute stop]
For more information on Jasper see pp147–55. If you hadn't planned to stop over in Jasper, you might well change your mind during the next 75 minutes. If you've already been to Banff, you'll be amazed by the complete absence of taxi drivers, tour guides and general clamour at the train station of this quieter, calmer town.

──────────────── RAILWAY SUBDIVISION ────────────────

JASPER TO KAMLOOPS

[MAP 14, p213]
Mile 17 [PT]: You're now going through the **Yellowhead Pass** which provides a gap through the **continental divide**. The continental divide is the line following the main ranges of the Rocky Mountains; on one side of the line rivers flow west to the Pacific, on the other side they drain into the Arctic or the Atlantic. It is also the border between Alberta and British Columbia and is the point at which you move from Mountain Time into Pacific Time.

Mile 22(S): The shimmering **Yellowhead Lake** appears, framed by Mount Fitzwilliam and Mount Rockingham. It's one of the most beautiful views of the journey.

Mile 24(S): Here you get your first glimpse of the **Fraser River**. It was named after Simon Fraser who in 1808 was the first European to journey the 1368km to the river's mouth.

As you follow the course of the Fraser River, spare a thought for the millions of salmon who don't have such a smooth ride on their way to the Pacific and back again. The headwaters of the river's tributaries are the spawning ground of millions of Pacific salmon. Around March the newly-hatched fry begin their migration down the Fraser River to the Pacific Ocean. Only a quarter will make it. The survivors spend the next two and a half years swimming around the North Pacific where quite a few more will meet their end. Then the ones that are left begin their incredible journey back to the place of their birth, where they will spawn and die. They swim (upstream) at an average speed of 30km per day and literally leap over the obstacles in their path. This amazing cycle takes around four years.

Mile 36 (S): Moose Lake The pale green waters of this lake reflect the passing train and surrounding peaks. The lake is full of rainbow trout and is said to be a popular watering spot for moose.

The Travelling Reverend was much taken with the place in 1872 and wrote: 'Moose Lake that we struck last night but only got a tolerable view of today, is a beautiful sheet of water, ten or eleven miles long, by three wide...The survey for the Railway is proceeding along the north side, where the bluffs, though high appear not so sheer as on the south. The hillsides of the country beyond support a growth of splendid spruce, black pine and Douglas fir, some of the spruce the finest any of us had ever seen. So far in our descent from the Pass, the difficulties in the way of the railroad are not formidable nor the grades likely to be heavy. Still, the work that the surveyors are engaged on requires a patience, hardihood, and forethought that few who ride in Pullman cars on the road in after years will ever appreciate.'

Mile 50 (S): Look out for a glimpse of the roaring waterfall at Glacier Creek.

Mile 52–60(N): Good views of **Mount Robson**, the tallest peak in the Canadian Rockies at 3954m. The native name for this mountain is 'Yuh Hai Has Hun' or 'Mountain of Spiritual Road.'

Mile 66: The tracks veer south and the snow-capped mountains of the **Premier Range** come into view (W). The eleven peaks are named after Canadian and British prime ministers. The dominant peak is Mount Sir Wilfrid Laurier, covered by a huge glacier which also spreads onto Mount Mackenzie King and Mount Arthur Meighen.

Mile 73(S): The mountain you're passing is the **Terry Fox Memorial Mountain**, named in honour of the brave man who attempted to run across Canada to raise money and awareness for cancer research. Fox had already lost one leg to cancer when he set out on his 'Marathon of Hope' from St John's in April 1980; 5373km further on, in Thunder Bay, it was discovered that the cancer had spread to his lungs and he was forced to abandon the run. He died in June the following year, having raised $24 million.

ROUTE GUIDES AND MAPS

British Columbia
This is Canada's most westerly province and quite possibly its most beautiful. Just short of a million square km in area, British Columbia embraces gentle ranch land, towering peaks, arid desert land and lush rainforest. About 70% of the province is covered by mountains, with most of this area unpopulated. British Columbians, numbering 3.9 million, tend to live near the south-west coast, the majority of them concentrated in Vancouver. BC's population is the third highest in Canada after Ontario and Quebec. It is also the third largest province in surface area, after Quebec and Ontario. Only one American state, Alaska, is bigger than British Columbia.

The province is home to an incredibly diverse range of communities, from the great British enclave in Victoria to the young and cosmopolitan crowd of Vancouver; and from the lumberjacks and miners of the interior to the North-West coastal tribes. The latter, which include the Haida, Kwakiutl and Nootka, are among the most culturally distinct native groups in Canada. Their art is currently undergoing a big renaissance, particularly the carving of totem poles.

Mile 74: Valemount* This little lumber town (population 1000) nestles in a wide valley between the Rocky, Cariboo and Monashee mountain ranges, at an elevation of 1100 metres.

Mile 91: Look west for a stunning view of the **Albreda Icefields Glacier**, over 10,000 feet thick.

Mile 106: The train meets the North Thompson River and follows it for 26 miles to Blue River.

Mile 113 (S): The sparkling **Pyramid Falls** tumble 90 metres from a lake on Mount Cheadle, falling in tiers towards the railtrack, enveloped in clouds of diaphanous spray. It's quite a spectacle and a great photo opportunity.

Mile 132: Blue River* This former railway centre has developed into a thriving outdoor resort specializing in heli-skiing in the Monashee Mountains at the cost of some $500 a day.

——————————— RAILWAY SUBDIVISION ———————————

Mile 5: As you leave Blue River the landscape begins to change from one of mountains and lakes into a distinctly more rugged terrain.

Mile 8 (E): For the next eight miles the **North Thompson River** narrows into a stretch of turbulent, treacherous rapids known as **Little Hell's Gate** or Porte d'Enfer. The train skirts the river until it joins up with the Fraser River near Lytton, making numerous crossings from one bank to the other following the path forced by engineers down the canyon.

Mile 15–20: Looking onto the mountainside across the river (S) you can see the large swathes of forest devastated by the great forest fire of 1998.

ROUTE GUIDES AND MAPS

Mile 20–21: Note the slide detectors along the wall of the mountain. Rock slides are common in this spot.

Mile 42: To the west you can make out the **Mad River Rapids**.

Mile 67: Clearwater* This logging and farming town provides a base for visitors to Wells Gray Provincial Park, one of the most beautiful wilderness and recreational areas in British Columbia.

Mile 72(W): An osprey nest balances on a telegraph pole. These birds cause so much trouble with the telegraph lines that false lines are erected where they can build their nests without disrupting the telecommunications network.

Mile 74: Blackpool Named, apparently, because of the dark waters in this stretch of the river, and not after the great city of lights in the north of England.

Mile 86: Before the highway came, the village of **Little Fort** used to operate a cable ferry across the Thompson River, powered only by the river's waters. You can still see the cables if it's not too dark.

Mile 114: Fishermen used to stretch nets across the rapids here to catch salmon. They're known as Fishtrap Rapids.

Mile 139: Kamloops   [35-minute stop]
Kamloops is one of BC's biggest cities, with a population of 87,000. It's the province's most important cattle centre. It has also served as a busy centre of the fur trade, with trading bases established by the Pacific Fur Company in 1812 and the Hudson's Bay Company in 1821. The earliest inhabitants of the area were the Shuswap tribe who named their settlement 'Cume-loups', meaning 'Meeting of waters': the North Thompson and South Thompson rivers meet here.

KAMLOOPS TO VANCOUVER

The portion of the journey between Kamloops and Vancouver takes place mostly overnight on both westbound and eastbound VIA trains. For a detailed description of this route, see *The Rocky Mountaineer* route guide on pp231–4.

MAP 14

ROUTE GUIDES AND MAPS

'As we drew near Kamloops, characteristics of a different climate could be noted with increasing distinctness. A milder atmosphere, softer skies, easy rolling hills; but the total absence of underbrush and the dry grey grass everywhere covering the ground were the most striking differences to us, accustomed so long to the broad-leaved underbrush and dark green foliage of the humid upper country. We had clearly left the high rainy ground and entered the lower arid region.'

Rev Grant, *Ocean to Ocean* (1873)

The Skeena:
Jasper to Prince Rupert

The Skeena takes you through some of the most beautiful wilderness in British Columbia – through the Rocky Mountains, into BC's Interior Plateau and up the Skeena Valley to Prince Rupert. On the way you'll pass snow-capped peaks, glaciers, fjords, waterfalls and Indian villages with their famed totem poles. The service now operates as a two-day, daylight-only journey, with an overnight stop in Prince George. The travelling time from Jasper to Prince George is 7hr 30 minutes, and from Prince George to Prince Rupert 12hr 30 minutes.

[MAP 15, p216]

Mile 0–44: The train follows the same track as *The Canadian* between Jasper and Redpass Junction – see pp210–11.

Mile 44: Redpass Junction Here *The Skeena* parts company with the route followed by *The Canadian*.

As you head north-west, look out towards the rear of the train (E) for superb views of **Mount Robson**, the highest peak in the Rockies at 3954 metres (12,972ft). The views are particularly stunning around Mile 10. Look out for bears and moose; it was here that I made my only bear-sighting from any train.

Mile 14.5: The train passes Swiftwater, an old Grand Trunk Pacific stop so named for the racing waters of all the glacial streams nearby.

Mile 17: Here the train crosses the **Fraser River**. To the west are the 10-metre-high Rearguard Falls. In summer you might be able to spot spawning salmon trying to leap over the falls to continue their epic journey up the river.

Mile 20: Taverna This marks the end of an extremely short railway division.

──────────── RAILWAY SUBDIVISION ────────────

Mile 4: Tête Jaune This little hamlet is named after Pierre Hatsinaton, an early 19th-century trapper who was known by all as Tête Jaune because of his famed golden locks (also celebrated in the name of the Yellowhead Pass).

The village was a stop on the route of the famous **Overlanders**, the name now given to a group of about 150 people who, in 1862, set out from Ontario to make their way to the British Columbian gold fields. The trans-Canada railway had not, of course, been built then; the Overlanders had to take steamships and American railways to get to Fort Garry (Winnipeg). This marked the end of public transport; from here they continued their arduous journey using horses and carts. They set off from Fort Garry at the beginning of June and arrived in Fort Edmonton on 21 July. This is where the going got really tough; they had to trade in their carts for pack horses and hire Indian guides to show them the paths through the Rockies.

The travellers arrived at Tête Jaune in late August. From here some rafted up the Fraser River to Fort George (Prince George); of these only six survived. Others rafted down to Kamloops, including the only woman of the party, Mrs Catherine Shubert, who was pregnant at the time! The day following the party's arrival in Kamloops, Mrs Shubert gave birth to her fourth child.

Mile 63: McBride This village stands on a high plateau in the shadow of the Rocky Mountains. It's named after Richard McBride, British Columbia's youngest ever premier (he was 33 when he was elected in 1903).

While the Grand Trunk Pacific was being built, this railway divisional point was a busy and booming little town. These days there are only about 700 people

---

Place names

The names of many places or geographic features in Canada are taken from native languages, especially on the west coast. The translations of these are often highly evocative. Take, for example, Yoho ('Awesome'); Kitimat ('People of the snow'); Skeena ('River of mists'); Cowichan ('Mountain warming its back'); Squalix ('Restful'), Toketic ('Beautiful place'); Chaumox ('Too hot'); Shawnigan ('Great battle') and Nanaimo ('Big strong tribe') – all in British Columbia. Manitoba takes its name from the Ojibwan words 'manito waba' which, referring to the rapids of Lake Manitoba, means 'The sound of the great spirit Manitou.' Its capital, Winnipeg, is derived from the word *win-nipi*, meaning 'murky waters'.

Other interesting Indian place names include Nipigon (Ontario) meaning 'Clear, fast water'; Oakshela (Saskatchewan), meaning 'Child'; Sintaluta (Saskatchewan) which means 'Tail of the red fox'; Shubenacadie (Nova Scotia) meaning 'The place where potatoes grow'; Stewiacke (Nova Scotia) meaning 'Oozing from dead water' and Nappan (Nova Scotia) which means 'Good place for wigwam poles.'

There are also some interesting English and French names. In Quebec there's Rivière-du-Loup (after the wolves that once gathered around the water); Chaudière (describing the rapids as a 'Boiling kettle'); Pointe-aux-trembles (after a host of trembling trees) and Grandmère (after a rock in the river looking like a crouching old woman). English names range from the poetic (eg Moonlight in Ontario) to the bizarre, such as Eyebrow in Saskatoon and Joe Batt's Arm and Come by Chance in Newfoundland. Naturally, you don't get a country with as much water as Canada without a wide variety of place names dedicated to the stuff, including Swift Current, Clearwater, Floods, Wolf Creek, Moose Lake, Canoe River, Mud Bay, Seal Cove and Ocean Pond, to name but a few.

MAP 15

JASPER

ALBERTA

BRITISH COLUMBIA

Fraser River

Mt Robson

Redpass Jct

Harvey

Dunster

McBride

Goat River

Loos

Dome Creek

Bend

Penny

Longworth

McGregor

Upper Fraser

Aleza Lake

PRINCE GEORGE

ROUTE GUIDES AND MAPS

left – though the little town recently enjoyed a burst of fame when it took part in a TV show called Hockeyville, where towns across Canada competed to see which showed the most spirit and support for the home hockey team.

McBride is the last scheduled stop before Prince George. There are several flag stops dotted along the desolate stretch of track in between but few people get on or off.

────────── **RAILWAY SUBDIVISION** ──────────

Mile 69: Penny* This tiny hamlet, with a population of just over 30 people, is typical of the sparsely populated communities along this section of the line.

Mile 79: Longworth* Unlike Penny this settlement doesn't even have a station; just a little shack marking the stop.

Mile 122: Giscome* This is a village come down in the world; it once had the biggest sawmill in northern British Columbia but this was shut down in 1974.

Mile 146: Prince George   [overnight stop]
The train goes over a half-mile-long bridge across the Fraser River on approaching Prince George. The city, with a population of 67,000, is British Columbia's third-largest and is situated at the junction of the Nechako and Fraser rivers, just under 800km north of Vancouver. Simon Fraser established the Fort George fur-trading post here in 1807. The place really took off when the GTP made it an important railway divisional point. Today the main industries are logging and mining.

There's an obligatory overnight stop in Prince George when travelling on *The Skeena*. The train station is conveniently located downtown. Hotels not too far away include the fairly basic ***Downtown Motel*** (☎ 250-563-9241 or ☎ 1-800-663-5729), 650 Dominion St at 6th Ave, and the smarter and more expensive ***Ramada Hotel Downtown Prince George*** (☎ 250-563-0055 or ☎ 1-800-663-6620), at 444 George St. There should be plenty of **taxis** at the train station but if not order one on ☎ 250-564-4444.

────────── **RAILWAY SUBDIVISION** ──────────

[MAP 16]

Mile 69: Vanderhoof This little town is named after Herbert Vanderhoof who was hired by the GTP to devise a huge advertising campaign to persuade Americans to move up and settle in the Canadian North West. Apparently his efforts were very successful, though it's hard to believe it travelling through the region today.

Mile 93: This is where the last spike was driven on the Grand Trunk Pacific Railway on 7 April 1914.

Mile 94: Fort Fraser* Like Prince George, this was originally a fur-trading post established by Simon Fraser. Today it's a lumbering village of about 400 people.

Mile 115: Endako With a population of just 100, Endako is a tiny railway divisional point. Its economy revolves around the mining of molybdenum (a metallic element with a very high melting point that's used to strengthen iron and steel). This strange substance is Canada's third most valuable metal after copper and gold.

—————— **RAILWAY SUBDIVISION** ——————

Mile 33: The train skirts Burns Lake (W); note the little island in the middle of the lake. This has been known as **Deadman's Island** ever since an explosion on the track during the construction of the railway caused the death of thirty men, fifteen of whom were standing on this island.

Mile 35: Burns Lake Settlers established a town here in the 1870s when the Overland Telegraph line to Alaska and Siberia was being built (the line was never completed). When the GTP arrived it began to grow quite rapidly and is still flourishing today with four mines, including a molybdenum mine, and two large sawmills.

Mile 51(E): Rose Lake's waters flow in two different directions: east through the Endako and Nechako rivers and west to the Bulkley River. The train now follows the Bulkley westwards.

Mile 85: Houston Originally called Pleasant Valley, the settlement was renamed in 1910 after

John Houston who established Prince Rupert's first newspaper. About 4000 people live here today, most of them employed in the town's sawmill or pulp mill.

Mile 105: Look north as the train travels up the Bulkley Valley for your first view of the snow-capped **Skeena Mountains**.

Mile 116: Telkwa* Another small settlement established by the Overland Telegraph as it advanced towards Alaska.

Mile 125: Smithers

Nestling in the Bulkley Valley and surrounded by four mountain ranges, this busy little town (population about 5000) has an idyllic setting. The mountains behind the station are part of the Skeena Range, and opposite the station you can see the Hudson Bay Range.

──────────── **RAILWAY SUBDIVISION** ────────────

Mile 3(E): This lake used to be called Chicken Lake but this was deemed inappropriate by the GTP who changed it to the somewhat duller Lake Kathlyn.

Mile 5: For some time the train has been getting closer and closer to Hudson Bay Mountain (W); at this point you get a superb view of the Kathlyn Glacier on the mountain, a giant slab of ice more than a hundred metres thick.

Mile 13: The train now takes you through a long tunnel after which it starts to climb high above the Bulkley River.

Mile 28–36: Some wonderful, soaring trestle bridges ahead: one over Boulder Creek at Mile 28, then another over Porphyry Creek at Mile 31. Both bridges sweep round to the north giving excellent views along the train.

At Mile 36 you cross a further trestle over Mud Creek – with magnificent mountain views on all sides.

Mile 40: *The Skeena* goes through a 630-metre-long tunnel, the longest of the journey. It's followed by two more tunnels; as the train travels between them look down for a quick glimpse of the Bulkley Gate, a huge 'gate' of rock jutting out into the river.

Mile 45: New Hazleton There are three Hazletons in the area: South Hazleton, New Hazleton and Hazleton. They all have a rich collection of totem poles. It is just after New Hazleton that the train finally joins up with the Skeena River.

Mile 50: Here the train crosses the Sealy Gulch bridge. It's 275 metres long and soars sixty metres above the water.

Once over the bridge the train makes its way into the Skeena Valley. The scenery is breathtaking from here to Prince Rupert.

[MAP 17]

Mile 73: Kitwanga* The translation of Kitwanga is 'The people of the place of plenty of rabbits'. No doubt the GTP were unaware of this or they would surely have changed it to something more seemly. This interesting Indian village is famous for its row of enormous, beautifully-preserved **totem poles**, some as high as eighteen metres. These poles are not visible from the train, but if you look south just after passing the station you can see some other less ornate ones. If you're going to Vancouver be sure to visit the art gallery where you can see some excellent paintings by Emily Carr of the totem poles in this region.

Mile 75. As you leave Kitwanga the view to the south is dominated by the striking Seven Sisters mountain. The jagged peaks remain in view for the next 20 miles or so.

Mile 81: Cedarvale* Founded in the 1880s by a missionary who converted all of the resident natives and turned the village into a hive of Christianity.

Mile 101: Dorreen* Dorreen has no road access so the railway provides a vital link for the few people who live in this remote community. It was an important site during the Omenica gold rush and a few locals still pan the rivers for elusive specks of gold.

Mile 107: Pacific* A former railway divisional point, Pacific was emptied almost overnight when the division was transferred to Terrace. For a long while it was an abandoned and derelict ghost town but it has begun to be repopulated.

Mile 119: Usk* Look out for Usk's ferry which uses the force of the waters to power the boat back and forth across the Skeena River.

Mile 121–123: The riverbanks give way to the solid rock of the Kitselas Canyon which the train cuts through in four tunnels. Just before you enter the first tunnel, look down to the river to see a whirlpool at the canyon's mouth.

Mile 131: Terrace With a population of over 10,000, Terrace is the first community for a long while that can safely be called a town. It was known by local natives as Kitimat but was renamed Terrace by white settlers because of the flat terraces of land lining the banks of the river.

ROUTE GUIDES AND MAPS

--------------------------- RAILWAY SUBDIVISION ---------------------------

Mile 45: Travelling through the **Coast Mountains**, the train moves into what is probably the most stunning landscape of the journey. To the south the **Skeena River** is dotted with numerous little islands. Immediately north are the fern-covered mountainsides, just a few metres from the track. Waterfalls plunge down the rock of the mountains, the most abundant and beautiful occurring

MAP 17

between miles 46 and 50. Look out also for the bald eagles that are very common in this area: about six swooped and circled around our train for almost a mile around this point.

Mile 48: Kwinitsa* This very picturesque station is located in a dangerous avalanche spot – note the snowsheds on the side of the mountain.

Miles 65–70: The views across the river (S) are extremely beautiful. The vivid green islands seem to loom out of the swirling mists of the Skeena, an Indian word meaning 'River of mists'. The whole thing looks like a travel brochure for the Norwegian fjords.

Mile 83(S): Smith Island was the location of a remote settlement at the turn of the 20th century, which stands as an abandoned ghost town today.

Mile 87: The train goes over the Zanardi Rapids and on to Kaien Island. Prince Rupert is located a few miles away.

Mile 92: Just before you get to Prince Rupert you pass the ferry terminals (S) from where passengers depart on their journey up to Alaska on the Alaska Marine Highway or down to Vancouver Island with British Columbia Ferries.

Mile 94: Prince Rupert
You'll notice the drop in temperature as soon as you get off the train: Alaska is, after all, just 40 miles away. The town (population around 16,000) is surrounded by deep-green mountains which seem to rise right out of the sea. The two tallest peaks are over 600 metres. There's not much to do here but it's a beautiful place to do nothing in.

● **Prince Rupert – Where to stay** Accommodation isn't too hard to come by in Prince Rupert though many places fill up with ferry arrivals in high season so it's worth booking ahead.

An excellent choice is the ***Inn on the Harbour*** at 720 1st Ave (☎ 250-624-9107, 🖳 www.innontheharbour.com) with modest but comfortable rooms (some with sea views) at around $80 a double. Similarly priced and another dependable option is the ***Aleeda*** at 900 3rd Ave (☎ 250-627-1367, 🖳 www.aleedamotel.bc.ca).

For more luxury, try the ***Crest Hotel*** at 222 West 1st Ave (250-624-6771, 🖳 www.cresthotel.bc.ca), where doubles go from around $120. Alternatively, seek advice on accommodation in Prince Rupert from VIA (☎ 250-624-5637) or Tourism BC (☎ 250-624-5637).

● **What to see** Points of interest in town include the **Kwinitsa Station Railway Museum**, steps from the VIA train station down at the harbourside, and the **Museum of Northern British Columbia**, currently annexed to the **Info-centre** (☎ 250-624-5637) on the corner of 1st Ave and McBride but due to be relocated. Check at the Info-centre for this and any other tourist information.

● **Moving on from Prince Rupert** For those in a hurry, **Air Canada** (☎ 1-888-247-2262, 🖳 www.aircanada.ca) flies twice daily to Vancouver from $214.

By far the most appealing options, however, are the ferries that head south to Vancouver Island and north to Alaska. The ferry terminal is at Fairview Dock, 2km south of Prince Rupert, and most easily reached by taxi.

BC Ferries (☎ 250-386-3431, or 1-888-223-3779 toll-free, 💻 www.bcferries .com) have services to Port Hardy on the north tip of Vancouver Island leaving three or four times a week from June to mid-October and once a week during the rest of the year. It's a 15-hour journey through spectacular fjordland; tickets cost around $170 in summer and around $130 in winter. **Alaska Marine Highway Ferries** (☎ 250-627-1744 or ☎ 1-800-642-0066, 💻 www.dot.state .ak.us) to Skagway in Alaska run four to six times a week from May to mid-October and twice a week in winter (around $170, less in winter). The journey takes about 36 hours.

The Hudson Bay: Winnipeg to Churchill

What possesses people to travel one thousand miles by train through bleak, monotonous landscape to Canada's freezing subarctic? There's not much to see (lakes, trees and tundra) but there's something curiously exciting about travelling through such desolation, going somewhere you can't get to by car, reaching the ultimate end of the line. Once there, travellers will really feel like they've come to the edge of the world   and will be rewarded with some fantastic opportunities to view northern wildlife.

The railway, built at great expense over many years and completed in 1929, was intended to transport grain up to Hudson Bay where it would be shipped off to Russia. The bay, however, is frozen over for nine months of the year which somewhat restricts ocean-going activity.

The line runs at an enormous loss and is probably one of VIA's biggest headaches but closure would be highly controversial as the train is the only connection with the outside world for the many native communities along the line. Still, it's hard to know how long the service will survive, so take the opportunity to go on this wonderful dinosaur of a journey while you can.

For a guide to Churchill, see pp182–6.

[MAP 18, p222]

Mile 0: Winnipeg You set out around 10pm from Winnipeg's Union Station (see p129 for details).

Mile 55: Portage-la-Prairie At this point *The Hudson Bay* leaves the tracks used by *The Canadian* to begin its lonely trek north.

Mile 91: Gladstone Dubbed 'Happy Rock' by the train's crew, this little town was originally called Palestine when it was settled by Ontario farmers in the 1870s. Today it's famous in the region for its large cattle auction.

MAP 18

WINNIPEG

Portage-la-Prairie

Gladstone

Plumas

Glenella

McCreary

Laurier

Ochre River

Dauphin

Gilbert Plains

Grandview

Roblin

MANITOBA

Togo

SASKATCHEWAN

Kamsack

ROUTE GUIDES AND MAPS

Mile 121: Dauphin This prosperous distribution and transportation centre is one of the oldest Ukrainian settlements in Canada (they established an agricultural community here in the 1890s). The Ukrainian influence continues to be strong and Dauphin hosts Canada's annual National Ukrainian Festival which has been going since the 1960s. Dauphin lies in a fertile valley between Riding Mountain and Duck Lake provincial parks.

———————— **RAILWAY SUBDIVISION** ————————

Mile 62: Roblin Situated on the banks of Goose Lake near the Manitoba/Saskatchewan border, this small agricultural town was founded by the Canadian Northern Railway after the arrival of the first train from Dauphin in 1903. One of Manitoba's first co-operative grain elevators was built here by local farmers.

Mile 79: Togo* Just on the other side of the Manitoba/Saskatchewan border lies this little mixed farming village.

Mile 100: Kamsack Named after a prominent local Indian, this village (population about 2500) was on one of the fur-trading routes for many years.

[MAP 19]
Mile 108: Veregin This town was founded by the Doukhobors in 1899 and named after the movement's leader, Peter Vasilevish Veregin. The Doukhobors were Russians who dissented radically from the Orthodox Church, believing that God is found not in churches but within each man. They rejected secular governments, advocated pacifism and believed that the Bible should be communicated orally rather than through the written word.

Following periodic persecution in Russia the Doukhobors were permitted to emigrate to Canada in 1898–99, in some part thanks to the efforts of Leo Tolstoy and the Quakers. Over 7000 sailed over, most of these settling in western Canada which the government was doing its best to populate at the time.

Mile 124: Canora Take the first two letters of each word in 'Canadian Northern Railway' and what do you get? Thus the town was established and named by the aforementioned company in 1904 when they located a divisional point here.

—————————— RAILWAY SUBDIVISION ——————————

93: Hudson Bay You've still got a long way to go before you get to the bay itself; this town was named by the Canadian Northern Railway in 1908 to commemorate the first phase of the Hudson Bay Railway.

—————————— RAILWAY SUBDIVISION ——————————

Mile 88: The Pas   [45-minute stop]

The Pas lies on the south bank of the Saskatchewan River and has been, in its time, an Indian settlement, a fur-trading centre and a fishing and lumbering town. The town-site was bought in 1906 from the Cree inhabitants who now live on the northern banks of the river.

The Pas' **Anglican Church of the Messiah** dates from 1840. Some of the furniture inside was carved by members of a rescue party searching for **Sir John Franklin** and his fellow explorers who'd disappeared on their search for the North-West Passage. European explorers had been looking for a water route through North America to the Orient ever since it was discovered that this continent blocked the way to Asia. Franklin's expedition was hoping to discover a route through the Arctic when it went missing in 1845; what followed was one of the largest ever rescue operations of its kind. Franklin was never found, and efforts to solve the mystery continued well into the 20th century. The bodies of some crew members were discovered buried on Beechy Island, perfectly preserved by the permafrost. In 1986 these were temporarily exhumed and analysed by scientists: they discovered evidence of scurvy and probably cannibalism among the men.

An earlier famous explorer in search of the elusive North-West Passage was **Henry Hudson** who set out to find it back in 1610. He took his expedition into the huge bay and sailed down the eastern coast, where he was forced to winter his boat.

When the ice broke up Hudson set about continuing the exploration to the dismay of his crew. A mutiny broke out and the rebels packed Hudson, his

MAP 19

Veregin
Mikado
Canora
Sturgis
Endeavour
Reserve
Hudson Bay
SASKATCHEWAN
MANITOBA
The Pas
Tremaudan
Tremaudan Lake
Orok
Atikameg Lake
Finger
Clearwater Lake
Budd
Cormorant Lake
Cormorant
Rawebb
Dyce
Paterson
Wekusko

ROUTE GUIDES AND MAPS

son and other supporters into a boat and set them adrift on the bay to die. It is in honour of this unfortunate leader that Hudson Bay is named.

──────────────── **RAILWAY SUBDIVISION** ────────────────

Mile 9: This is where the lakes start. Current scheduling has northbound trains travelling through this stretch at night but if you're on a southbound train in summer it should still be light enough to see outside. The first one you pass is **Tremaudan Lake** (E). Next, at Mile 13 (W), is **Clearwater Lake**. Then at Mile 31 comes **Cormorant Lake** (W). This is an important nesting habitat for waterfowl; keep your eyes open (daylight permitting) for geese, teal and crow-ducks. You'll pass many more lakes along this stretch. If you're travelling in spring or summer, look out for the numerous wild flowers growing alongside the track: tiger lilies, brown-eyed Suzies, pink lady's slippers and honeysuckle are particularly abundant. The ground is punctuated by curious limestone rock formations.

Mile 29: The little village of Budd was named after Henry Budd, the first native in western Canada to be ordained as an Anglican Minister (in 1853).

Mile 37: The train passes two large osprey nests on the top of telegraph poles right by the side of the track (E).

Mile 41: Cormorant This was one of the first settlements to spring up along the line once the railway was completed. There'll probably be quite a few people getting on or off here, mainly Indian or Inuit families. Note that the word 'Eskimo' is not a polite way to refer to an Inuit – it means 'Eater of raw flesh' in the Algonquian language. 'Inuit', on the other hand, simply means 'People'.

Mile 55: Rawebb You'd be forgiven for thinking Rawebb was an Indian place name. The village was named after a former mayor of Winnipeg, Ralph Webb.

Mile 81: Wekusko This tiny settlement of around 50 people is located on one of the few roads in the region, a 35-mile link to the nearby town of Snow Lake.

[MAP 20]

Mile 90: The limestone rock gives way to *muskeg* (an Algonquian word meaning 'grassy bog'). Muskeg is organic terrain which produces peat deposits. Where there's muskeg there's often permafrost, which the train will be moving into presently.

Mile 136: Wabowden Situated between tiny Bowden and Rock Island lakes, Wabowden serves as a supply centre for the communities in northern Manitoba. Between here and Thicket Portage look out for pelicans and bald eagles.

Mile 177: Hockin This village was named in honour of Corporal CH Hockin of the North West Mounted Police who was killed in 1897 in a shoot-out with a Cree outlaw known as **Almighty Voice** (or **Kah-kee-say-mane-too-wayo**).

───

(Opposite) Top: The Columbia Icefields (see p154) make an interesting excursion from Jasper. (Photo © HG). **Bottom**: If you go to Churchill between October and May you can try out a sled ride (see p185). Each dog is capable of hauling up to 180lbs. (Photo © MG).

Almighty Voice had been imprisoned for stealing a cow and when he escaped from jail he killed a mountie in the process. Police hunted him for almost two years before cornering him with a couple of young relatives. The Indians were up against a hundred police and civilians but they put up a fierce fight, killing three men (including Hockin). In the end the fugitives were killed, and the incident has become a symbol of the tragically violent confrontation between the Indians and the whites in North America.

Back in 1872, Butler wrote: 'Terrible deeds have been wrought out in that western land; terrible heart-sickening deeds of cruelty and rapacious infamy – have been I say? No, are to this day and hour, and never perhaps more sickening than now in the full blaze of nineteenth century civilization. If on the long line of the American frontier, from the Gulf of Mexico to the British boundary, a single life is taken by an Indian, if even horse or ox be stolen from a settler, the fact is chronicled in scores of journals throughout the United States, but the reverse of the story we never know. The countless deeds of perfidious robbery, of ruthless murder done by white savages out in these Western wilds never find the light of day. The poor red man has no telegraph, no newspaper, no type, to tell his sufferings and his woes. My God, what a terrible tale could I not tell of these dark deeds done by the white savage against the far nobler red man!' (*The Great Lone Land*).

Mile 184: Thicket Portage Fur traders used this as a land crossing between the lakes and streams which connect Lake Winnipeg to the Nelson River (which goes up to Hudson Bay).

One of the crew told me that back in the '70s the mayor of Thicket Portage was given a large sum of money to have a road constructed in the area. Instead, he took off to Hawaii with his friends for a holiday. The locals were furious and practically lynched him on his return. For a while he was reduced to trapping and selling furs to earn his crusts but when it became clear that no one else was willing to do the job, he found himself reinstated as mayor!

(Opposite) Top: *The Canadian* approaching the Rockies (Photo © SJB). **Bottom**: Vancouver (pp165-81, photo © EK).

MAP 20

Turnbull
Ponton
Button
Dunlop
Pipun
Wabowden
Medard
Lyddal
Odhill
La Perouse
Hockin
Thicket Portage
Thompson
Sipiwesk
Pikwitonei
Bridgar
Wilde
Arnot
Mile 238.3
Boyd
Munk
Ilford
Nonsuch

ROUTE GUIDES AND MAPS

MAP 21

Wivenhoe
Luke
Gillam
Kettle Rapids
Bird
Amery
Charlebois
Weir River
Lawledge
Thibaudeau
Herchmer
Kellet
O'Day
Back
M'Clintock
Belcher
Cromarty
Chesnaye
Lamprey
Bylot
Digges
Tidal
CHURCHILL
Hudson Bay

ROUTE GUIDES AND MAPS

Mile 200: At Sipiwesk the train leaves the main line to follow a 30-mile branch to Thompson and back.

Mile 30: Thompson   **[one-hour stop]**
This busy industrial city of 15,000 people is something of a surprise after all the remote communities and stretches of wilderness you've been through. It was created from scratch following the discovery of abundant nickel deposits in 1956 and named after John F Thompson, the chairman of INCO.

Unfortunately the railway station is a few miles from the city so there's very little to do here in the one-hour stop unless you're prepared to take a taxi into town and back. The attractions aren't, however, worth the risk of being left behind by the train.

Mile 200: Here you are back in **Sipiwesk** – a depressing lack of advancement.

Mile 213: Pikwitonei This name is taken from the Cree word meaning 'Broken mouth' though no one seems to be sure why. Perhaps another bust-up between mounties and natives?

Mile 230: Wilde This place name definitely does come from another Indian-NWMP confrontation, this time in 1886. Sergeant WB Wilde was killed in the incident and the village name commemorates him.

Mile 238.3: This flag stop is known simply by its mileage.

Mile 269: Munk Named after Jens Munk, the first European to discover what is now Churchill. The Danish navigator arrived in September 1619 with two ships and forty-eight men. They were forced to spend winter there and suffered an outbreak of scurvy. Only three men survived; Munk was one of them.

Mile 295: Nonsuch This village is named after the famous ship owned by the Hudson's Bay Company.

[MAP 21]
Mile 326: Gillam With a population of nearly 2000, this is the biggest community since Thompson. The town's economy is based on its three hydroelectric power stations on the Nelson River.

Mile 350: Around here the train leaves the Laurentian Plateau and moves into the Hudson Bay lowlands. From here onwards the muskeg is permanently frozen, a condition known as permafrost. The frost extends about 12 metres down, making engineering work extremely difficult. The telegraph wires have to be supported by three poles forming a tripod. Night will be falling as you advance through this increasingly desolate landscape.

Mile 440–80: When morning breaks you'll probably be travelling through the Barren Lands. Pull up your blinds and prepare to be dazzled by snow (for most of the year, anyway). The trees have nearly all vanished and the ones that are left are stunted and shrivelled. You've gone beyond the tree line into the sub-arctic tundra. Look out for Arctic ptarmigan and silver fox.

Mile 509: Churchill At long, long last!

The Rocky Mountaineer

The privately owned Rocky Mountaineer runs along four different routes:

- 'First Passage to the West' from Vancouver to Banff/Calgary
- 'Journey Through the Clouds' from Vancouver to Jasper
- 'Rainforest to Goldrush' from Whistler to Jasper
- 'Whistler from Sea to Sky Climb' from Vancouver to Whistler

First Passage to the West (Vancouver-Banff/Calgary)
This is a two-day daylight-only journey with overnight accommodation in a hotel included in the package. Trains from Vancouver to Banff/Calgary and Jasper follow the same track from Vancouver to Kamloops, in the Rockies, where passengers spend the night. After Kamloops, travellers take the original, southern route on CPR tracks. This is the only passenger train to travel along part of Canada's first transcontinental line, completed in 1885. In this book the journey is described in a westbound direction, in common with all the VIA Rail routes described in this guide.

'Journey Through the Clouds' (Vancouver-Jasper)
As with the above, this is a two-day journey with overnight accommodation in a hotel in Kamloops included in the package. Jasper-bound trains take the northern route through the Rockies via the Yellowhead Pass (along the same track as The Canadian). Once again, this book describes the journey in a westbound direction.

'Rainforest to Goldrush' (Whistler to Jasper)
Yet another two-day journey with overnight accommodation included, the Whistler–Jasper route follows the old Pacific Great Eastern (which later became BC Rail) tracks along what was called the 'Cariboo Dayliner' line to Prince George, where it joins the tracks used by The Skeena between Prince George and Jasper. In this guide the route is described in a northbound direction (ultimately heading east) following the direction of construction and the mile markers.

Whistler from Sea to Sky Climb' (Vancouver to Whistler)

Much shorter than the others, this is a three-hour trip – so no local accommodation is required. As with the Rainforest to Goldrush (p227), the route is described in a northbound direction (ultimately heading east).

CALGARY/BANFF TO VANCOUVER – 'FIRST PASSAGE TO THE WEST'

Calgary/Banff to Kamloops

[Map 22]

Mile 0: Calgary (MT) For more information on Calgary see pp155–64. Home of cowboys, stampedes and oil-wells, Calgary is Canada's most famous prairie city. It's also the city closest to the Rocky Mountains that has an international airport, with plenty of scheduled and charter flights arriving from all over the world.

Mile 16(S): Look to the front of the train for your first glimpse of the Rocky Mountains, which are about 70km away.

Mile 24: Cochrane Just beyond the station is the Cochrane Landmark, a bronze statue of a cowboy riding his horse.

Mile 45: The peaks loom closer and closer as the train advances towards the mountains. To the north you can see Saddle Peak and Orient Peak and to the south you can see Heart Mountain.

Mile 54: Kananaskis The name of this village is Indian for 'Man with a tomahawk in his head' and is named after a local native who survived this experience.

Mile 66(S): The Three Sisters Mountain was given this name by the brother of Major AB Rogers, the explorer who discovered Rogers Pass, because he thought its peaks looked like three nuns.

Mile 71: Banff National Park At this point the train crosses the eastern boundary of Banff National Park. It was originally known as the Rocky Mountain National Park when it was founded in 1887 (when there were just two other national parks in the world).

It was when the railway was being constructed that Banff's famous hot springs were discovered, prompting immediate claims to the land by men hoping to reap a profit. The Canadian Government decided that the area must be protected from commercial development and established the park. Today it encompasses 6640 sq km and is Canada's most heavily visited national park, attracting almost three million visitors each year.

ROUTE GUIDES AND MAPS

Mile 73(S): For the next eight miles the train skirts the towering **Mount Rundle**.

Mile 81: Banff The station was originally known as 'Siding 29' by the railway men building the line; it was renamed in 1880 by Donald Smith of the CPR.

Today the town (population 4600) is a busy (and some would say over-crowded) base for thousands of tourists, providing them with an impressive quantity of hotels, restaurants and shops.

Its most famous hotel is the exclusive *Banff Springs Hotel*, formally opened by William Cornelius Van Horne for the CPR back in 1888. You can see the green turrets of its copper roof as you pass it on the train at Mile 82 (S).

Mile 99(N): There are excellent views of **Castle Mountain**, with its broad, flat top, from here. The mountain was originally named in the 1850s by the explorer, James Hector, but it was officially changed to Mount Eisenhower in 1946. This change of name was strongly resisted by local people who lobbied to have it changed back. In 1979 the government duly restored the mountain's original name, allotting Eisenhower Peak to its highest point.

Mile 116(S): Watch out for a quick flash of **Victoria Glacier**. You can't see much of it from the train but fear not: you will see its image rising over Lake Louise thousands of times on thousands of postcards, calendars and tea towels before you get out of Canada.

Mile 116.5(S): Lake Louise Station This is no longer used by the railways; the beautifully preserved log building now serves as a restaurant.

Mile 122: Stephen [PT] At 1625 metres above sea level, this is the highest point on the CPR line. It's also the point at which the train crosses the Continental Divide.

Mile 128: Spiral Tunnels Here the train goes through the extraordinary Spiral Tunnels. When the CPR decided to build the track through the Kicking Horse Pass they hadn't quite reckoned on the steepness of the drop on the western side of Mount Stephen. There was no time or money for building tunnels, so the track plunged straight down for eight miles at a dizzying 4.5% gradient – more than twice the grade normally permitted by the government.

This hazardous stretch of track was known as the **Big Hill**. Trains made it to the top only with the help of four specially designed locomotives with 154-tonne engines; two pulled at the front, and another two pushed from behind. Most dangerous, though, was the trip down the hill. All passenger trains stopped at the top so that the brakes could be thoroughly checked before the heart-stopping descent began. Safety switches were operated to divert runaway trains onto uphill tracks. Nonetheless, many lives were lost as a result of trains getting out of control.

The danger was finally eliminated when the **Spiral Tunnels** were built in 1909, reducing the gradient to 2.2%. This was achieved by curving the track 250 degrees through the Upper Spiral, and then 230 degrees through the Lower Spiral. The train loops around in a sort of figure of eight, in such a way that the rear of the train crosses over the front of the train, several feet below.

ROUTE GUIDES AND MAPS

Mile 136: Field Once a busy railway divisional point, Field's economy now revolves around the tourism industry in Yoho National Park.

———————————— **RAILWAY SUBDIVISION** ————————————

Mile 20: The train, following the course of the **Kicking Horse River**, enters the Kicking Horse Canyon. The river takes its name from an incident in which Dr James Hector, a member of the Palliser expedition commissioned to explore western Canada in 1857–60, was thrown off his horse when he rode it into the river's rushing waters. Hector was badly injured by a kick from the frightened horse but he continued with the expedition.

Mile 35: The Kicking Horse River meets the Columbia River. To the south you can see the Beaverfoot Range and to the north the Van Horne Range.

Mile 62: Beavermouth This was the location of the riots by a group of striking railwaymen, desperate for their long-overdue wages in the middle of the CPR's financial crisis of 1884. It's reputed to be a good place for sighting bears.

[Map 23]

Mile 70: Photo opportunities abound as the train crosses a series of high bridges. First is the 183-metre-long **Mountain Creek Bridge**. Then, at Mile 74, is a bridge over **Surprise Creek**, over 50 metres below. Finally you reach the climax, the crossing of the highest bridge on the CPR line: **Stoney Creek Bridge** at Mile 76. It's 147 metres long and curves 99 metres over the water. For the next twenty miles you'll be surrounded by breathtaking mountain vistas as you travel through the heart of the Selkirks.

Mile 80: The train enters the five-mile-long **Connaught Tunnel**, built to avoid the dangerous avalanches that plagued the route over Rogers Pass. It was completed in 1916 and until 1988 was the longest tunnel in North America. This record is now held by the **Mount McDonald Tunnel**, nine miles long and built underneath the Connaught Tunnel. It is used by westbound freight trains.

Mile 94: Note the concrete snowsheds above the train (N); there are frequent avalanches in this area.

Mile 125: Revelstoke This small city of around 8000 people was named after Lord Revelstoke, an English banker who helped bail the CPR out of their financial difficulties in 1884.

———————————— **RAILWAY SUBDIVISION** ————————————

MAP 23

Mile 5: The train is now on its way up the last big climb, this time up the Monashee Mountains which it will cross via Eagle Pass. There are waterfalls at this point on both sides of the train.

Mile 28: Craigellachie No fanfare marked the occasion when, on 7 November 1885, Donald Smith drove in the last spike of the CPR trans-Canada railway here in **Eagle Pass**. The only monument to that triumphant completion is a plaque on a cairn by the side of the track (N).

Mile 44: For the next 25 miles the train skirts the Salmon Arm of **Shuswap Lake**, which boasts prodigious quantities of Dolly Varden and kokanee salmon. Note the colourful houseboats moored in the lake.

Mile 82: Look south for a glorious view over Shuswap Lake.

Mile 100: At this point the train starts to move away from the forested mountains into a landscape of gently rolling hills.

Mile 103(N): Look out for the **hoodoos** standing on the hillside. These fantastic pillars of rock have been eroded into strange shapes by wind, rain and running water.

Mile 111(S): If you're wondering what's growing in these fields it is, in fact, ginseng. Once grown only in Korea and Manchuria, this plant is now thriving in British Columbia.

Mile 114: This is the site of Bill Miner's least successful train robbery. Miner, known as the Gentleman Bandit, was a famous Canadian train robber in the early 20th century. In 1904 he had robbed a CPR train near Mission (BC) of $7000 but when he tried to pull off the same stunt at this spot two years later he got the wrong train and ended up with only $15 and a bottle of pills.

The robber, getting on for 60 by now, was obviously losing his touch: he was captured by police and sent to jail for 25 years. He did, however, manage to escape a year later taking off to the US where he spent the rest of his days robbing more trains.

Mile 128: Kamloops This is where you get off *The Rocky Mountaineer* for your overnight stay at a nearby hotel. A brief description of Kamloops is on p213.

———————————— **RAILWAY SUBDIVISION** ————————————

Kamloops to Vancouver [Map 24, p232]
Mile 1: The train follows the South Thompson River (S) as far as Lytton, 97 miles away. The track is carved into the rocky cliffs of the Thompson Canyon and switches back and forth across the river.

The colours of the canyon walls are muted reds and browns and the desert-like landscape contrasts sharply with the lush mountains you passed on your previous day's journey.

Mile 49: Ashcroft* This is one of Canada's driest towns, with an average annual rainfall of just 18cm.

MAP 24

KAMLOOPS

Ashcroft — Kamloops Lake

Thompson River

Lytton

Fraser River — Boston Bar

Hope

Chilliwack

Port Coquitlam — Matsqui

VANCOUVER

Rev Grant was not charmed by the place when he was here in 1872 and wrote: 'The country about Ashcroft is sparsely peopled, and men accustomed to the rich grassy plains on the other side of the mountains might wonder at first sight that it is peopled at all. In appearance, it is little better than a vast sand and gravel pit, bounded by broken hills, bald and arid except on a few summits that support a scanty growth of scrub pines. The cattle had eaten off all the bunch-grass within three or four miles of the road, and a poor substitute for it chiefly in the shape of a bluish weed or shrub, called 'sage grass' or 'sage brush' has taken its place.'

Mile 85–90: The canyon narrows into what is known as **Jaws of Death Gorge**. Look down to the racing waters of **Suicide Rapids** at Mile 87.

Mile 90–95: Rainbow Canyon The walls of the cliffs are suddenly striped with pinks, greens and greys creating a beautiful rainbow effect.

Mile 97: Lytton This is where the Thompson River meets the Fraser River, which the train follows nearly all the way to Vancouver through the **Fraser Canyon**. It is said that you can sometimes see a clear line dividing the Thompson's clear waters from the Fraser's murky waters for some distance after they meet.

In *The Queen's Highway* Cumberland described the impressive scene in 1887: 'Six miles below Lytton a gulch, deeper and broader than any of the preceding ones, presents itself. To cross it by an ordinary bridge would be impossible, and a cantilever bridge, 96 feet above low-water mark, has been constructed at a great cost for the purpose.

'As one crosses the bridge a magnificent scene presents itself in thus being suspended over the surging, maddening river, increased in force by the waters of the North Thompson River, and with a full view of the gloomy canyon through which we have passed.'

Mile 103: The train crosses the Fraser River on one of the **Cisco Bridges**, a spectacular crossing high above the river's turbulent waters. There are two bridges side by side – one built by the CPR in the 1880s, the other by the CNR about thirty years later. As you cross the CNR bridge, look behind for a view of the beautiful cantilever CPR bridge.

Totem Poles

Everyone knows what a totem pole is but not everyone knows that they are made almost exclusively in North-West British Columbia by Indian tribes. Contrary to popular belief these carved cedar logs are not used for religious worship. Their functions are as diverse as marking a grave, supporting a roof, celebrating a house-moving or ridiculing a local individual, whose likeness is painted upside down.

The tallest, brightest and most elaborately carved totem poles tell of family histories or legends using a complicated series of symbols, often in the form of animals or spirits. Each family has its own symbols, so interpretation of the story on a totem pole usually requires a narrator from the family that constructed it. Unfortunately the poles have a relatively short life span since the moisture of the climate rots the wood.

Mile 125: Boston Bar* This village was established by fortune-seekers of the Fraser River gold rush of 1858.

———————————————— RAILWAY SUBDIVISION ————————————————

Mile 7: Don't miss the dramatic **Hell's Gate** where the river is forced to squeeze through the narrowest point of the gorge at high speed.

The narrowing was caused by a huge landslide triggered off by an explosion during the construction of the CN line. The landslide, blocking the sockeye salmon run that annually ascends the river, had a catastrophic effect on the fishing industry; fishways have since been constructed in an attempt to remedy the problem.

Mile 27: Keep an eye out for Lady Franklin Rock lying in the Fraser River, named after English explorer Sir John Franklin's wife who came searching for him after he disappeared in 1845 (see p223).

Mile 40: Hope* A fur-trading post was established here in 1848 but it was from the 1858 gold rush that the town grew affluent. At Hope the rugged rocks of the Fraser Canyon recede into the fertile Fraser Valley, surrounded by verdant mountains.

Mile 71: Chilliwack* This is a busy agriculture-based city of around 42,000 people. Its name is thought to mean 'Going back up' (probably from the river) in a local native language.

Mile 87: Matsqui* This stop is close to the town of **Mission**, originally settled in 1862 by a Roman Catholic priest who aimed to convert the Indians. It was also the site of Canada's first train robbery.

Mile 111: Port Coquitlam The train passes an enormous CP railyard here (N); it covers 468 acres and can hold 3700 rail cars.

Mile 131: Vancouver The journey ends in Canada's third-largest and fastest growing city. For more information on Vancouver, see pp165–81.

JASPER TO VANCOUVER – 'JOURNEY THROUGH THE CLOUDS'

The route from Jasper to Vancouver is not described here as it is covered elsewhere: you will find a description of the section from **Jasper to Kamloops** in the guide to *The Canadian* on pp210–13, while the section from **Kamloops to Vancouver** is described in the guide to the 'First passage to the West' route (pp231–4).

WHISTLER TO JASPER – 'RAINFOREST TO GOLDRUSH'

[Map 25]

Mile 73.7: Whistler (MT) The old 'Cariboo Dayliner' route (operated by Pacific Great Eastern/BC Rail) actually began in North Vancouver, not Whistler – and that's why Whistler is Mile 73.7 and not mile 0. Today, the first portion of the 'Cariboo Dayliner' route is covered by the 'Whistler from Sea to Sky Climb'; see p236–7 for a description.

When the line was constructed in the early twentieth century, Whistler – in the heart of the Coast Mountains – was a little mountain hideaway visited by in-the-know locals; these days it's one of the largest and most famous ski resorts in North America and hosted the Winter Olympics with Vancouver in 2010. The resort also offers plenty of summer activities too, such as whitewater rafting, mountain biking and golf.

Heading out of Whistler, the train follows the **Green River** down into the lush Pemberton Valley, home to Douglas fir, hemlock and cedar.

Mile 80: Look out for the glacier-fed **Green Lake** (W), with its vivid jade-green water.

Mile 87: The valley narrows to a slender canyon; Green River's waters hurtle down the dramatic **Nairn Falls** at Mile 91 (E).

Mile 95: Pemberton An agricultural town famous for its enormous potatoes and turnips.

Mile 99.4: Mt Currie The Mount Currie Reservation is BC's largest native reserve, home to the Lillooet people.

ROUTE GUIDES AND MAPS

Mile 100: The train climbs up towards the town of **Birken**, alongside the salmon-rich Birkenhead River.

Mile 113: Shortly after passing **Birkengates Lake** (E), the train begins its descent into the dry side of the Coast Mountains, characterized by its desert-like landscape. The brown sagebrush and tumbleweed form a striking contrast with the lush temperate rainforests on the coastal side of the mountains

Mile 123.8: Keep your camera at the ready for the beautiful **Anderson Lake** (E), which the track skirts for 15 miles.

Mile 141: The train follows the banks of another picturesque lake, the moss-green **Seton Lake** (W), flanked by vertical cliffs looming over the tracks.

Mile 157.5: Lillooet In the 1850s and 60s, Lillooet sprang up as a base for prospectors who headed first for the gold-rich sand bars of the Fraser River, and then for British Columbia's Cariboo region when gold strikes in 1862 precipitated the **Cariboo gold rush**. The town's boom-and-bust years led to a lot of fortunes being made and lost overnight. Just outside town, the macabre 'hanging tree' was the site of desperate suicides, as testified by several nearby graves.

———————————— **RAILWAY SUBDIVISION** ————————————

Mile 160–192: Leaving Lillooet behind, the train crosses the 242m/800ft-long Fraser River Bridge onto the east side of the Fraser River and climbs steeply up the Fraser Canyon – by Mile 180 you are vertiginously high above the river, on one of the most dramatic stretches of rail track in the Rockies.

Mile 192.2: Kelly Lake Overlooked by the beautiful Marble Mountains, this lake (W) makes a striking sight.

Mile 203: Clinton Once a major stagecoach stop on the Cariboo Trail from Lillooet (a wagon road built by prospectors during the gold-rush days), Clinton marks the beginning of the **Cariboo Plateau** – a flat, wide-open area between two mountain ranges, home to many ranches. The most common tree found on the plateau is the trembling aspen, whose leaves turn a dazzling golden colour in autumn.

Mile 206: A long trestle bridge takes you over the Fiftyone Creek canyon.

Mile 215.2: As you cross the Sixtyone Creek Bridge, look east for a brief glimpse of the ten-thousand-year-old **Painted Chasm**: a deep channel cut through the rock by the meltwater from receding glaciers. The walls of the Chasm are streaked by many vivid colours thanks to the rich minerals of the rock.

Mile 236.3: The **Flying U Ranch** is Canada's oldest working guest ranch. Look east and you might spot a few ranch-hands riding their horses along the trail that runs parallel to the train track.

Mile 273.4: The train skirts the shore of **Lac La Hache** (E), whose exceptionally transparent waters are packed with trout. The wetlands around the lake also provide a home to many birds, including the loon, which appears on the $1

coin. Loons, incidentally, are said to be reliable predictors of storms – when one is on its way, a loon will often become very agitated, flap wildly above the lake and fly into the wind.

[Map 26]

Mile 302.9: This tiny stop originally served the Cariboo Indian School, established by missionaries in the 19th century.

Mile 313.9: Williams Lake A busy livestock centre, Williams Lake is famous for its annual stampede held here every July.

──────────── RAILWAY SUBDIVISION ────────────

Mile 330: Snaking its way up the Fraser Canyon, the train crosses the dramatic **Deep Creek Bridge**, the second-highest railway bridge in North America at 94.5m/312ft above the water.

Mile 384: Quesnal This is where you get off the train for your **overnight stop** in a nearby hotel. The largest town in the Cariboo region, Quesnal (pronounced 'Kwa-Nell') is a big sawmill and pulp-mill centre. It was the 'temporary' terminus of the rail line for 30 years, due to the difficulty of getting the track over the Cottonwood River.

Mile 398: Fourteen miles north of Quesnal, the **Cottonwood River** held up the completion of the rail line for three decades, owing to the difficulties of building a bridge on the unstable river banks. The bridge you cross was finally built in 1952 at a cost of $1 million.

Mile 462.4: Prince George When the track from Quesnal to Prince George was completed on 31 October 1952 (forty years behind schedule), celebrations were held throughout the city. For a brief description of the town today, see p216.

On to Jasper: From Prince George, *The Rocky Mountaineer* continues east to Jasper along the tracks used by VIA Rail's *The Skeena*: you will find a route guide for this portion of the journey on p214-6.

VANCOUVER TO WHISTLER – 'WHISTLER FROM SEA TO SKY CLIMB'

The 'Whistler from Sea to Sky Climb' follows the first portion of the old Pacific Great Eastern (later BC Rail) 'Cariboo Dayliner' route from Vancouver to Prince George, started in 1912 and not completed until 1956. The three-hour journey to Whistler covers 73 miles of glorious scenery, including the stunning Howe Sound.

ROUTE GUIDES AND MAPS

[MAP 27]

Mile 1: As you pull away from the North Vancouver terminus, look out for the totem poles in Stanley Park (see p177) to the south. You can also admire the fantastic waterfront houses of West Vancouver.

Mile 11: The train goes through the 1700-foot-long **Horseshoe Bay Tunnel**, deemed so long that a special rule was created for it: 'Train crews are limited to a maximum of 45 minutes in the tunnel. If this time is exceeded, self-containing breathing apparatus must be used. All windows are to be kept closed and crewmen walking in the tunnel should go in pairs (buddy system).'

Mile 14–39: For 25 miles, the train hugs the shore of **Howe Sound**, a stunning fjord studded with islands. It's a fabulous stretch of track: on one side (E) the Coast Mountains rise steeply above you; on the other, the views across the fjord to the mountains are breathtaking.

Mile 36.1: Look east for a good view of the **Shannon Falls**, the third-highest in BC at 335m/1100ft.

Mile 40.4: Squamish The train passes through the rail yards of the West Coast Railway Heritage Park, home to the famous *Royal Hudson* **steam train** which for many years travelled between Vancouver and Squamish during the summer season – until BC Rail (who operated it) was sold to CN Rail in 2003, with all passenger services discontinued.

Mile 40–75: The train begins its climb over the Coast Mountains, gaining almost 610m/2000ft. At Mile 47, look west as you cross the Cheekye River for stunning views onto the snow-capped **Tantalus mountain range**, which takes its name from the Greek myth of Tantalus, tortured by Hades and plunged into ice cold water with fruit dangled just out of his reach (giving rise to the word 'tantalize'). Far below, you can make out the whitewater rapids pounding through the canyon.

Mile 53: There are dizzying views for the next three miles as the track clings to a vertiginous ledge carved out of the side of the sheer **Cheekamus Canyon**.

Mile 65.3: Brandywine Falls (E) This is the only bit of rail track in Canada to cross over the top of a waterfall – look down for great views onto the thundering water.

Mile 73.7: Whistler The journey ends at the first-class ski resort (and year-round holiday resort) of Whistler. For comprehensive details on accommodation, things to do and other information, check Tourism Whistler's own website at 🖳 www .tourismwhistler.com.

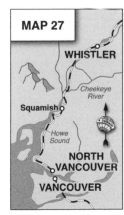

MAP 27

WHISTLER

Cheekeye River

Squamish

Howe Sound

NORTH VANCOUVER

VANCOUVER

APPENDIX A: TIMETABLES

The timetables given below are the latest available but are, of course, subject to change. Check with VIA and the Rocky Mountaineer. VIA's website (💻 www.viarail.ca) has downloadable timetables in pdf format. Note also that although VIA give distances in kilometres, the CN subdivisions are still marked by mileposts at the side of the track.

OCEAN: HALIFAX–MONTREAL

Station name	Km from Halifax	Westbound Day 1 Ex Tue	Eastbound
Halifax	0	12.30	16.35
Truro	103	14.01	15.05
Springhill Jct*	200	15.17	13.40
Amherst	227	15.42	13.18
Sackville	243	16.59	13.02
Moncton	304	Ar 16.52	Dp 12.13
		Dp 17.07	Ar 11.58
Rogersville*	397	18.18	10.51
Miramichi	433	18.57	10.13
Bathurst	504	20.06	09.09
Petit Rocher*	521	20.25	08.43
Jacquet River*	549	20.48	08.19
Charlo*	574	21.09	07.58
Campbellton	605	21.56 (AT)	07.22 (AT)
Matapédia	624	21.48 (ET)	05.38 (ET)
Causapscal*	681	22.38	04.09
Amqui	703	23.00	03.48
Sayabec*	727	23.22	03.25
Mont-Joli	774	00.11	02.40
		Day 2	
Rimouski	803	00.46	02.02
Trois-Pistoles	864	02.01	00.48
Rivière-du-Loup	907	02.54	00.06
			Day 2
La Pocatière	975	03.37	23.20
Montmagny*	1035	04.09	22.46
Charny	1099	Ar 04.57	Dp 21.54
		Dp 05.12	Ar 21.39
Drummondville	1246	06.57	20.10
Saint-Hyacinthe	1292	07.31	19.28
Saint-Lambert	1339	08.06	18.55
Montreal	1346	08.29	18.30
			Day 1 Ex Tue

* Flag stop. The train will stop here only when someone wants to get on or off.
AT = Atlantic Time, ET = Eastern Time

CORRIDOR: MONTREAL–TORONTO (WESTBOUND)

Station name	Km	No 53 Ex Sun	No 57 Daily	No 61 Ex Sat	No 65 Daily	No 67 Ex Sat	No 69 Daily
Montreal	0	06.30	09.40	11.35	15.40	17.00	18.05
Dorval	19	06.55	10.06	11.59	16.04	17.25	18.30
Cornwall	111	07.44	10.59	12.49	16.54		19.22
Brockville	204		11.47				20.08
Gananoque	249						
Kingston	285	Ar 09.04	12.30	14.10	18.15		20.50
		Dp 09.07	12.34	14.14	18.19		20.53
Belleville	357		13.18				21.34
Cobourg	426		13.58				22.13
Oshawa	488	10.47	14.36		20.00	21.07	22.49
Guildwood	518		14.55	16.08			23.07
Toronto	539	11.17	15.13	16.24	20.29	21.34	23.23

CORRIDOR: TORONTO–MONTREAL (EASTBOUND)

Station name	Km	No 52 Ex Sun	No 56 Ex Sat	No 60 Daily	No 64 Daily	No 66 Ex Sat	No 68* Ex S/S*
Toronto	0	07.05	09.30	11.35	15.15	17.00	18.35
Guildwood	21	07.25	09.48	11.56			18.54
Oshawa	51	07.45	10.06	12.16	15.47	17.32	19.13
Port Hope	101						19.42
Cobourg	113	08.20	10.39	12.53			19.51
Trenton Jct.	163						20.19
Belleville	182	08.57	11.16	13.32	16.54		
Kingston	254	Ar 09.32	11.51	14.10	17.28		21.09
		Dp 09.36	11.55	14.14	17.32		21.12
Gananoque	290						21.34
Brockville	335	10.32	12.51	15.02			22.00
Cornwall	428	11.17	13.35	15.51	18.57		22.47
Dorval	520	12.05	14.22	16.41	19.46	21.14	23.37
Montreal	539	12.23	14.42	17.02	20.05	21.32	23.57

* **Ex S/S** = excluding Saturday and Sunday
* **No 68** = replaced by Train 668 on Sat & Sun; dep Toronto at 18.35, arr Montreal at 00.05

CANADIAN: TORONTO–VANCOUVER

Station name	Km	Westbound	Eastbound
		Day 1	
		Tu Th Sa	
Toronto	0	22.00	09.30
		Day 2	
		We Fr Su	
Washago*	143	00.40	07.05
Parry Sound*	241	02.42	05.10
Sudbury Jct*	422	05.13	02.20
Capreol	444	Ar 05.38	Dp 01.50
		Dp 06.08	Ar 01.20
Laforest*	493	07.12	00.15
McKee's Camp*	494	07.15	00.04
			Day 5
			Sa Tu Th
Felix*	521	07.35	23.36
Ruel*	527	07.54	23.30
Westree*	547	08.24	22.54
Gogama*	583	09.03	22.35
Folyet*	683	11.16	20.50
Elsas*	739	12.14	19.50
Oba*	859	14.20	17.50
Hornepayne	921	Ar 15.15	Dp 16.50
		Dp 15.50	Ar 16.15
Hillsport*	989	17.02	15.10
Caramat*	1046	17.54	14.20
Longlac*	1084	18.26	13.50
Nakina*	1133	19.09	13.05
Auden*	1222	20.24	11.50
Ferland*	1265	21.18	11.10
Mud River*	1273	21.28	11.06
Armstrong*	1314	22.19 (ET)	10.25 (ET)
Collins*	1348	22.05 (CT)	08.50 (CT)
Allanwater Bridge*	1401	22.49	08.05
Flindt Landing*	1421	23.08	07.50
Savant Lake*	1440	23.23	07.30
		Day 3	
		Th Sa Mo	
Sioux Lookout	1537	Ar 00.56	Dp 06.05
		Dp 01.16	Ar 05.45
Richin*	1621	02.34	04.35
Red Lake Road*	1652	03.15	03.45
Canyon*	1682	03.45	03.15
Farlane*	1720	04.24	02.40
Redditt*	1735	04.41	02.23
Minaki*	1758	05.07	02.00
Ottermere*	1780	05.31	01.39
Malachi*	1784	05.36	01.35
Copeland's Ldng*	1788	05.40	01.31
Rice Lake*	1796	05.49	01.22
Winnitoba*	1801	05.54	01.17

CANADIAN: TORONTO–VANCOUVER (cont'd)

Station name	Km	Westbound	Eastbound
Ophir*	1806	06.00	01.13
Brereton Lake*	1826	06.21	00.56
Elma*	1854	06.52	00.35
			Day 4
			Fr Mo We
Winnipeg	1943	Ar 08.01	Dp 23.30
		Dp 12.00	Ar 20.30
Portage la Prairie*	2032	13.24	19.15
Rivers*	2173	15.13	16.30
Melville	2394	18.42	13.25
Watrous*	2602	21.48	10.36
Saskatoon	2702	Ar 23.22	Dp 09.10
		Dp 23.47	Ar 08.45
		Day 4	
		Fr Su Tu	
Biggar	2792	01.14	07.30
Unity*	2885	02.29 (CT)	05.55 (CT)
Wainwright*	3017	03.15 (MT)	03.00 (MT)
Viking*	3089	04.19	01.55
			Day 3
			Th Su Tu
Edmonton	3221	Ar 06.37	Dp 23.45
		Dp 07.37	Ar 23.00
Evansburg*	3331	08.55	21.38
Edson*	3430	10.13	20.20
Hinton*	3518	11.24	18.55
Jasper	3600	Ar 13.00	Dp 17.30
		Dp 14.30 (MT)	Ar 16.00 (MT)
Valemount*	3721	16.07 (PT)	12.50 (PT)
Blue River*	3814	18.27	10.50
Clearwater*	3923	20.44	08.46
Kamloops	4038	Ar 23.09	Dp 06.35
		Dp 23.44	Ar 06.00
		Day 5	
		Sa Mo We	
Ashcroft*	4117	01.27	04.02
Boston Bar*	4240	04.14	
North Bend*	4265		01.16
Hope*	4305	05.43	**Day 2**
			We Sa Mo
Katz*	4308		22.47
Chilliwack*	4355	06.40	
Agassiz*	4360		22.33
Abbotsford*	4380	07.08	
Mission*	4405		22.05
Vancouver	4466	09.42	20.30
			Day 1
			Tu Fr Su

* Flag stop. Requires 48-hours advance notice
ET = Eastern Time, CT = Central Time MT = Mountain Time, PT = Pacific Time

SKEENA: JASPER–PRINCE RUPERT

Station name	Km	Westbound Day 1 We Fr Su	Eastbound
Jasper	0	12.45 (MT)	18.30 (MT)
Harvey*	106	13.38 (PT)	14.54
Dunster*	142	14.12	14.05
McBride	174	14.44	13.48
Goat River*	217	15.41	12.52
Loos*	232	15.58	12.37
Dome Creek*	262	16.32	12.03
Bend*	265	16.36	12.02
Penny*	285	16.56	11.43
Longworth*	301	17.11	11.29
Hutton*	314	17.24	11.18
Sinclair Mills*	319	17.30	11.14
McGregor*	331	17.43	11.03
Upper Fraser*	341	17.52	10.55
Aleza Lake*	349	18.01	10.47
Willow River*	378	18.31	10.18
Prince George	409	Ar 19.08 Day 2 Th Sa Mo Dp 08.00	Dp 09.45 Day 2 Th Sa Mo Ar 20.29
Vanderhoof	520	09.55	18.35
Fort Fraser*	560	10.32	17.57
Endako	594	10.50	17.25
Burns Lake	650	11.58	16.32
Houston	734	13.08	15.22
Telkwa*	780	13.52	14.37
Smithers	795	14.20	14.24
New Hazelton	869	15.37	12.58
Kitwanga*	912	16.27	12.08
Cedarvale*	933	16.51	11.44
Dorreen*	957	17.12	11.19
Pacific*	967	17.21	11.07
Usk*	988	17.40	10.48
Terrace (Kitimat)	1007	18.05	10.25
Kwinitsa*	1084	19.09	09.17
Prince Rupert	1160	20.25	08.00 (PT) Day 1 We Fr Su

* Flag stop. The train will stop here on demand only.

HUDSON BAY: WINNIPEG–CHURCHILL

Station name	Km	Northbound Day 1 Tu Su	Southbound
Winnipeg	0	12.05	16.45
Portage la Prairie	88	13.15	15.37
Gladstone	148	14.07	14.51
Plumas	169	14.44	14.06
Glenella	191	15.16	13.34
McCreary	224	15.57	12.54
Laurier	238	16.15	12.38
Ochre River	262	16.36	12.20
Dauphin	283	17.06	12.06
Gilbert Plains*	315	17.44	11.32
Grandview*	331	18.00	11.12
Roblin	385	18.55	09.14
Togo*	412	19.22	09.37
Kamsack	446	19.59	08.58
Veregin	459	20.12	08.43
Mikado	473	20.22	08.30
Canora	484	20.46	08.18
Sturgis	520	21.21	07.24
Endeavour	549	21.54	06.55
Reserve*	586	22.34	06.09
Hudson Bay	636	23.32 Day 2 We Mo Fr	05.27
The Pas	777	Ar 01.45	Dp 03.15 Day 3 Sa Mo
		Dp 02.30	Ar 23.30
Cormorant	843	04.06	21.32
Wabowden	996	07.30	18.30
Thicket Portage	1073	09.26	16.30
Thompson	1149	Ar 12.00	Dp 14.00
		Dp 13.00	Ar 13.00
Pikwitonei	1220	15.13	10.56
Ilford	1337	17.59	08.23
Gillam	1401	Ar 19.30	Dp 07.00
		Dp 20.00	Ar 06.30
Weir River	1477	22.34 Day 3 Th Tu Sat	03.55
Herchmer	1540	01.42	00.47 Day 2 We Fr Su
Churchill	1697	07.00	19.30 Day 1 Tu Th Sa

* Flag stop. The train will stop here on demand only.

APPENDIX B: FRENCH WORDS AND PHRASES

Many travellers are astonishingly ignorant about the importance of the French language in Canada. A group of backpackers I met in Toronto were flabbergasted when I introduced them to a Quebecker whose English was quite poor – they had assumed that all Canadians speak English as their main language. The fact is that, in theory at least, French has equal status with English; they are the country's two official languages. Over six million Canadians speak French as their first language. These are concentrated in, but not confined to, Quebec. There are also sizeable groups of Francophones in parts of Nova Scotia, New Brunswick, Ontario and Manitoba.

Apart from being a matter of common courtesy, speaking (or attempting to speak) French to a Francophone displays a cultural sensitivity that will be greatly appreciated by your listener, especially in Quebec. Even the clumsiest efforts will be rewarded with smiles and encouragement and will definitely enhance your experience of French Canada.

MEETING PEOPLE

Hello	*Bonjour*
Good evening	*Bonsoir*
How are you?	*Ça va?* (informal); *Comment allez-vous?* (polite)
I'm fine, thanks	*Ça va bien, merci*
Yes	*Oui*
No	*Non*
Maybe	*Peut-être*
Please	*S'il vous plaît/s'il te plaît*
Thank you	*Merci*
You're welcome	*De rien/bienvenu*
Excuse me (in a crowd)	*Pardon*
Sorry	*Je m'excuse*
Okay	*D'accord*
No problem	*Pas de problème*
I'm called...	*Je m'appelle...*
What's your name?	*Comment vous-appelez vous* (polite)
	Comment t'appelles-tu? (informal)
I'm British/American	*Je suis Anglais(e)/Américain(e)*
I'm Australian/Japanese	*Je suis Australien(ne)/Japonais(e)*
I'm from New Zealand	*Je suis de la Nouvelle-Zélande*
I'm Swiss/Swedish	*Je suis Suisse/Suédois(e)*
I'm Italian/German	*Je suis Italien(ne)/Allemand(e)*
I'm Dutch/Danish	*Je suis Hollandais(e)/Danois(e)*

DIRECTIONS

I'm looking for the tourist office	*Je cherche le bureau de tourisme*
Where is the ...?	*Où est le/la ...?*
train station	*la gare*
town centre	*le centre-ville*
airport	*l'aéroport*
bus stop	*l'arrêt d'autobus*
metro	*le métro*
museum	*le musée*
washroom (toilets)	*les toilettes*

DIRECTIONS (cont'd)

Is it far to walk?	*C'est loin à pied?*
straight ahead	*tout droit*
near to	*près de*
in front of	*devant*
behind	*derrière*
to the right	*à droite*
to the left	*à gauche*
here	*ici*
street	*la rue*
bridge	*le pont*
square	*la place*
building	*l'immeuble*

ACCOMMODATION

hotel	*l'hôtel*
youth hostel	*l'auberge de jeunesse*

Do you have a room for	*Est-ce que vous avez une chambre pour*
one/two people	*une personne / deux personnes?*
for one night / two nights	*pour une nuit / deux nuits*
with a bathroom?	*avec salle de bain?*

Is breakfast included?	*Est-ce que le petit-déjeuner compris?*
How much is it?	*C'est combien?*
Do you have anything cheaper?	*Est-ce que vous avez quelque chose moins cher?*
May I see the room?	*Pourrais-je voir la chambre?*
I'll take it.	*Je la prends.*

NUMERALS

1	*un(e)*	14	*quatorze*	60	*soixante*
2	*deux*	15	*quinze*	70	*soixante-dix*
3	*trois*	16	*seize*	71	*soixante-et-onze*
4	*quatre*	17	*dix-sept*	72	*soixante-douze*
5	*cinq*	18	*dix-huit*	80	*quatre-vingt*
6	*six*	19	*dix-neuf*	90	*quatre-vingt-dix*
7	*sept*	20	*vingt*	91	*quatre-vingt-onze*
8	*huit*	21	*vingt-et-un*	100	*cent*
9	*neuf*	22	*vingt-deux*	105	*cent-cinq*
10	*dix*	30	*trente*	200	*deux cents*
11	*onze*	31	*trente-et-un*	500	*cinq cents*
12	*douze*	40	*quarante*	1000	*mille*
13	*treize*	50	*cinquante*	1000,000	*un million*

MONEY

bank	*la banque*
money	*l'argent*
travellers' cheques	*chèques de voyages*
credit card	*une carte de crédit*
ATM	*distributeur automatique*

FOOD AND DRINK

water	*de l'eau*
orange/pineapple juice	*un jus d'orange/ananas*
wine	*du vin*
beer	*la bière*
(white) coffee	*café (au lait)*
tea	*le thé*
menu	*le menu*
salmon	*le saumon*
chicken/pork/ham	*le poulet/porc/jambon*
vegetables	*les légumes*
eggs	*des oeufs*
salt/pepper	*sel/poivre*
milk/sugar	*lait/sucre*

RAILWAY

timetable	*l'indicateur / horaire*
reservation	*une réservation*
connection	*une correspondance*
platform	*le quai*
ticket	*le billet*
ticket office	*la billetterie*
one way	*aller simple*
return	*aller retour*
sleeper class	*la classe voiture-lits*
Silver & Blue class	*la classe Bleu-Argent*
economy class	*la classe économique*
conductor	*le chef de train*
an upgrading	*un surclassement*
a refund	*un remboursement*
cancel	*annuler*
checked luggage	*bagages enregistrés*
hand luggage	*bagages à main*
luggage trolley	*un chariot à bagages*
bedding	*la literie*
late	*en retard*
on time	*à l'heure*

APPENDIX C: BIBLIOGRAPHY

Beattie, Owen and Geiger, John *The Fate of the Franklin Expedition 1845-48*
Berton, Pierre *The National Dream* and *The Last Spike* (1975)
Butler, W F *The Great Lone Land* (1872)
Cumberland, Stuart *The Queen's Highway* (1887)
Dorin, Patrick *Canadian Pacific Railway* (1974)
Dumond, Don *The Eskimos and Aleuts*
Gibbon, J M *Steel of Empire* (1935)
Grant, Rev George M *Ocean to Ocean* (1873)
Hurtig, Mel *The Betrayal of Canada* (1992)
Innes, H A *A History of the Canadian Pacific Railway* (1923)
Lavallée, Omer *Van Horne's Road* (1974)
Lotz, Jim and McKenzie, Keith *Railways of Canada*
MacEwan, G *The Battle for the Bay* (1975)
Macmillan, Alan *Native Peoples and Cultures of Canada*
McKee, Bill and Klassen, G *Trail of Iron*
McNaught, Kenneth *The Penguin History of Canada* (1988)
Mitchell, David *All Aboard* (1995)
Morton, Desmond *A Short History of Canada* (1994)
Pullen-Burry, B *From Halifax to Vancouver* (1912)
Radwanski, George and Luttrell, Julia *Awakening the Canadian Spirit* (1992)
Richler, Mordecai *Oh Canada! Oh Quebec!* (1992)
Roper, Edward *By Track and Trail Through Canada* (1891)
Stephens, D E *Iron Roads* (1972)
Stevens, G R *Canadian National Railways* (1960)
Woodcock, George *A Social History of Canada*

Map key

♠ Where to stay	⊞ Library/bookstore	⊕ Bus station	
○ Where to eat and drink	⊙ Internet	━☐━ Rail line & station	
⊠ Post Office	⊤ Museum/gallery	⛴ Ferry	
ⓘ Tourist Information	✚ Church/cathedral	▬ Park	
	● Other		

INDEX

TRAILBLAZER'S LONG-DISTANCE PATH (LDP) WALKING GUIDES

We've applied to destinations which are closer to home Trailblazer's proven formula for publishing definitive practical route guides for adventurous travellers. Britain's network of long-distance trails enables the walker to explore some of the finest landscapes in the country's best walking areas. These are guides that are user-friendly, practical, informative and environmentally sensitive.

● **Unique mapping features** In many walking guidebooks the reader has to read a route description then try to relate it to the map. Our guides are much easier to use because walking directions, tricky junctions, places to stay and eat, points of interest and walking times are all written onto the maps themselves in the places to which they apply. With their uncluttered clarity, these are not general-purpose maps but fully edited maps drawn by walkers for walkers.

● **Largest-scale walking maps** At a scale of just under 1:20,000 (8cm or 3¹/₈ inches to one mile) the maps in these guides are bigger than even the most detailed British walking maps currently available in the shops.

● **Not just a trail guide – includes where to stay, where to eat and public transport** Our guidebooks cover the complete walking experience, not just the route. Accommodation options for all budgets are provided (pubs, hotels, B&Bs, campsites, bunkhouses, hostels) as well as places to eat. Detailed public transport information for all access points to each trail means that there are itineraries for all walkers, for hiking the entire route as well as for day or weekend walks.

Coast to Coast *Henry Stedman* ISBN 978-1-905864-30-0, £11.99
4th edition, 256pp, 109 maps & town plans, 40 colour photos

Cornwall Coast Path *Edith Schofield* ISBN 978-1-905864-19-5, £9.99
3rd edition, 256pp, 112 maps & town plans, 40 colour photos

Cotswold Way *Tricia & Bob Hayne* ISBN 978-1-905864-16-4, £9.99
1st edition, 192pp, 60 maps & town plans, 40 colour photos

Hadrian's Wall Path *Henry Stedman* ISBN 978-1-905864-14-0, £9.99
2nd edition, 208pp, 60 maps & town plans, 40 colour photos

Offa's Dyke Path *Keith Carter* ISBN 978-1-905864-06-5, £9.99
2nd edition, 208pp, 88 maps & town plans, 40 colour photos

North Downs Way *John Curtin* ISBN 978-1-873756-96-6, £9.99
1st edition, 192pp, 60 maps & town plans, 40 colour photos

Peddars Way & Norfolk Coast Path *Alexander Stewart* £9.99
1st edition, 192pp, 60 maps & town plans, 40 colour photos   **Due late 2010**

Pembrokeshire Coast Path *Jim Manthorpe* ISBN 978-1-905864-27-0, £9.99
3rd edition, 224pp, 96 maps & town plans, 40 colour photos

Pennine Way *Keith Carter & Chris Scott* ISBN 978-1-905864-02-7, £11.99
2nd edition, 272pp, 135 maps & town plans, 40 colour photos

The Ridgeway *Nick Hill* ISBN 978-1-905864-17-1, £9.99
2nd edition, 192pp, 53 maps & town plans, 40 colour photos

South Downs Way *Jim Manthorpe* ISBN 978-1-905864-18-8, £9.99
3rd edition, 192pp, 60 maps & town plans, 40 colour photos

West Highland Way *Charlie Loram* ISBN 978-1-905864-29-4, £9.99
4th edition, 192pp, 53 maps, 10 town plans, 40 colour photos

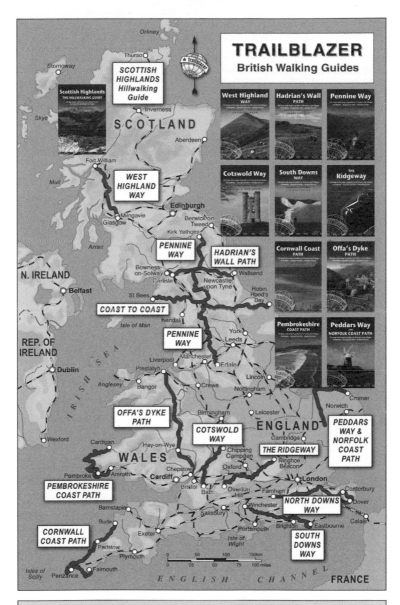

'The same attention to detail that distinguishes its other guides has been brought to bear here'. **The Sunday Times**

Trans-Siberian Handbook *Bryn Thomas*
7th edn, 480pp, 60 maps, 40 colour photos
ISBN 978 1 873756 94 2, £13.99, US$19.95
First edition short-listed for the **Thomas Cook Guidebook Awards**.
Seventh edition of the most popular guide to the world's longest rail
journey. How to arrange a trip, plus a km-by-km guide to the routes.
Updated and expanded to include extra information on travelling inde-
pendently in Russia. New mapping. *'The best guidebook is Bryn
Thomas's "Trans-Siberian Handbook"'* **The Independent (UK)**

Japan by Rail *Ramsey Zarifeh*
2nd edn, 480pp, 60 maps, 30 colour photos
ISBN 978 1 873756 97 3, £13.99, US$19.95
The real secret to travelling around Japan on a budget is the Japan
Rail Pass, as explained in this guide. Includes selected routes, strip
maps, where to stay and where to eat, practical information. Km-by-
km route guides. *'Excellent guide'* – **The Sunday Times**

Australia by Rail *Colin Taylor*
5th edn, 304pp, 70 route maps & town plans, 30 colour photos
ISBN 978 1 873756 81 2, £12.99, US$21.95
Fifth edition of this long-running guide. With 65 strip maps covering all
rail routes in Australia, city guides (Sydney, Melbourne, Brisbane,
Adelaide, Perth, Darwin and Canberra), and now includes the new
Ghan line from Alice Springs to Darwin. *'Benefiting from Taylor's 30
years of travel on Australia's trains.'* **The Sunday Times**

Indian Rail Handbook *Nick Hill & Royston Ellis*   (late 2010)
1st edn, 256pp, 30 colour, 10 B&W photos, 80 maps
ISBN 978 1 873756 87 4, £12.99, US$19.95
India has the most comprehensive railway network in the world, with
almost all tourist attractions accessible by rail. For most visitors travel by
train is the preferred means of transport, the ideal way to see the coun-
try. This new book is a wholly inclusive guide for rail travellers in India.
● Fully-indexed **rail atlas** of 80 maps with all 7326 railway stations
● **Rail travel for all budgets**, **special trains** and **railway history**
● **Timetables, suggested itineraries** and how to book tickets

Kilimanjaro: the trekking guide to Africa's highest mountain
Henry Stedman, 3rd edition, 368pp, 40 maps, 30 photos
ISBN 978-1-905864-24-9, £12.99, US$19.95
At 19,340ft the world's tallest freestanding mountain, Kilimanjaro is
one of the most popular destinations for hikers visiting Africa. It's pos-
sible to walk up to the summit: no technical skills are necessary.
Includes town guides to Nairobi and Dar-Es-Salaam, excursions in the
region and a colour guide to flora and fauna. **Includes Mount Meru.**

Adventure Cycle-Touring Handbook *Stephen Lord*
2nd edn, 320pp, 28 colour & 100 B&W photos
ISBN 978-1-905864-25-6, £14.99, US$21.95
The guide for anyone planning (or dreaming) about taking a bicycle on
a long-distance adventure. This comprehensive manual will make that
dream a reality whether it's cycling in Tibet or pedalling from Patagonia
to Alaska. Part 1 covers Practicalities; Part 2 includes Route outlines;
and Part 3 has Tales from the Saddle.*'The definitive guide to how,
where, why and what to do on a cycle expedition'* **Adventure Travel**

TRAILBLAZER GUIDES – TITLE LIST

www.trailblazer-guides.com

Rail Routes – Key Map

Numbers refer to route maps on the following pages: